M000302722

Clearing and Settlement of Derivatives

Clearing and Settlement of Derivatives

David Loader

ELSEVIER
BUTTERWORTH
HEINEMANN

AMSTERDAM ● BOSTON ● HEIDELBERG ● LONDON ● NEW YORK ● OXFORD
PARIS ● SAN DIEGO ● SAN FRANCISCO ● SINGAPORE ● SYDNEY ● TOKYO

Elsevier Butterworth-Heinemann
Linacre House, Jordan Hill, Oxford OX2 8DP
30 Corporate Drive, Burlington, MA 01803

First published 2005

Copyright © 2005, Elsevier Ltd. All rights reserved

No part of this publication may be reproduced in any material form (including
photocopying or storing in any medium by electronic means and whether or not
transiently or incidentally to some other use of this publication) without the written
permission of the copyright holder except in accordance with the provisions of the
Copyright, Designs and Patents Act 1988 or under the terms of a licence issued
by the Copyright Licensing Agency Ltd, 90 Tottenham Court Road, London, England
W1T 4LP. Applications for the copyright holder's written permission to reproduce any
part of this publication should be addressed to the publisher

Permissions may be sought directly from Elsevier's Science and Technology
Rights Department in Oxford, UK: phone: (+44) (0) 1865 843830;
fax: (+44) (0) 1865 853333; e-mail: permissions@elsevier.co.uk. You may also
complete your request on-line via the Elsevier homepage (www.elsevier.com),
by selecting 'Customer Support' and then 'Obtaining Permissions'

British Library Cataloguing in Publication Data
A catalogue record for this book is available from the British Library

Library of Congress Cataloguing in Publication Data
A catalogue record for this book is available from the Library of Congress

ISBN   0 7506 6452 5

For information on all Elsevier Butterworth-Heinemann publications
visit our website at http://books.elsevier.com

Typeset by Integra Software Services Pvt. Ltd, Pondicherry, India
www.integra-india.com
Printed and bound in Great Britain

Working together to grow
libraries in developing countries

www.elsevier.com | www.bookaid.org | www.sabre.org

ELSEVIER   BOOK AID
            International   Sabre Foundation

Contents

Preface

Derivatives aren't dangerous, only the people who use them without understanding their characteristics and how to clear, settle and manage the operational risk.

The world of derivatives is sometimes viewed as a highly technical and somewhat mystical area of the financial markets. It also has, in some quarters anyway, a poor reputation following various high-profile situations involving rogue dealing and large losses on transactions. The reality is that derivatives are a product that is primarily designed to transfer risk and without the use of derivatives in commerce, commodities, investment and finance, there would be extensive fluctuations in supply and prices plus increased uncertainty.

The derivatives industry is therefore fundamental to the economic well-being of such diverse entities as governments and farmers, global corporate entities and fund managers, bankers and manufacturers, and the individual as well, not that the latter may always be aware of their affinity with derivatives. Derivatives are fundamental to the well-being because they allow risk to be avoided, reduced or increased, thereby offering both protection and opportunity.

Everyday life is influenced by supply and demand, prices, disaster, wealth and numerous other factors. Risk is always there but not always evident. Few investors will be aware, for instance, that a fund manager that hedges against a fall in the stock market through the use of derivatives has in fact protected, to some degree anyway, their investments. The shopper in the supermarket is probably unaware that the price of the jar of coffee they buy is affected by how effective the producer was in 'locking in' the price of coffee beans some time in the past.

Both the investor and the shopper may, however, be aware of a young man who broke the bank, literally through his uncontrolled and seemingly unnoticed activities in derivatives in Singapore. Both the shopper and investor would be unlikely to risk not insuring their house or car and yet mention the use of derivatives, and the chances are they would be either confused or fearful or indeed both!

Such is the ignorance of derivatives in many quarters that in the wake of the Nick Leeson debacle there were calls, many from leading politicians and the so-called experts to make them illegal. How little these politicians and 'experts' understand the real world.

Derivatives did not cause the collapse of Barings Bank, but abysmal management and inadequate controls did. Call for a ban on derivatives use and in effect you are calling for a ban on insurance policies.

Thankfully in spite of, or maybe because of, episodes like Leeson there is today a greater understanding of derivatives, how they work and what they do, but it is still the case that to many within and without the financial services industry they are shrouded in mystery.

Many peoples' first real awareness of derivatives then was when Nick Leeson famously destroyed a 200-year-old UK Bank. Perhaps more surprising was the fact that many of those people worked in the financial markets. In the aftermath of the collapse of Barings in 1995, many wild and somewhat ludicrous assertions were made about derivatives by the so-called experts who had suddenly materialised. They collectively blamed derivatives for nearly every problem in the world, bandied around words and phrases like 'catastrophe', 'disaster', ' highly dangerous products', 'total gambles', etc. No doubt this sensationalism made good news stories in the media but just like so much news it was just media hype.

The bank went bust because of poor management and non-existent and ineffective controls, as simple as that. Derivatives were simply the products Leeson traded. It might have been fair to say that the characteristics of the product made it possible for the loss to accumulate in a relatively short time, but other than that derivatives were incidental and not the cause of the problem.

Another misconception bandied around was that these were 'new' products. But they were not; in fact they are products whose origin can be traced back to the days before cash when 'trades' were an exchange of goods or what today we might call a commodity swap. Much later, in the 1800s a more formalised style of trading in commodities saw the creation of futures contracts that could be traded on an organised exchange, the Chicago Board of Trade, which was established in 1848 for the trading of contracts on grains.

The creation of these standardised contracts and an organised market enabled farmers and merchants to hedge against risk by locking in the price they would receive or pay in advance of the actual time of delivery of the commodity. The system worked well creating certainty where, before that, there was no way of knowing what the price would be until harvest time. Speculators took the risk that hedgers wanted to get rid of. They were hoping to profit from a rise in price or to be able to trade their positions benefiting from price changes. Not surprisingly the volume of trading in these contracts increased, as more and more people recognised the benefits of using futures.

However, it was not until the 1970s that users of the financial markets needing to manage risk being generated by fluctuating interest rates and currency exchange rates turned to futures contracts to enable them to hedge against the risk.

The impact was quite dramatic. The number and variety of financial-based futures contracts that were introduced not only on markets in Chicago but also elsewhere in the world increased massively, so too did the use of another derivative, option contracts, so that by the late 1980s the global volume of traded contracts had grown from under 10 million annually to over 800 million. The popularity and spectacular growth in the use of exchange-traded products overshadowed the over-the-counter (OTC) or negotiated market for derivatives. This market was also popular as trades were made in products that were not available on exchanges and also when a more bespoke product was needed rather than a standardised one. However, there were issues like counterparty risk and the need for documentation every time a trade was entered into. Later these would, to a large extent, be resolved, and so a massive exchange-traded and OTC derivative market came about.

The increase in the use of derivatives is easily explained.

As the world became a global market place and as the residual impact of the Second World War faded, the risk in terms of fluctuating prices, interest rates and foreign exchange rates increased enormously. Once again there was uncertainty and the need to be able to hedge against that uncertainty became important. Futures and options and various OTC products met that demand and so in commerce, banking and investment, expansion took place and volumes in derivatives increased, which created liquidity, encouraged expansion, etc.

When Barings happened, although there was much negative comment very little was heard about how for years derivatives had been used successfully by numerous organisations. Few thought about how everything from the price of coffee to the interest rate on their fixed-rate mortgage was in no small way directly or indirectly affected by the derivatives markets.

Just like with any product or market, there will be times when someone probably has a bad experience using derivatives. This needs, however, to be looked at in the context of the size of the market. Losses attributable to errors, strategy or operational, and problems with using derivatives is a tiny figure compared to the value of all the derivatives traded. This may be of no comfort to those who suffer such an experience but it is important when hype and sensationalism so often seems to be aimed at the derivatives industry.

Today, contracts of several billions are traded; over-the-counter activity of many trillions of dollars, in value terms, occurs; and the growth continues.

Naturally market, credit and operational risk are features of using derivatives. Effective processing and controls on derivatives business are therefore critically important. Exchange-traded derivatives, and some OTC derivatives benefit from the fact that they are traded in a significantly regulated environment and are cleared and settled by a clearing house that is not only efficient at administering transaction processing but also an expert at managing risk.

The member firms of these clearing houses, usually banks and brokers, need to meet strict criteria to have such status. This is a comfort for the customers who deal with them, as the bank/broker is effectively their 'clearing house' and is often referred to as the 'clearing broker'. Counterparty risk is an issue with the off-exchange transactions but here highly effective documentation offers both parties to such a trade a legal comfort that the terms will be honoured.

The bottom line is that today derivatives use is taking place in a mature and highly professional environment with regulation, sophisticated systems and by and large competently managed organisations. New entrants to the derivatives markets are able to benefit from the experience of the mature participants and also from an extensive range of education and training products.

Much of the comfort factor in using derivatives stems from being sure that controls over the activity are strong and that the administration of the transactions is efficient. The role of the derivatives operations team is therefore a significant one being both a protector of profit and also a major contributor to controlling the risk.

In this book and the accompanying CD-ROM the reader will see what the various roles and functions are, who the participants are and how different products require different processes, procedures and controls. If nothing else it should dispel the myths that existed after Barings and still exist to some extent today. The book will help to explain why derivatives came about, how they get used and the settlement and other issues that occur when derivatives are used.

Anyone not familiar with these products is, we think, going to be pleasantly surprised as they read through the book. The myths will be removed and we hope the interest stimulated.

Derivatives aren't dangerous, only the people who use them without understanding their characteristics and how to clear, settle and manage the operational risk.

David Loader
April 2005

Acknowledgements

I would like to thank the many various parties who helped with advice and input to the content of this book and also the exchanges, clearing houses and other organisations whose websites, brochures, etc. provided so much help and excellent information.

I would also like to extend my thanks to Joanna Scott and Mike Cash at Butterworth for their incredible patience and to my wife Pat for her encouragement and acceptance of my being 'absent' for so many hours!

I would like to thank Jaya Nilamani, Project Manager at Integra Software Services Pvt. Ltd, Pondicherry, India and Jeremy Loader for their extended help to produce this book.

David Loader

Disclaimer

In this book there are references to derivative products, trading, clearing and settlement strategies, procedures, etc.

There are also references to information obtained from external sources.

The author and publishers wish to make it clear that this book is for educational purposes and none of the content howsoever sourced, including sourcing externally, is not intended to be any kind of recommendation for investment or trading.

Clearing and settlement, or management decisions based on the content of this book must take into account and recognise that the content is compiled from reliable sources and is believed to be correct at the time of publication; however, things change frequently in the derivatives industry, and before any action or decision is made it is important to check with the relevant exchanges and clearing houses, regulatory bodies, etc. for the current situation.

1

The development of futures and options and OTC derivatives

What are derivatives?

'Derivatives' is a generic term used to describe a wide range of products that *derive their price or have their value linked in some way to some other product.*

As a result the derivative product can be used as a synthetic version of that other product, often referred to as the underlying, and this enables many different strategies to be developed, including hedging and speculative ones. For instance if we think the price of say BP shares is likely to move sharply upwards but it would equally be possible that something might happen to make the shares fall in price, we may be reluctant to commit funds to buying the shares. On the other hand if there is a product that allows us to have an exposure to the BP share price but without, at this stage, committing to paying the full value we would be more inclined to back our judgement. This is because we would know that if we were wrong we would not have committed all the required funds needed to buy the shares themselves but if we were right the product, a derivative of BP, would tend to move in the same way as the price of BP shares and we would profit from it.

Two derivative products that were established early on were the futures contract and the options contract. It is not easy to determine exactly when these products or similar types of product first saw the light of day but one thing for sure is that today, futures and options markets are global and trade contracts on a wide range of products encompassing currencies, commodities, interest rates, shares, indices, insurance; in fact you can find derivatives on just about anything.

We do know that this vast array of products traded today would seem unbelievable to the farmers and merchants of the Midwest of the United States of America who first started trading futures contracts, in a form similar to today, in the mid-1800s.

What is a futures contract?

A futures contract is a legally binding agreement to buy or sell a predetermined amount of a defined product at or by a set date for an agreed price.

Did derivatives exist before the 1800s?

The development of futures markets can be traced back at least as far as the Middle Ages and revolved around the supply and demand of people like farmers and merchants. The early contracts were, therefore, for delivery of 'underlying' products like grains, e.g. oats, corn and wheat. These trades took place for either immediate settlement ('spot' trades) or settlement at some time ahead ('forward' trades). They were not without problems. To establish the current price for say wheat, farmers would take their harvested crops to the major towns and visit each merchant in turn to find out who would pay the best price. Picture the scene as hundreds of farmers going back and forth across the town. Often many ended up dumping all or some of their crops as they could not manage to find a buyer, especially when there were bumper harvests. Even when the farmer had reached agreement with a merchant before harvest time, as there was no regulations in place there was no guarantee that the agreement would be honoured and both parties were potentially the 'guilty' ones to the default if prices moved in their favour.

The first futures market

The Chicago Board of Trade (most exchanges use mnemonics/ abbreviations and in this case the one used is CBOT or in speech sometimes 'the Board') was established in 1848 to standardise the size, quality and delivery date of these commodity agreements that were forwards contracts into a contract that could be traded on an exchange.

Once established, the standardisation of the terms of the contract enabled contracts to be readily traded as what we call today 'futures contracts'. Thus the forerunner of today's markets was born and farmers or merchants who wanted to hedge against price fluctuations, caused by poor or bumper harvests, bought and sold futures contracts with traders or market makers who were willing to make a different price for buying and selling. Speculators, who wanted to gamble on the price going up or down without actually buying or selling the physical grains themselves, were also attracted to the market. Therefore liquidity in the contracts was created, as many buyers and sellers came together to trade. The trader was able, if they wanted, to lay off the risk they had assumed from buying and selling with the hedgers, by doing the opposite, that is buying and selling with the speculators. The trader's profit was the difference between buying and selling the contracts.

Another important result of the creation of the CBOT was the ability to discover the price of a commodity. As buyers and sellers joined together on the floor of the exchange to trade and quoted prices to each other, the 'real' price for, say, soybeans was established. Price discovery helps to create a stability in price because anyone, buyer or seller, can immediately see by looking at the futures price what price the supply and demand for the underlying is generating.

In essence, today's markets do the same job as the original concept back in 1848 but in hundreds of different products. The CBOT, for instance, trades a wide range of contracts on commodities, like soybeans and silver as well as financials like Treasury Bonds and Notes.

In 1874, following in CBOT's footsteps, the Chicago Produce Exchange provided the market for perishable agricultural products like butter and eggs. After some upheaval in 1898, certain traders broke away and formed what is now known as the Chicago Mercantile Exchange (CME). In 1919 the CME was recognised to allow futures trading. Futures on a variety of commodities have since come to the exchange, including pork bellies, hogs and cattle as well as financials like currencies and index products.

The emergence of financial futures and options markets

In 1972 the CME established a division known as the International Monetary Market (IMM). Its purpose was to enable trading in futures contracts based on foreign currencies. In 1982 the CME started trading futures contracts on the S&P 500 Stock Index and now trades many different index products.

In the United States, prior to 1975, nearly all contracts traded were agricultural. Volume in these contracts was less than 10 million per year. However, by 1994 the figure had risen to almost 700 million contracts and by the end of 2003 to a staggering 8.1 billion contracts.

From the end of Second World War until the early 1970s there was a very stable economic environment in the United States helped by the Bretton Woods Agreement, which kept interest rates in a narrow range. However, when the US dollar was devalued, partly as a consequence of the funding of the Vietnam War and a heavy domestic spending programme, uncertainty and fluctuation in interest rates replaced the economic stability. Europe and Japan had also recovered in economic terms from the re-building effects of Second World War and, with their economies growing, the Dollar came under severe pressure. The need to be able to hedge (or to protect) against the risk associated with volatile currencies and interest rates became critical for many businesses and industries. The result was the birth of the first financial contracts, which became the cornerstone of the futures and options industry, as we know it today.

It was in 1975 that the CBOT launched the first futures contract on a financial instrument, the Ginnie Mae Mortgage Bond future, followed by the CME, which listed a Eurodollar contract. Shortly, the CBOT listed what was to become one of the world's most heavily traded futures contract, the Treasury Bond future.

Since then, the growth in volume of futures and options contracts in the United States and the rest of the world has been quite phenomenal, as more and more exchanges have opened and a plethora of financial products were developed and listed to meet the demand for risk-hedging mechanisms.

This process continues today as new markets open in the developing countries. However, the emergence of futures and options markets outside the United States has seen a change in the make-up of the overall volume of business traded. Today Eurex, formed from the amalgamation of the German Deutsche Terminborse and the Swiss Options and Financial Futures Exchange, is one of the largest exchanges in the world by volume of contracts traded. The Euro Bund future traded on Eurex is one of the heaviest traded futures contracts in the world and, to illustrate the global nature of today's market, the Kospi option traded on the Korea Stock Exchange was in 2003 the heaviest traded derivatives contract in the world (Table 1.1).

Mergers and alliances between derivative markets and stock exchanges has been common in recent times and today we have Euronext, the combined stock and derivative markets of France,

Table 1.1   Global futures and options volume.

2003 Rank	2002 Rank	Exchange	2002 Volume	2003 Volume	% Change
1	1	Korea Stock Exchange	1,932,749,868	2,899,937,895	50.04
2	2	Eurex	801,200,873	1,014,932,312	26.68
3	3	Euronext	696,323,560	694,970,981	−0.19
4	4	Chicago Mercantile Exchange	558,447,820	640,209,634	14.64
5	5	Chicago Board of Trade	343,882,529	454,190,749	32.08
6	6	Chicago Board Options Exchange	267,616,496	283,946,495	6.10
7	8	International Securities Exchange	152,399,279	244,968,190	60.74
8	7	American Stock Exchange	186,039,445	180,074,778	−3.21
9	11	Bovespa	90,884,897	177,223,140	95.00
10	14	Mexican Derivatives Exchange	84,274,979	173,820,944	106.25
11	9	New York Mercantile Exchange	133,744,435	137,225,439	2.60
12	10	BM&F	101,615,788	120,785,602	18.86
13	12	Philadelphia Stock Exchange	88,955,247	112,705,597	26.70
14	15	Tokyo Commodity Exchange	75,413,190	87,252,219	15.70
15	13	Pacific Exchange	85,426,649	86,152,637	0.85
16	18	Dalian Commodity Exchange	48,407,404	74,973,493	54.88
17	17	London Metal Exchange	58,634,004	72,308,327	23.32
18	16	OM	60,920,817	72,137,347	18.41
19	21	Sydney Futures Exchange	36,243,524	44,755,340	23.49
20	33	National Stock Exchange of India	13,287,113	43,081,968	224.24
21	34	Shanghai Futures Exchange	12,173,083	40,079,750	229.25
22	19	Tel-Aviv Stock Exchange	41,419,705	38,098,479	−8.02
23	22	Singapore Exchange	32,887,395	35,648,224	8.39

Source: Futures Industry Association.

Belgium, Portugal and the Netherlands together with the main derivative market in the United Kingdom, the London International Financial Futures & Options Exchange (LIFFE, pronounced 'life'). Other merged markets include, The Singapore Exchange (SGX), formed from the merger of the Singapore International Monetary Exchange (SIMEX) and the Stock Exchange of Singapore and the joining of the Hong Kong Stock Exchange and the Hong Kong Futures Exchange to create HKEx.

Other significant developments have included the approval by the US Regulators and the launch by Eurex, the German-based exchange, of a new exchange in the United States, Eurex US, to directly compete with the established Chicago markets.

Also in the United States was the combining of the clearing for the two largest futures markets, the CBOT and the CME, with resulting efficiencies and cost savings for members.

The first options markets

Like futures, the use of options can be traced back to the eighteenth century, and in certain forms as far back as the Middle Ages. In the eighteenth century, options were traded in both Europe and the United States, but unfortunately due to widespread corrupt practices the market had a bad name. These early forms of options contracts were traded between the buyer and the seller and had only two possible outcomes. The option was delivered (i.e. the underlying product changed hands at the agreed price) or it expired without the buyer taking up his 'option' to exercise the contract for delivery. In other words there was no 'trading' of the option positions and, still worse, in the early days just as we saw with forward trades there was no guarantee that the seller would honour his obligation to deliver the product if the buyer exercised his option.

However, there was little doubt that options were considered highly flexible and desirable products and therefore in April 1973 the CBOT proposed a new exchange, the Chicago Board Options Exchange (CBOE), to trade stock options in a standardised form and on a recognised market where performance of the options contract on exercise was guaranteed. This was the birth of what we call today 'traded options'.

Since 1973, option markets have grown in the United States and of course globally. Like futures markets they cover a wide range of products, including options on futures, a derivative with another derivative as the underlying. Although options have been trading on exchange for a shorter time than futures, they are nevertheless extremely popular with both hedgers and speculators alike.

The Australian Options Market (now owned by the Australian Stock Exchange) opened in 1976. In 1978, the first traded options markets started trading in Europe. The European Options Exchange opened in Amsterdam followed soon after by the London Traded Option Market (now owned by the LIFFE).

Other futures and options markets followed. The London International Financial Futures & Options Exchange opened for business in 1982, the Singapore International Monetary Exchange in 1984 and the Hong Kong Futures Exchange in 1985. Many new markets in the Americas, Europe and the Far East followed these during the late 1980s and the early 1990s.

Today, as we have already noted, the derivatives industry is truly global. To illustrate just how big the industry is we only need to look at the volume of contracts traded on worldwide derivatives exchanges during 2003, which totalled a staggering 8 billion-plus contracts.

We must also take into account the derivatives business that is not traded on exchanges. In 2003, the market in the interest rate segment of OTC derivatives was estimated by the Bank for International Settlements (BIS) to be valued at $142 trillion.

Over-the-counter derivatives tend to be more specialised products that are negotiated and very much tailored to the user's requirements. Swaps, forwards and forward rate agreements (FRAs) are traded over-the-counter and so too are many different types of options making the combined on- and off-exchange volume of business in options massive.

The industry, both exchange-traded and OTC, continues to grow with new exchanges and new products providing users with the medium to control risk.

More recently, products introduced on- and off-exchange include credit derivatives, weather derivatives, share futures, flex options and 'mini' (smaller contract size than the standard futures contract) contracts on, for instance, various equity indices.

As the table of the world's leading exchanges (Table 1.1) and the graph of OTC values (Table 1.2) illustrates, today the derivatives industry is truly global and also enormous. Equally it is a diversified industry as the following list of the 20 highest volume contracts in the first half of 2004 shows (Table 1.3).

Table 1.2 Global OTC derivatives market turnover by instrument.[1]

Instrument	Average daily turnover in April, in billions of US dollars			
	1995	1998	2001	2004
A. Foreign exchange instruments	45	97	67	140
Currency swaps	4	10	7	21
Options	41	87	60	117
Other	1	0	0	2
B. Interest rate instruments[2]	151	265	489	1025
FRAs	66	74	129	233
Swaps	63	155	331	621
Options	21	36	29	171
Other	2	0	0	0
C. Estimated gaps in reporting	4	13	19	55
D. Total	200	375	575	1220
Memo				
Turnover at April 2004 exchange rates[3]	180	410	690	1220
Exchange-traded derivatives[4]				
Currency instruments	17	11	10	22
Interest rate instruments	1204	1371	2170	4521

[1] Adjusted for local and cross-border double-counting.

[2] Single currency interest rate contracts only.

[3] Non-US dollar legs of foreign currency transactions were converted into original currency amounts at average exchange rates for April of each survey year and then reconverted into US dollar amounts at average April 2004 exchange rates.

[4] *Sources*: FOW TRADEdata; Futures Industry Association; various futures and options exchanges.

As can be seen, there are many diverse products in the list and yet all of them with the exception of No. 1 soybean futures on the DCE are financial-based products. This does not mean that commodities are not important products; for instance, according to the latest data for the first six months of 2004 from the FIA, global agriculture trading has increased by 31.5 per cent to 177.3 million contracts.

In the United States, agricultural products traded 40.0 per cent higher in the first half of 2004, with 70.1 million contracts. Outside the United States, agricultural commodities were up by 24.2 per cent to 107.3 million contracts.

The top global agriculture contract, Dalian Commodity Exchange's soybean futures, was up by 10.8 per cent to 31.5 million contracts.

Table 1.3 Top 20 Contracts by volume (in millions of contracts).

Contract	Exchange	Jan.–Jun. 04	Jan.–Jun. 03	% Change
Kospi 200 Options	Kofex	1,347.50	1,372.40	−1.80
3-Month Eurodollar Futures	CME	139.7	100.1	39.60
Euro-Bund Futures	Eurex	119.4	129.3	−7.70
TIIE 28 Futures	MexDer	100.6	93.0	8.10
10-Year T-Note Futures	CBOT	94.6	66.5	42.20
E-mini S&P 500 Index Futures	CME	85.8	83.4	2.80
3-Month Euribor Futures	Euronext	84.6	70.1	20.70
Euro-Bobl Futures	Eurex	83.7	78.3	6.90
Euro-Schatz Futures	Eurex	66.0	59.6	10.70
3-Month Eurodollar Options	CME	65.3	55.1	18.50
DJ Euro Stoxx 50 Futures	Eurex	62.5	62.0	0.80
Interest Rate Futures	BM&F	53.0	24.1	120.10
Five-Year T-Note Futures	CBOT	49.3	33.2	48.30
E-mini Nasdaq 100 Futures	CME	38.6	32.1	20.20
DJ Euro Stoxx 50 Options	Eurex	37.0	30.9	19.80
3 Month Euribor Options	Euronext	36.7	33.6	9.40
CAC 40 Index Options	Euronext	36.3	36.3	0.00
T-Bond Futures	CBOT	35.5	30.5	16.50
No. 1 Soybean Futures	DCE	31.5	28.4	10.80
Kospi 200 Futures	Kofex	27.8	33.4	−16.80

Source: Futures Industry Association.

Soymeal futures at the same exchange-traded 47.1 per cent higher, reaching 11.3 million contracts traded. At the Tokyo Grain Exchange, non-GMO soybean futures nearly tripled in volume, up by 195.1 per cent to 5.6 million contracts.

Corn futures at the CBOT were the most widely traded US agricultural commodity, up by 51.2 per cent to 13.8 million contracts in the first half. This contract also had the greatest absolute volume increase within global agricultural products, up by 4.7 million in the first six months of 2004.

While trading in precious metals was up in the United States by 41.0 per cent to 13.9 million contracts in the first half, trading in these products outside the United States declined by 14.5 per cent to 19.4 million contracts. Gold futures at the New York Mercantile Exchange rose by 29.9 per cent to a total of 7.7 million contracts in the first half, while gold options trading at Nymex climbed by 41.1 per cent to 2.4 million contracts. Silver futures trading at Nymex also grew, up by 47.8 per cent to 2.7 million contracts for the same period.

The decline outside the United States was mainly due to a slowdown in gold futures trading at the Tokyo Commodity Exchange, where volume in that contract declined by 30.0 per cent to 10.2 million contracts in the first half.

Non-precious metals trading jumped by 36.3 per cent globally to 55.9 million contracts. At the Shanghai Futures Exchange, copper futures trading increased by 203.0 per cent to 11.0 million contracts, while aluminium futures trading climbed by 455.9 per cent to 4.9 million contracts. The largest contract in this category was the London Metal Exchange's aluminium futures, up by 12.3 per cent to 14.7 million contracts.

Outside the United States, energy trading fell 6.2 per cent to 52.3 million contracts, but within the United States trading in energy commodities grew 8.4 per cent to 62.2 million contracts. Crude oil futures at Nymex, the world's most actively traded energy contracts, gained by 12.0 per cent to 25.7 million contracts in the first half of 2004. Unleaded regular gas futures at Nymex were also up by 15.0 per cent to 6.7 million contracts. Gasoline futures were down globally by 27.2 per cent at the Central Japan Commodities Exchange to 6.8 million contracts, by 11.9 per cent at the Tokyo Commodities Exchange to 11.5 million contracts, and by 15.3 per cent at Nymex to 8.3 million contracts.

It is also an industry undergoing continuous development and change; for instance, the growth of electronic trading and the emergence of new exchanges to challenge the traditional established markets. Once again, according to the FIA several new exchanges successfully began operating in the first half of 2004 in direct competition with existing US derivatives exchanges. Eurex US launched Treasury futures trading in February.

In Europe, Euronext.liffe successfully introduced futures on the Eurodollar in March 2004, with an opening monthly volume of 64 036. By June, monthly volume had reached 351 252 contracts.

The Boston Options Exchange began trading in February. Volume grew from 241 319 contracts in the first month to 1.4 million contracts in June. By June, the exchange's market share had grown to 1.8 per cent of the US options trading volume.

The following excerpts from an article by Will Acworth editor of Futures Industry magazine published by the FIA in the Sep./Oct. 2004 edition (the whole article can be found on www.futuresindustry.org) illustrate what has been happening in the options markets over the last few years.

Electronic Trading Sweeps Options Industry

What a difference six years has made in the U.S. options industry.

In 1998 the market was effectively divided into exclusive franchises. Very few options traded on more than one exchange, and all trading was conducted in traditional open outcry environments dominated by crowds of specialists. Prices were indicative, and there was a gentlemen's agreement to limit competition.

Today the situation is radically different. Starting in August 1999, the exchanges began to compete directly for order flow across a broad range of options classes, and multiple listings rapidly became the order of the day. A new all-electronic exchange entered the business and captured more than a third of the market, and the four incumbent exchanges began rapidly developing and installing electronic trading systems for their most active products. Spreads tightened substantially, market-making both expanded and consolidated, and customer transaction fees were drastically reduced, if not eliminated altogether.

Not all of these changes came about as a direct result of electronic trading. The government also was involved, in the form of antitrust investigations by the Justice Department and regulatory edicts from the Securities and Exchange Commission that forced greater competition among the exchanges. But electronic trading, and in particular the formation of International Securities Exchange, was one of the central catalysts for change.

Perhaps the best measure of its importance is that all four of the incumbent exchanges, even the most resistant to change are building electronic trading platforms to replace at least some part of their floor-based markets. They are moving cautiously, migrating only a few options classes at first and then gradually expanding the coverage, and seeking to preserve a role for floor-based trading within the system.

The Chicago Board Options Exchange is now entering the second phase of its hybrid trading system. As of mid-August, six electronic specialists were active on the system, and the exchange expects to begin allowing remote market makers in the near future, pending SEC approval. As of July 31, the exchange had made 960 out of a total of 1450 classes available for trading on its hybrid system, which integrates floor and screen trading.

The Philadelphia Stock Exchange received SEC approval in July to launch trading on its XL platform and has scheduled 10 classes for conversion in August. Pacific Exchange has begun rolling out its PCX Plus system, and the American Stock Exchange is developing its own electronic trading system, ANTE.

No figures are available on the overall ratio of electronic to open outcry trading, but the trend is clear: an increasing amount of orders are being matched electronically as each exchange moves farther along the curve.

The all-electronic ISE has grown steadily since its start in May 2000 and continues to gain market share at the expense of the other exchanges. It pulled past the CBOE earlier this year and now ranks as the largest exchange in the world for individual equity options, with 176.4 million contracts traded in the first half of 2004.

Even so, ISE still has only a third of the total volume in the U.S. market. In contrast to the experience of futures exchanges, competition among the U.S. options exchanges has not resulted in a winner-take-all outcome. As of June, Amex had around 19 per cent of the market, down from 23 per cent in December 2002, and Pacific Exchange was holding onto 8 per cent of the market, down from 11 per cent in December 2002. Their market shares are declining, but they remain competitive.

Last but not least, there is a new exchange in the marketplace. The Boston Options Exchange (BOX), a joint venture of the Boston Stock Exchange, Interactive Brokers and the Montréal Exchange, began trading in February and has traded 6.8 million contracts in its first six months. Compared to the other exchanges, it's still tiny, with less than 2 per cent of the overall market at the end of June, but BOX says its market share in individual names has been as high as 10 per cent.

Source: FIA.

Summary

The derivatives industry continues to be innovative and to grow. New products, new exchanges, growing use of OTC products all of this is creating a massive challenge to the firms and infrastructure that supports the industry, and the growth is not confined to the United States and European markets.

In the first six months of 2004 the Asia-Pacific region, which includes Australia and New Zealand, took 37.4 per cent of the total global volume in futures and options, 5 per cent ahead of North America (32.3 per cent) and over 10 per cent ahead of Europe (24.6 per cent).

The challenges that operations teams face is also diversified with technology, product awareness and adequate controls to manage operational risk as key issues.

2

Derivative products

'Derivatives' is the generic term used for a whole host of products that are traded either as listed products on an exchange or as bespoke, tailored products negotiated over-the-counter (directly between the counterparties).

There are many thousands of derivative products yet most of them fall into categories that identify the underlying such as 'interest rate', 'commodity' or 'currency', or the specific instrument characteristic such as 'interest rate swap', 'cocoa futures', etc. This categorisation is then used to produce everything from statistics (Table 2.1) to identifying the division within a market that trades the products.

Table 2.1 Volume by category (in millions).

	2003	2002	Change	% Change
Global				
Equity indices	3960.87	2791.18	1169.69	41.91
Interest rate	1881.27	1478.44	402.83	27.25
Individual equities	1558.52	1354.70	203.82	15.05
Ag commodities	261.15	199.39	61.77	30.98
Energy products	217.56	209.37	8.19	3.91
Non-precious metals	90.39	71.57	18.82	26.29
Foreign currency/index	77.85	60.56	17.28	28.53
Precious metals	64.46	51.26	13.2	25.75
Other	0.66	0.8	−0.14	−17.14
Total	8112.73	6217.28	1895.45	30.49

Continued

Table 2.1   Volume by category (in millions)—cont'd

	2003	2002	Change	% Change
US				
Individual equities	791.64	679.7	111.94	16.47
Interest rate	678.3	579.21	99.09	17.11
Equity indexes	420.55	327.72	92.82	28.32
Energy products	112.4	115.93	−3.53	−3.05
Ag commodities	107.86	97.7	10.16	10.40
Foreign currency/index	36.1	26.07	10.03	38.46
Precious metals	21.76	14.91	6.85	45.94
Non-precious metals	3.25	2.92	0.33	11.24
Other	0.66	0.73	−0.07	−9.85
Total	2172.52	1844.90	327.62	17.76
Non-US				
Equity indices	3540.32	2463.46	1076.87	43.71
Interest rate	1202.97	899.23	303.74	33.78
Individual equities	766.88	675.01	91.88	13.61
Ag commodities	153.29	101.69	51.6	50.75
Energy products	105.16	93.44	11.72	12.54
Non-precious metals	87.14	68.65	18.49	26.93
Precious metals	42.7	36.35	6.35	17.47
Foreign currency/index	41.74	34.49	7.25	21.03
Other	0	0.07	−0.06	−98.80
Total	5940.22	4372.38		

Source: Futures Industry Association.

Even where a derivative product is seemingly the same, the actual characteristics may differ considerably so a bond futures contract is different from an equity index future as illustrated by the differences in the two example contract specifications for the FTSE 100 Index and Long Gilt futures contracts listed on Euronext.liffe shown below.

FTSE 100 Index Futures

Unit of Trading	Contract Valued at £10 per index point (e.g. value £65,000 at 6500.0)
Delivery Months	March, June, September, December (nearest four available for trading)

Quotation	Index points (e.g. 6500.0)
Minimum Price Movement (Tick Size & Value)	0.5 (£5.00)
Last Trading Day	10:30:30 Third Friday in delivery month[1]
Delivery Day	First business day after the Last Trading Day
Trading Hours	08:00–17:30

[1] In the event of the third Friday not being a business day, the Last Trading Day shall normally be the last business day preceding the third Friday.

Trading Platform
- LIFFE CONNECT® Trading Host for Futures and Options.
- Algorithm: Central order book applies a price-time trading algorithm with priority given to the first order at the best price.
- Wholesale Services: Asset Allocation, Block Trading, Basis Trading.

Exchange Delivery Settlement Price (EDSP)
The EDSP is based on the average values of the FTSE 100 Index every 15 seconds between (and including) 10:10 and 10:30 on the Last Trading Day. Of the 81 measured values, the highest 12 and lowest 12 will be discarded and the remaining 57 will be averaged to calculate the EDSP. Where necessary, the calculation will be rounded to the nearest half index point.

Contract Standard
Cash settlement based on the Exchange Delivery Settlement Price.

Economic and Monetary Union/Euro
Please refer to the full contract specification on the LIFFE web site at www.liffe.com.

Unless otherwise indicated, all times are London times.

Long Gilt Futures

Unit of Trading	£100,000 nominal value notional Gilt with 6 per cent[1] coupon
Delivery Months	March, June, September, December, such that the nearest three delivery months are available for trading

Quotation	Per £100 nominal
Minimum Price Movement (Tick Size & Value)	0.01 (£10)
First Notice Day	Two business days prior to the first day of the delivery month
Last Notice Day	First business day after the Last Trading Day
Last Trading Day	11.00 – Two business days prior to the last business day in the delivery month
Delivery Day	Any business day in delivery month (at seller's choice)
Trading Hours	08:00–18:00

Trading Platform
- LIFFE CONNECT™ Trading Host for Futures and Options.
- Algorithm: Central order book applies price/time priority trading algorithm.
- Wholesale Services: Asset Allocation, Block Trading, Basis Trading.

Exchange Delivery Settlement Price (EDSP)
The LIFFE market price at 11.00 on the second business day prior to Settlement Day. The invoicing amount in respect of each Deliverable Gilt is to be calculated by the price factor system. Adjustment will be made for full coupon interest accruing as at Settlement Day.

Contract Standard
Delivery may be made of any gilts on the List of Deliverable Gilts in respect of a delivery month, as published by the Exchange on or before the tenth business day prior to the First Notice Day of such delivery month. Holders of long positions on any day within the Notice Period may be delivered against during the delivery month. All gilt issues included in the List will have the following characteristics:

- having terms as to redemption such as provide for redemption of the entire gilt issue in a single instalment on the maturity date falling not earlier than 8.75 years from, and not later than 13 years from, the first day of the relevant delivery month;

- having no terms permitting or requiring early redemption;
- bearing interest at a single fixed rate throughout the term of the issue payable in arrears semi-annually (except in the case of the first interest payment period which may be more or less than six months);
- being denominated and payable as to the principal and interest only in pounds and pence;
- being fully paid or, in the event that the gilt issue is in its first period and is partly paid, being anticipated by the Board to be fully paid on or before the Last Notice Day of the relevant delivery month;
- not being convertible;
- not being in bearer form;
- having being admitted to the Official List of the London Stock Exchange; and
- being anticipated by the Board to have on one or more days in the delivery month an aggregate principal amount outstanding of not less than £1.5 billion which, by its terms and conditions, if issued in more than one tranche or tap or issue, is fungible.

Recent Changes
- For the March 1998 delivery month (and previous delivery months), the notional coupon was 9 per cent.
- Up to and including the June 1998 delivery month, the unit of trading was £50,000 nominal.
- The tick size for the June 1998 delivery month switched to 1/100th of a point from the close of business on 8 May 1998 from 1/32.
- The tick value for the June 1998 delivery month, from the close of business on 8 May 1998 until expiry, was £5. Up to 8 May, the tick value was £7.8125.
- Prior to December 98 contract maturity bracket 10 to 15 years.

[1] For December 2003 delivery month (and previous delivery months), notional coupon was 7 per cent.

Unless otherwise stated, all times are London times.

Source: Euronext.liffe.

As we can see, one contract, the bond future, has a delivery standard that requires physical delivery of a bond that is on the list of deliverable bonds published by the exchange, whilst the other contract, the index future, is cash-settled with reference to an exchange published price. Notice also how the bond future specification has been subject to changes.

More details about the contract terms and administration terms are contained in the full contract specification, the above examples being 'summary' specifications, and a copy of the specification for the FTSE 100 Index Future is contained in the Appendices.

Standardised products that are traded on exchanges are developed by the exchange to meet perceived requirements of the exchange members and their clients. OTC derivatives are developed by firms to meet the need of their clients or even the specific requirement of a single client. Fundamental differences exist between the exchange-traded and the OTC derivatives products including the counterparty risk situation, liquidity, suitability and costs. Another key area where significant differences occur is in the settlement process.

Settlement terms for exchange-traded products are set out by the clearing house of the exchange concerned and the clearing member is subject to many disciplines including the time of payment of obligations, delivery and managing the settlement process with their clients. Any failure to meet the disciplines successfully can cause significant problems and may even result in the clearing member being put into a default by the clearing house, usually terminal for the firm.

Over-the-counter derivatives are different in the sense that the settlement terms are negotiated along with the rest of the terms of the transaction. Although some settlement terms are based on the market standard or convention for the product concerned, the two parties to a trade can negotiate quite different terms if needed. For example, in an interest rate swap where two parties agree to exchange the fixed and floating interest flows, resets will take place when the rates will be confirmed and the settlement then takes place based on those agreed and confirmed rates. The two parties could agree to do this every quarter, semi-annually, annually or they could reset the floating rate quarterly and the fixed rate annually or any other combination that suits both parties. They would also need to agree on the reference standard for the floating rate, in the above example, if the reset was semi-annual, maybe the 6-Month London Inter Bank Offered Rate (LIBOR) (Figure 2.1).

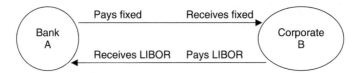

Figure 2.1 Example Interest Rate Swap

The terms are negotiated and a confirmation detailing the terms is then exchanged and should be agreed. An Interest Rate Swap (IRS) confirmation for a fixed/floating transaction would contain information such as:

Confirmation from mega bank	To: Interbank Inc.
Interest rate swaps	
Transaction date	19 June 2004
Effective date	21 June 2004
Maturity date	21 December 2004
Terms	ISDA
Currency/Amount	USD 5 000 000
We pay	5.76%
Frequency	Annual
Calculation basis	Actual/365
We receive	6-Month LIBOR
Frequency	Semi-annual
Calculation basis	Actual/360

There are other pieces of information that can or will be added to this such as frequency being modified following convention.

In contrast, an exchange-traded option will have predetermined exercise procedures; however, with an off-exchange option these will be negotiated and could be variable. For example, a Bermudan style option will have exercise rights at periodic times agreed by the two parties whereas for an exchange-traded call option the exercise rights are set out in the contract specification and apply uniformly to all the contracts. In the latter there is no room for argument between parties whereas that is not true of the former where one party's 'understanding' of the terms may differ from the others.

We can look at some of the characteristics and differences between products by looking at the table below:

Product	Exchange traded	OTC	Liquidity exchange	Liquidity OTC	Duration
Interest rate swap	Yes – swap futures, contract size typically £	Yes – usually in amounts of £50 000 or $100 000 or greater		Good in 'common' durations and type of swap	2–50 years OTC
Bond futures	Yes – contract size varies Liffe Long Gilt is £100 000, CBOT US Treasury Bond is $ and the Eurex Eurobund is €	Not usually	Can range from excellent to poor. Eurobund on Eurex can trade around a million contracts per day	N/A	Nine months
Property derivatives	No	Yes	N/A	Few participants and depends on the type of product required	Negotiable
Stock options	Yes	Yes	Good but equally can be poor in some low volatility stocks and markets	Good in some stocks and baskets of stocks	ETD, from nine months to 2/3 years

There are many other differences and even quirks associated with derivative products, some driven by the underlying on which the derivative is based or the broad market conventions, or local market practices and, in the case of OTC derivatives, the client needs.

So, for example, we have forward swaps that have terms agreed today but that will not take effect for maybe 20 years, currency options on an exchange rate between two currencies but settled in a different currency and weather derivatives where the delivery is a compensating monetary amount, not the underlying weather!

Standard derivative products are where there is either a standard-ised contract or a negotiated but common structure, sometimes called 'vanilla' products and examples would be:

- Futures
- Forwards
- Traded options
- Interest rate swaps
- Currency swaps
- Call and put options.

More specialist derivative products are where there are very bespoke terms or complex structures involved; sometimes these are called 'exotic' products, and examples would be:

- Caps, floors, collars
- Barriers (Knock in/Knock out options)
- Amortising swaps
- Forward swaps
- 'Asian' style or Average price options.

These products and the terminology is covered in more detail in other chapters of the book.

It should be noted that although there may be different complexi-ties in the structure of the products it does not always follow that there is any particular complexity in the settlement or accounting for these products. For example, an 'exotic' option will often have a premium that is paid by the buyer in exactly the same way as a conventional call or put option has a premium that is paid by the buyer.

The exercise rights attached to the option may however be different and a particular trigger may cause the exercise, delivery or even ter-mination of the option.

Exchange-traded options have contract specifications determined by the exchange and an example is shown below:

Euronext.liffe Individual Equity Option Contracts

Unit of Trading	One option normally equals rights over 1000 shares*
Expiry Months⁺	January Cycle (J): means the 3 nearest expiry months from Jan, Apr, Jul, Oct cycle

	February Cycle (F): means the 3 nearest expiry months from Feb, May, Aug, Nov cycle
	March Cycle (M): means the 3 nearest expiry months from Mar, Jun, Sep, Dec cycle
Quotation	Pence/share
Minimum Price Movement (Tick Size and Value)	0.5 pence/share (£5.00) 0.25 pence/share (£2.50)**
Exercise Day	Exercise by 17:20 on any business day, extended to 18:00 for all series on a Last Trading Day
Last Trading Day	16:30 Third Wednesday in expiry month/ Third Friday in expiry month***
Settlement Day	Settlement Day is four business days following the day of exercise/ Last Trading Day
Trading Hours	08:00–16:30

+ From Thursday 18 April 2002, serial contract months and further dated quarterly months were introduced in VOD options, resulting in the extension of the maximum expiry to two years and the addition of two serial expiry months such that the first three calendar months are always available for trading. Further information is available in the Vodafone enhancement information sheet.

In addition, to become effective following the Mar 03 expiry on Wednesday 19 March 2003, serial longer-dated expiry months will be introduced in the following options: AstraZeneca plc (AZA), Aviva plc (CUA), Barclays plc (BBL), BP plc (BP), BT Group plc (BTG), Diageo plc (GNS), GlaxoSmithKline plc (GSK), HSBC Holdings plc (HSB), Lloyd TSB Group plc (TSB), Prudential plc (PRU), Royal Bank of Scotland Group plc (RBS) and Shell Transport & Trading Co. plc (SHL). Full details are available in the UK Equity Option product enhancements pages.

* Due to corporate action contract adjustments some equity options series may have a non-standard contract size. The unusual contract sizes page contains current details.

** The minimum price movement for the following equity options price is now 0.25 pence: British Airways plc (AWS), Invensys plc (BRT), BT Group plc (BTG), Cable & Wireless plc (C+W), Colt Telecom Group plc (CTM), Legal & General Group plc (LGE), Marks & Spencer Group plc (M+S), mmO$_2$ plc (OOM), Sainsbury (J) plc (SAN), Corus Group plc (STL), Tesco plc (TCO) and Vodafone Group plc (VOD). In addition, with effect from Monday 17 March 2003, the tick size of the following equity option contracts will be reduced from 0.5 pence to 0.25 pence: BAE Systems (AER), Barclays plc (BBL) and Shell Transport & Trading Co. plc (SHL).

*** The Last Trading Day of all UK equity options will change from the current third Wednesday of the expiry month to the third Friday of the expiry month. All maturities from the Jan 04 contract month onwards (with the exception of the Jan 04, Apr 04 and Oct 04 expiry months in VOD) will have the new third Friday Last Trading Day.

Trading Platform
- LIFFE CONNECT™ Trading Host for Equity Options.
- Algorithm: Central order book applies a price-time trading algorithm with priority given to the first order at the best price.
- Wholesale Services: Block Trading.

Contract Standard
Delivery will be 1,000 shares (or other such number of shares as determined by the terms of the contract).

Exercise Price Intervals
The interval between the exercise prices is set according to a fixed scale determined by the Exchange.

Introduction of new exercise prices
Additional exercise prices will be introduced after the underlying index level has exceeded the second highest, or fallen below the second lowest, available exercise price.

Option Premium
is payable in full by the buyer on the business day following a transaction.

Economic and Monetary Union/Euro
Please refer to the full contract specification on the LIFFE web site at www.liffe.com.

Unless otherwise indicated, all times are London times.

In the United States these products may only be offered and sold to prescribed entities under specified conditions.

Source: Euronext.liffe.

It is important to note that the expiry cycle of the Euronext.liffe individual equity options have been standardised to the March, June, September and December cycle. From the clearing and settlement point of view, there is a concentration of both activity, as the options series approaches maturity and closing transactions take place, in the exercise and assignment of positions.

A full list of the individual equity options and their tick size can be found at www.liffe.com.

From a settlement point of view it is also important to note the comment in the specification that relates to how the terms of the specification might change due to a corporate action event on the underlying. This is covered in more detail later in the book.

One very important aspect of the derivatives products available today is the demand by market participants. In the exchange-traded environment this is reflected by the liquidity in the products. Liquidity must be there for the users to have confidence that the obligations they have entered into can be terminated by 'closing out' the position by entering into an equal and opposite trade. For example, the seller of a future who creates a short position has an obligation to go to delivery and can remove that obligation only by purchasing a futures contract and then closing out the two offsetting positions. The details, with the exception of the price, must be the same, i.e. the maturity or delivery month.

It is vitally important that all closeouts are done correctly and immediately if unwanted delivery is to be avoided.

Example	
15th Jan. Sell 10 Mar. Widget futures @ $200	Position: Short 10 contracts
20th Feb. Buy 5 Mar. Widget futures @ $180	Position: Long of 5 contracts, short of 10 contracts
Close out 5 contracts	Position: Short 5 contracts
3rd Mar. Buy 5 Mar. Widget futures @ $150	Position: Long of 5 contracts, short of 5 contracts
Close out 5 contracts	Position: Flat (i.e. no obligations remain)

One way that an investor can ascertain the liquidity in an exchange-traded contract is to look at the data published by the exchange that shows the volumes traded and also the 'open interest'. The latter is the number of contracts held open and which therefore will either be traded out before maturity or will, in the case of futures, go to delivery. High daily volume but a very low open interest might indicate that there is little institutional client activity in that particular contract, i.e. fund managers hedging portfolios and therefore holding open positions. Most of the trading is speculative and is termed as 'day trading'. If volatility falls, so too will the volume being traded.

There are also some marked differences between financial and commodity derivatives. Producers and users of the relevant commodity, to enable a reduction in risk and forward planning on supply and demand, have traditionally used commodity derivatives. To some degree they are perhaps a more technical market place with a very specific user base. Today, given the demand to generate returns on investment and poorly performing equity markets and fairly stable interest rates, commodities are an asset class that fund managers have to look at and so the user base is widening.

Later in the book we will look at commodity derivatives in more detail but by comparing the following contract specification of an oil future with that of the index and bond future earlier in the chapter we will see how some characteristics of the contract are similar to a financial derivative whilst others are somewhat different.

IPE BRENT CRUDE FUTURES CONTRACT

BACKGROUND
The IPE Brent Crude futures contract provides a highly flexible hedging instrument and trading mechanism. It is tailored specifically to meet the oil industry's need for an international crude oil futures contract and is an integral part of the Brent pricing complex, which also includes spot and forward markets.

The Brent pricing complex is used to price over 65 per cent of the world's traded crude oil. The IPE Brent Crude futures contract is a deliverable contract based on EFP delivery with an option to cash settle.

FEATURES OF THE CONTRACT

Increased flexibility
By providing a contract parallel to the physical market, the oil industry has the opportunity to separate its pricing from supply arrangements by means of EFPs and basis trading, giving greater control and flexibility with regard to the timing of purchases and sales.

Price transparency
Real-time prices are available through the major data vendors. As a result, the price at which a particular contract is trading can be known instantly by all participants.

IPE Brent Weighted Average (BWAVE)

The IPE Brent Weighted Average is produced on a daily basis. It represents the average price of all trades executed on the market floor for each contract each business day. Following its introduction in November 1999, the BWAVE has itself become a benchmark price in its own right.

As well as being the basis for EFP, EFS and OTC transactions, it is used directly by several major oil producing nations as the basis for crude exports into Europe.

The BWAVE is published each day after the close of business for that day. It was first published on 16 November 1999. An average for each traded month is published in the prices section of this site. The average is calculated for each traded month using trades executed during IPE opening hours. All trade types are included in the calculation except EFPs, EFSs, settlement and contra trades which are excluded.

The calculation for each contract month is:
Sum (Trade Volume * Trade Price) Divided by – Total Daily volume (less EFP, EFS, Settlement & Contra Volume)

Due to the nature of the above calculation, the IPE does not publish a real-time BWAVE. The IPE does not support any unofficially generated BWAVE Index. The official Brent Weighted Average is updated once each business day.

Small parcel trading

The contract provides the opportunity to trade in small parcels (multiples of 1,000 barrels) of less than the standard cargo size necessary on the physical market.

Contract security

The London Clearing House Ltd (LCH) acts as the central counterparty for trades conducted on the London exchanges. This enables it to guarantee the financial performance of every contract registered with it by its members (the clearing members of the exchanges) up to and including delivery, exercise and/or settlement. LCH has no obligation or contractual relationship with its members' clients who are non-member users of the exchange markets, or non-clearing members of the exchanges.

CONTRACT SPECIFICATION

Date of launch
23 June 1988.

Trading hours
Open 02:00 Close 22:00(20:30 Fridays) – local time, electronic
Open 10:02 Close 19:30 – local time, open outcry.

Unit of trading
One or more lots of 1,000 net barrels (42,000 US gallons) of Brent
crude oil.

Specification
Current pipeline export quality Brent blend as supplied at Sullom
Voe.

Quotation
The contract price is in US dollars and cents per barrel.

Minimum price fluctuation
One cent per barrel, equivalent to a tick value of $10.

Maximum daily price fluctuation
There are no limits.

Daily margin
All open contracts are marked-to-market daily.

Trading period
Twelve consecutive months then quarterly out to a maximum
twenty-four months and then half yearly out to a maximum thirty-
six months.

Position limits
There are no limits to the size of position.

DELIVERY MECHANISM

Cessation of trading
Trading shall cease at the close of business on the business day
immediately preceding the 15th day prior to the first day of the
delivery month, if such 15th day is a banking day in London. If the
15th day is a non-banking day in London (including Saturday),

trading shall cease on the business day immediately preceding the first business day prior to the 15th day.

These dates are published by the Exchange.

Delivery/settlement basis

The IPE Brent Crude futures contract is a deliverable contract based on EFP delivery with an option to cash settle against the published settlement price i.e. the IPE Brent Index price for the day following the last trading day of the futures contract. If the contract is to be subject to the cash settlement procedure notice must be given (in accordance with LCH procedures) up to one hour after cessation of trading.

The IPE Brent Index

The Exchange issues, on a daily basis at 12 noon local time, the IPE Brent Index which is the weighted average of the prices of all confirmed 21 day BFO deals throughout the previous trading day for the appropriate delivery months. These prices are published by the independent price reporting services used by the oil industry.

The IPE Brent Index is calculated as an average of the following elements:

1. First month trades in the 21 day BFO market.
2. Second month trades in the 21 day BFO market plus or minus a straight average of the spread trades between the first and second months.
3. A straight average of all the assessments published in media reports.

Payment

Payment for contracts subject to the cash settlement procedure takes place through LCH within two business days of the cessation of trading.

Exchange of Futures for Physical (EFP) and Exchange of Futures for Swaps (EFS)

EFPs or EFSs may be reported to the Exchange during trading hours and registered by LCH up to one hour after the cessation of trading in the delivery month in which the EFP or EFS is traded. These allow more effective hedging opportunities for market participants with over-the-counter positions.

Law

The contract is governed by English law and includes provisions regarding force majeure, trade emergency and embargoes.

CLEARING AND REGULATION

Clearing

LCH guarantees financial performance of all IPE contracts registered with it by its clearing Members. All IPE Floor Member companies are either members of LCH, or have a clearing agreement with a Floor Member who is a member of LCH.

Regulation

The IPE is regulated in the UK by the Financial Services Authority (FSA) as a recognised investment exchange (RIE) under Part XVIII of the Financial Services and Markets Act 2000 (FSMA). Further, in April 2003, the IPE received no-action relief from the US Commodity Futures Trading Commission under Sections 5 and 5a of the Commodity Exchange Act to make all of its contracts available in the UK on the ICE Platform during the course of the entire trading day.

In accordance with the FSMA, all IPE General Participants based in the UK will be authorised and regulated by the FSA. Where General Participants are incorporated overseas, they will be regulated by the relevant regulatory authority in that jurisdiction.

Source: International Petroleum Exchange.

Derivative products can be of the same type and category, i.e. energy future, index options but it is important to stress that it cannot and must not be assumed that they are the same.

Over-the-counter derivatives

OTC derivatives as noted are negotiated or non-standardised products.

The advantages are the ability to tailor the product to meet a specific need or to transact in a single trade the required hedge or exposure strategy.

Over-the-counter derivatives are a large market, estimated by the International Swaps and Derivatives Association (ISDA) as being in trillions of US dollars in value. The combined OTC and exchange-traded markets can be reasonably said to be the largest market in the world.

How do OTC derivatives differ from exchange-traded products?

We have seen how exchange-traded products are standardised into contracts such as futures or options and that they are actively traded in the secondary market, i.e. someone who buys a futures contract can sell it in the market to someone else.

However the standardisation of the contracts does cause some problems when it comes to their use as hedging instruments, as the amount of an asset to be hedged is often different to the size of the derivative contract which is of course fixed by the standardisation process.

Also the hedger may want to hedge the position for say 12 months and the asset may be a combination of different classes of the asset.

Example

A fund manager has a portfolio of UK equity shares in a combination of FTSE 100 stocks and smaller companies and wants to hedge the portfolio for twelve months. The value of the portfolio is £2 425 000 and the FTSE 100 Index Future is currently trading at 5823.5.

If the fund manager decides to use the FTSE 100 Index Future there are some problems.

First, the most liquid contract will be the nearest maturity, a maximum of three months away. Therefore the futures position will need to be 'rolled' over through different maturities in the course of the 12-month period.

Secondly, the FTSE 100 Index Future is based on the 100 Stock Index and will therefore move in price according to the movement in the 100 stocks and will not take into account the change in value of the smaller companies not in the index. The hedge correlation is therefore not right.

Thirdly, the number of contracts required to hedge the portfolio would be:

$$\text{Portfolio}/£10 \times \text{Index Point} = 2\ 425\ 000/£10 \times 5823.5$$
$$2\ 425\ 000/58235 = 41.64 \text{ contracts}$$

You cannot trade 41.64 contracts so the fund manager must trade either 41 or 42 contracts. In either case the portfolio is not precisely hedged.

It is because of these kind of issues that hedgers often look to arrange an deal with a counterparty, usually a bank if it is a financial product that can be tailored to meet the precise hedging requirement.

On the other hand the fund manager knows that there is a counterparty risk in an OTC transaction and there is usually no clearing house guarantee, possibly a capital adequacy issue as a result of the exposure and that it is usually difficult or expensive to trade out of the position if the fund manager changes their mind.

Therefore both OTC and ETD derivatives can and often are used by the same organisation and the choice will depend on the strategy, risk appetite, liquidity, cost and ability to close the position if desired.

Characteristic	Derivative product	
	OTC	ETD
Contract terms	Tailored, negotiated, flexible and confidential	Standardised quantity, grade and maturity
Delivery	Negotiable dates and very often go to delivery	Defined delivery dates and terms but majority of contracts are closed out before delivery
Liquidity	Negotiated so can take time and can be limited by available counterparties	Usually very good for main contracts
Credit risk	Risk is with counterparty although some OTC products are now cleared by clearing houses Collateral is also used to reduce the risk	Clearing house becomes counterparty to all trades and manages risk through daily revaluations and margin calls

With the terms of OTC derivatives being totally negotiated, the operations function is different to that of the exchange-traded products.

Instead of standardised settlement processes and procedures, like daily variation margin (VM) calls, we have periodic or event-driven settlement.

We can illustrate this, as we look at some of the products traded over-the-counter in more detail later in the book.

To summarise derivative products we can say that derivatives are widely used instruments designed to transfer risk, at the same time offering opportunities to arbitragers, speculators, corporate treasurers and investors like fund managers and private clients.

Derivatives can be either exchange-traded, where they are standardised products, or, where they are negotiated and bespoke. Some types of derivative instruments are available in both forms. As versatile products, whether traded on an exchange or over-the-counter they have differing characteristics, uses and of course settlement conventions.

The clearing and settlement process will be either via a clearing house (exchange-traded and some types of OTC transactions) or from counterparty to counterparty (OTC). The clearing house provides a central guarantee and manages the counterparty risk as well as the settlement and delivery processes. Documentation and events tend to drive the settlement process in OTC transactions.

As with all types of transactions in financial markets, reconciling trade details, positions, cash movements, etc. is absolutely vital. With derivatives the problems of errors are magnified by the gearing or leverage characteristics so that any unresolved errors and unreconciled trades or positions are potentially going to lead to significant loss.

That said, many millions of derivative transactions take place daily around the world without problems occurring because the user understands the product and the processes involved.

Derivative markets continue to grow steadily and in some locations spectacularly. New products are constantly being designed and requested and the infrastructure in the industry changes constantly to meet these challenges.

3

The role of the clearing house

In the derivatives industry we find different terminology being used around the world. This is true with the description used to identify the organisation appointed by or incorporated into the exchange to manage the clearing, settlement and risk of the exchange and its members.

Clearing house is commonly used but equally we might come across clearing corporation, clearing organisation as well as 'clearer', clearing firm or clearing member but the latter three refer to members rather than the exchange clearing entity.

For simplicity we will use the term 'clearing house'.

In general terms the role of the clearing house is to act as a counterparty to both sides of the trade thereby breaking the direct counterparty relationship between the two trading counterparties. It is fundamental to the integrity and credibility of the market for which it operates, as its purpose is to guarantee the performance of each and every transaction.

By assuming the legal responsibility for the trade, the clearing house removes any risk on each other that the two original counterparties might have had.

In addition the clearing house also acts as risk manager, and provides the settlement routing and data to members, and statistical and other data to the exchange and external parties often including regulators.

There are two main types of clearing house; those that are a division of the exchange itself and indistinguishable from the exchange who own them, and those that are independent of the exchange with their own financial backing. In most cases, for these independent clearing houses, shareholders, the members of the markets and the clearing house, or a combination of these three provide the necessary financial backing.

The London Clearing House (now LCH.Clearnet) and the Options Clearing Corporation (OCC) in Chicago are examples amongst clearing houses of ones that clear business for more than one exchange.

This can be advantageous for the broker as clearing members of, for instance, Euronext.liffe, London Metal Exchange (LME) and IPE because it means only one point of settlement for all of their trading in these markets as LCH.Clearnet is the clearing house for these exchanges.

Clearing houses must be financially robust in order to sustain a default in the market(s) for which they operate. The financial standing of the clearing house is a very important consideration for brokers when they are contemplating becoming clearing members of an exchange. It is also an important issue for companies researching the potential of trading in the market, as they need to know that their trades will be efficiently settled and that their positions will be secure in the event of another unrelated party causing a default in the market.

In the United Kingdom the FSA have designated LCH.Clearnet as a Recognised Clearing House and regulate it. This gives the members and users of the market comfort that it is a properly organised and approved clearing house. Of course the members of LCH.Clearnet must also adhere to the rules and regulations laid down by the clearing house. Any failure to do so would almost certainly be deemed to put a firm in breach of these rules and regulations and in turn it would constitute a default. That would result in the firm concerned being banned from acting as a clearing house member not only in the market concerned but in all probability would result in curtailment or suspension of the status in relation to other markets.

The LCH.Clearnet also has registration as a Designated Clearing Organisation (DCO) granted by the US regulator The Commodity Futures Trading Commission (CFTC).

When did the first clearing house come into existence?

One of the oldest clearing houses is that established by the Chicago Board of Trade as the following statement illustrates:

The Chicago Board adopted a motion suggesting that it establish a modern clearinghouse. Probably no more progressive and far-reaching step was ever taken to insure prices accurately reflecting supply and demand. I believe it will be effective.

Secretary of Agriculture William Jardine in a Report to President
Calvin Coolidge, 1925

Source: The Clearing Corporation.

Originally formed as the 'Board of Trade Clearing Corporation' it is
today called The Clearing Corporation (CCorp) and provides services
to the Eurex US electronic derivatives market. Its importance in the
history and development of the clearing of derivatives exchanges can
be seen by the following extract taken from their website:

In the history of the world's financial markets, perhaps no single
entity has had a greater impact on the safety and soundness of the
clearing process than The Clearing Corporation (CCorp). Based on
a tradition of independence, integrity, and innovation, The Clearing
Corporation has established itself as the model for the majority of
the world's clearinghouses.

September 3, 1925 is among the most important dates in the history of the futures industry. It was on that day, more than 75 years
ago, that the Board of Trade Clearing Corporation, now named The
Clearing Corporation, was founded by the Chicago Board of Trade
(CBOT®) membership.

The Clearing Corporation is one of the oldest independent clearinghouses in the world. It has not only survived, but flourished,
through the Great Depression and periods of recession, war, and
rapid technological and economic change. Its world-class standing
has been and will continue to be built upon three fundamental
concepts: Independence, Integrity, and Innovation.

The importance of its independence as a corporate entity cannot be
overestimated. This quality has allowed The Clearing Corporation
to make objective decisions during periods of substantial stress
with one goal in mind–financial integrity for the clearing and
settlement process.

Integrity goes hand-in-hand with independence. Clearing members
know that The Clearing Corporation makes decisions based on
safety and soundness for the marketplace and nothing else.

The financial integrity of the marketplace also has been aided
through The Clearing Corporation's commitment to innovation
since its founding. This commitment is evidenced by its history as
an industry leader–from its first use of computers in 1963 to the

development of on-line trade entry and risk analysis systems. The Clearing Corporation continues to make every effort to enhance the clearing and settlement process for its members.

Source: Clearing Corporation website.

The statement above sums up many of the attributes of a clearing house in general and today the many clearing houses that operate do so with efficiency, cost effectiveness and security of the markets and members as their primary objectives.

We can look at some of the clearing houses and in doing so build up a picture of the role of these important organisations in the market infrastructure.

We can start with a clearing house closely linked to the CCorp through the Eurex exchange.

Eurex AG

To be eligible for clearing membership of Eurex, an organisation must be a financial institution located within the European Union or Switzerland authorised to operate custody business, credit operations and receipt of margin by customers in the form of securities and cash. Applicants must have a prescribed level of proven equity capital as well as contribute a specific amount to the Eurex Clearing AG clearing fund.

Clearing Members can be either General Clearing Member (GCM) or Direct Clearing Members (DCM). General Clearing Members are authorised to clear their own transactions as well as those of their customers and those of Non Clearing Members clearing through them. Direct Clearing Members are entitled to carry out the clearing for their own transactions, those of their customers and of affiliated NCMs. Although the clearing member is responsible for settlement, there is the possibility to stipulate a separate settlement institution for the settlement of transactions.

There are prerequisites for settlement, which include an account at the Bundesbank (of the Federal Republic of Germany) and a securities account at one central depository recognised by Eurex Clearing AG. These accounts are to be held either by the settlement institution or by the clearing member with the necessary power of attorney. Importantly one of the requirements is that the Settlement Institution shall use appropriate technical equipment including back-office systems in order to guarantee the correct recording, accounting and supervision of all transactions. A combination of the functions of trading, clearing and settlement are possible within a financial institution.

The structure and relationships possible with Eurex AG are shown below in Figures 3.1 and 3.2.

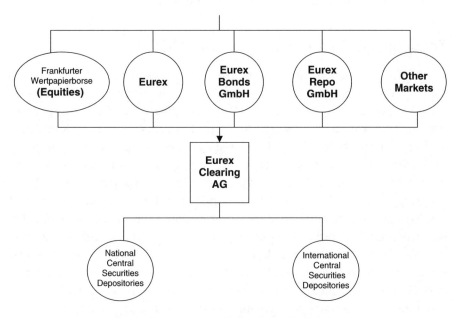

Figure 3.1 Eurex AG Structure. *Source*: Eurex.

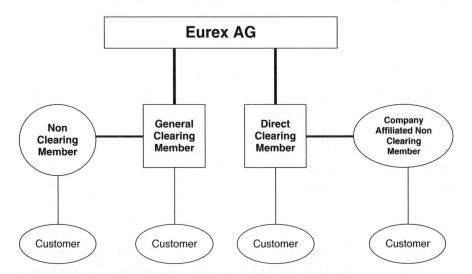

Figure 3.2 Eurex AG Structure. *Source*: Eurex AG.

As we can see, the GCM and DCM have a direct relationship with the clearing house. The DCM can only clear business of an affiliated company who is a NCM of Eurex whereas the GCM can clear business for any NCM.

Customers can have a relationship with the GCM, DCM, an affiliated NCM of the DCM or any NCM of the exchange.

The Options Clearing Corporation (OCC)

Options Clearing Corporation is the largest clearing organisation in the world for options and was the first clearing house to receive an AAA rating from Standard & Poor's Corporation. Operating under the jurisdiction of the Securities and Exchange Commission (SEC) and the CFTC, OCC clears US-listed options, futures and options on futures on a number of underlying financial assets including stocks, currencies, stock indexes and interest rate products. The OCC's Clearing Membership consists of approximately 130 of the largest US broker/dealers, US futures commission merchants and non-US securities firms representing both professional traders and public customers. The American Stock Exchange, the Chicago Board Options Exchange, the International Securities Exchange, the Pacific Exchange and the Philadelphia Stock Exchange share equal ownership of OCC.

It has in recent years developed and introduced a completely new clearing system called ENCORE.

The ENCORE has enabled real-time processing capabilities, increased flexibility by accommodating growth in options volume and new products, and provided secure Internet access to OCC's customers.

LCH.Clearnet

There are several key stages in the 'clearing process' much of which is generic across clearing houses.

A key stage is when and how the counterparty relationship between the two parties to the trade on the exchange converts to a relationship between the clearing house and each of the trade participants. That stage is often referred to as novation.

Novation

The process of creating the trade in the name of the clearing house as counterparty to each member is called novation. In this process the clearing house becomes buyer to every seller of each transaction and seller to every buyer of each transaction. At this point, the clearing member has no counterparty risk in the market for their trade other than with the clearing house. All open positions are only held with the clearing house and it becomes irrelevant which market member the trader dealt with originally. Once this process is completed, the clearing house is in a position to effect settlement of the two transactions (Figures 3.3 and 3.4).

Settlement takes place between the Members and the clearing house, not with each other. Counterparty risk between the members has been removed.

The settlement process on LCH.Clearnet is secured by the use of a direct debit system, known as the Protected Payment System (PPS).

Protected Payments System

LCH.Clearnet Limited operates PPS for the transfer of funds to and from Clearing members. A Clearing member is required to maintain a PPS bank account(s) in London in Great Britain Pounds (GBP) and for each currency in which it incurs settlements at one of the participating PPS banks. Different banks can be used for different currencies. Clearing Members are also required to maintain a USD account at one of the specified banks for PPS in the United States. Any bank charges arising from the operation of a PPS account are for the account of the Clearing member. A PPS mandate must be completed, the original of which is held at the PPS bank and a copy lodged with LCH.Clearnet Limited.

Figure 3.3 Trade Relationship

NOVATION

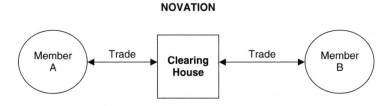

Figure 3.4 Novation

Clearing Process System (CPS)

First, we can look at the CPS for Euronext.liffe and IPE. The CPS is an extension of the Trade Registration System (TRS), using the same computer terminals and the data processed by TRS.

TRS functions

The following functions are performed within TRS:

- Trade matching
- Presentation of particulars to LCH for registration
- Allocation and designation of trades to a position-keeping account, for example house/principal account, client account, NCM account.

Recorded trades flow into CPS throughout the trading day. Any correction to trade data is performed within TRS and results in the automatic amendment of the trade in CPS. Trade details can be disseminated to Members via the Trade Status Change Stream (TSCS).

CPS functions

The following functions are performed within CPS:

- Settlement
- Position keeping
- Account transfers
- Calculation of margin
- Option exercise
- Tender notification and delivery/option allocation.

Trade Registration System provides Members with the facility to print reports which include TRS, CPS and LCH.Clearnet banking reports.

Now let us look at the situation regarding the LME.

The LME Clearing System is an extension of the LME Matching System, using the same computer terminals and the data processed by the Matching System.

Matching System functions

The following functions are performed within the Matching System:

- Trade matching and designation of trades to a position-keeping account
- Trade suspension and acceptance outside a lots or price range limit
- Trade confirmation and presentation of trades to LCH for registration.

Clearing System functions

The following functions are performed within the Clearing System:

- Settlement
- Position maintenance
- Margin calculation
- Deliveries (values, batch allocations) and option exercise allocation processing.

The TRS and CPS facilities allow a clearing member to reconcile and monitor the transactions being created and placed into their account at the clearing house and for which they will be liable for settlement the next day.

Risk management

A very significant role of the clearing house is managing the risk created by the transactions on the exchange. From setting the criteria for membership of the clearing house to establishing default rules, using margin systems and requiring daily settlement of resulting obligations of all members, the clearing house controls the risk that the exchange, the members and the users of the market face.

We will look at margin in more detail in another chapter, but it is as much about the risk management tools like margin as it is about the technology and risk management skills of the clearing house itself.

Globally, clearing houses daily manage trillions of dollars of derivatives transactions and it is a testament to their skills and professionalism that when a member does default, it is managed in such a way that the exchange and its members are not usually affected.

Summary

Without a clearing process the transactions on an exchange would not get to the stage of settlement. However, the role of the derivative clearing house is not just about preparing trades for settlement and then making sure that happens, it is about managing risk as well.

The clearing house is responsible to the exchange and its own members to protect them from unnecessary risks created by parties failing to meet their obligations generated by their derivative activities. It provides a central clearing counterparty to the clearing members and establishes the rules and regulations under which its member firms must operate.

The clearing house is a regulated and recognised professional risk management organisation and as such it rightly demands high levels of professionalism and capabilities from its members, as well as adequate financial status to be able to meet the obligations of its activities.

These requirements extend to the quality of systems, the quality and experience of the management, effectiveness of operational risk controls and competence in the operations teams.

It is not difficult to see that the teams working within clearing members must be fully aware of and able to meet the high standards that the clearing house demands.

That way *everyone* is protected.

4

Futures processing

Futures contracts are margined instruments. This means that the full value of the contract is not exchanged at the time of the trade but instead the open position that the transaction creates is marked to market. This revaluation process creates a profit or loss on the position on a daily basis, which is in turn due for settlement. Futures contracts also attract what is known as an initial margin or deposit that is required from the holders of open futures positions.

Futures are designed to go to delivery and the contract standard published by the exchange informs users whether the delivery is in physical form, i.e. if the underlying asset is deliverable, or if it is cash-settled or if there is an alternative delivery process.

The futures contract specification is, therefore, a key document that also includes details of the maturity months available, the unit of trading and other important information related to the contract. Each exchange publishes contract specifications and also 'summary' specifications that outline the main details of the contract. Each exchange not surprisingly has its own style.

From an operations point of view these specifications contain essential static data such as the minimum price movement and value, maturity months, etc. Terminology used in different markets is evident in the details contained in the specifications; for example, in the CME the Point Description describes what in the UK would be called the minimum price movement and value (commonly called the tick size).

An example of the Eurodollar futures contract listed on the CME is shown below.

Eurodollar Futures

Trade Unit	Eurodollar Time Deposit having a principal value of $1,000,000 with a three-month maturity.
Point Descriptions	1 point = .01 = $25.00
Contract Listing	Mar, Jun, Sep, Dec, Forty months in the March quarterly cycle, and the four nearest serial contract months.
Strike Price Interval	N/A
Product Code	Clearing = ED Ticker = ED GLOBEX = GE

Trading Venue: Floor

Hours	7:20 a.m.–2:00 p.m.Holidays LTD(Monday 5:00 a.m.)^ See note*	
Listed	All listed series	
Strike	N/A	
Limits	No Limit	
Minimum Fluctuation	Regular	0.01 = $25.00
	Half Tick	0.005 = $12.50
	Quarter	0.0025 = $6.25 for nearest expiring month.

Trading Venue: GLOBEX®

Hours	Mon/Thurs 5:00 p.m.–4:00 p.m. & 2:00 p.m.–4:00 p.m.; Shutdown period from 4:00 p.m. to 5:00 p.m. nightly; Sun & Hol 5:00 p.m.–4:00 p.m. LTD-5:00 a.m.
Listed	All listed series
Strike	N/A

Limits	200 points	
Minimum Fluctuation	Regular	0.01 = $25.00
	Half Tick	0.005 = $12.50
	Quarter	0.0025 = $6.25 for nearest expiring month.

Trading Venue: SGX

Hours	Sun/Thur 9:20 p.m.–4:00 a.m.	
Listed	All listed series	
Strike	N/A	
Limits	No Limit	
Minimum Fluctuation	Regular	0.01 = $25.00 Months 11 thru 40
	Half Tick	0.005 = $12.50 Months 2 thru 10
	Quarter	0.0025 = $6.25 for nearest expiring month.

Source: CME.

We can compare this contract specification with that of the Eurodollar Future listed on Euronext.liffe:

Three Month Eurodollar Interest Rate Futures Contract

Unit of Trading	Interest rate on three month deposit of $1,000,000
Delivery Months	March, June, September, December and four serial months, such that 24 delivery months are available for trading, with the nearest six delivery months being consecutive calendar months
Quotation	100.000 minus rate of interest

Minimum Price Movement (Tick Size & Value)	0.005 ($12.50) for all delivery months
Last Trading Day	11:00 London time – Two London business days prior to the third Wednesday of the delivery month
Delivery Day	First business day following the Last Trading Day
Trading Hours	07:00 to 21:00 London time
Daily Settlement	Positions settled to nearest 0.005 20:00 London time

Trading Platform
- LIFFE CONNECT® Trading Host for Futures and Options.
- Algorithm: Central order book applies a pro-rata algorithm, but with priority given to the first order at the best price subject to a minimum order volume and limited to a maximum volume cap.
- Wholesale Services: Asset Allocation, Block Trading, Basis Trading.

Exchange Delivery Settlement Price (EDSP)
Based on the British Bankers' Association offered rate (BBA US$ LIBOR) for three month US$ deposits at 11:00 London time on the Last Trading Day. The settlement price will be 100.000 minus the BBA US$ LIBOR. Where the EDSP Rate is not an exact multiple of 0.001, it will be rounded to the nearest 0.001 or, where the EDSP Rate is an exact uneven multiple of 0.0005, to the nearest lower 0.001 (e.g. BBA US$ LIBOR of 1.53750 becomes 1.537).

Contract Standard
Cash settlement based on the Exchange Delivery Settlement Price.

Source: Euronext.liffe.

Apart from terminology some of the differences in these two contracts are fundamental; for instance the CME contract is traded on the CME trading floor, on the electronic system Globex and also in Singapore on SGX.

To fully understand the structure of the markets and the associated processes involved, let us start by looking at the situation in the exchange and clearing house environment.

Futures trading

Futures are traded on exchanges either by an electronic dealing system or by an open outcry in designated trading areas on an exchange floor. In some cases futures are traded by both mechanisms, for instance on the CBOT, but a majority of the major markets are today solely electronic.

Prices and the volume of contracts traded of the futures available for trading are distributed by the exchange and major information systems like Bloomberg on a continuous basis during the trading period.

At the close of trading each day the exchange publishes a closing price and that price is used to compute the VM and value positions held in portfolios or trading books.

A trade is made between two members of the exchange through the relevant trading mechanism.

The trade details will be matched, automatically on an electronic exchange and through a matching system on an open outcry market. The matching fields will be:

Contract	The reference or identifier of the relevant listed contract, often numeric or alpha
Quantity	The number of contracts the trade represents
Maturity	The month in which the contract will mature
Price	The price traded by the two parties
Buy/Sell	The act of either being the buy or the sell side of the transaction
Time of trade	Time at which the trade is recorded as being carried out
Counterparty	The person on the opposite side of the trade often identified by a standard mnemonic

In the case of an electronic exchange these details are automatically captured from the trader's action on the dealing screen. In the case of an open outcry market, either the details are input into an electronic matching system by the trader or alternatively a deal ticket is completed and is then passed to support staff for input to the exchange matching system.

Members are advised of the trades that have successfully matched and those that have not, as well as trades that are alleged against the member. This is either in a trade match system or through reports made available during the trading day at intervals to members. There will be a deadline by which time an unmatched/alleged trade must have been resolved by amendment or deletion. Fines will be applied to members failing to resolve these problems by the prescribed time.

Once matched the trade is passed to the clearing system.

Clearing process

In the clearing process the trade details are enhanced and placed into the account of the clearing member. The enhancement may be the identification of 'house' and 'client' trades for posting to the respective account or closeout instruction indicating that the trade should be used to closeout (offset) an existing position either entirely or partially. In some markets much of this enhancement is carried out in trade match systems and the enhanced trade details then move into the clearing system.

The clearing house provides each member with the details of their updated positions and the member will reconcile these to their own position records.

The clearing house will calculate the extent of the obligations of the member's positions and will settle these usually on T + 1 (trade day + 1). The obligations to be settled will be:

1. The VM generated by the open positions being marked to market and closeouts
2. The initial margin created by new open positions
3. The return of initial margin on closed-out positions
4. Any settlement amount related to delivery of futures
5. Any fees related to activity.

The settlement of the obligations is made via a secured payment system to and from an account specifically designated and held at an approved bank on the list published by the clearing house.

The structure in the market is shown in Figure 4.1.

The exchange member may also be a clearing house member. If they are not then they will need to appoint a clearing member to settle their trades with the clearing house.

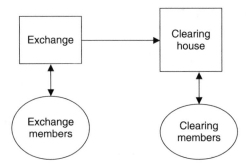

Figure 4.1 Member Relationships

Where a client is trading onto the futures market, the relationship might look like that in Figure 4.2.

In Figure 4.2 the client is trading through an exchange member and settling with a clearing member. It should be noted that (a) the client could trade and settle with the exchange member irrespective of whether that exchange member was also a clearing member of the clearing house and (b) it is common for clients to use several exchange members to undertake transactions on their behalf but to have those trade settled with a single broker, referred to as clearing broker, global clearing broker or even central clearing broker (the Figure 4.2 would be applicable in a central clearing arrangement and the whole process is explained in more detail later in the book).

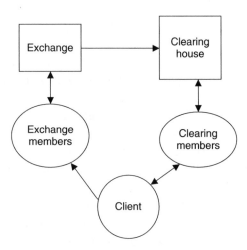

Figure 4.2 Client Relationships

To summarise the exchange and clearing process environment we can say that:

1. Trades take place between exchange members.
2. Trades are made via the trading mechanism applicable to the exchange.
3. Trades are matched either via the dealing system or through a matching process.
4. The status of trades is often available in real time through a trade processing/registration system or at a minimum by periodic reports from the exchange.
5. Unmatched/alleged trades need to be resolved and repaired within a set time frame or a member will incur fines.
6. Once matched both the buy and the sell elements of the trade passes to the clearing system.
7. The clearing system allows clearing members to see the updated positions and settlement obligations they have with the clearing house.
8. The obligations are settled automatically at a predetermined time via a secured payment system with a designated bank.
9. A failure to meet obligations to the clearing house would result in the member facing 'being put into default'.
10. The clearing member reconciles the positions and settlement obligations shown by the clearing house to their own records.

Use of futures

Futures contracts are used for a variety of reasons such as speculation or hedging, as well as strategies like asset allocation in fund management and also for arbitrage opportunities.

If we consider that futures contracts are synthetic versions of the underlying on which they are based we can easily see how they are used by speculators and hedgers alike.

Take the case of a fund manager who is worried about the direction of the equity market. Let us suppose that the equity exposure of the fund is mainly in FTSE 100 stocks with a current value of £15 000 000. If the index falls, the fund's current good performance will be affected. The fund manager believes that the UK equity market will fall gradually over the next three months but then will recover to its current level.

The manager could sell the equity portfolio at the current level and then repurchase the shares at the lower level. There are two problems here. First, costs to the fund in terms of the broker's commission for selling and buying the shares. Secondly, what if the index does not fall?

The manager looks at the Euronext.liffe futures market where the FTSE 100 Index Futures contract is listed. The manager knows from the contract specification issued by the exchange that the size of the contract is £10 × the index point and the futures are trading at 5495, which means one contract equals a value of £54 950. The manager works out that to cover the portfolio value of £15 000 000 they will need £15 000 000/£54950 or 272.97 rounded to 273 futures contracts.

The manager sells (goes short) the futures contracts and in doing so has 'locked in' a value for index of 5495 and thus the portfolio value of the equity asset class. Now, if the index does fall, the loss on the shares in the portfolio is offset by the gain on the short position in the futures. If the index does not fall, the fund manager will buy back the futures contracts as the hedge is no longer needed.

The advantages for the fund manager are that the portfolio itself has not been disturbed, the commission on the futures trades will be less than if the shares had been sold and then repurchased, and if the market moves unexpectedly upwards the fund manager can very quickly close out the futures and leave the fund to benefit from the rise in the market. That would be more difficult and potentially expensive if selling and then repurchasing the shares were involved.

So futures contracts helped the fund manager hedge. Now let us look at the case of the speculator.

Suppose you are generally bullish of the equity market but at the moment you have only limited funds available, how can you benefit from the rise in the market you are anticipating?

We saw above that a FTSE 100 Index Futures contract is trading at 5495 and the contract represents an exposure with a value of £54 950. Because the contract is not settled on the basis of its full value but instead it works on a margin basis in the form of a deposit plus a daily settlement of the revaluation of the position, it will cost far less than £54 950 to buy the same exposure to the market.

So the speculator gets an initial exposure worth £54 950 for a seemingly ridiculous low outlay. Well that is absolutely true but, and it is a big 'but', the speculator must be prepared and able to settle immediately any losses that might occur. Let us look at an example:

The speculator buys 1 FTSE futures contract with a maturity in Sep. @ 5495 at 10.00 a.m. in the morning. Around lunchtime there is very bad news from America and the FTSE responds to the news by falling quite rapidly to close at 5450, a fall of 45 points.

From the contract specification the speculator sees that each half-point fall is the equivalent of £5 per contract. The speculators position is now valued 45 points lower than the purchase value, or in monetary terms 90 half-points (called ticks) × £5 or £450. In addition there is a deposit, or initial margin, that needs to be paid of maybe £3000.

The speculator must pay to their broker this loss plus the deposit tomorrow. Even worse, the next day the FTSE futures fall by 200 points to 5250, which equates to 400 ticks × £5 = £2000. Again this must be settled with the broker the next day.

The speculator has accumulated a loss of £2450 in two days and has to settle that loss plus they have to provide £3000 in cash or acceptable collateral to cover the initial margin requirement.

So the speculator has the advantage of a very large exposure gained at a fraction of the true cost but has, nevertheless, to provide over £5000 in just two days to settle the deposit and losses.

Of course the index and the futures might have risen instead of falling and the speculator now has a profit of £2450 but still has to provide the deposit amount of £3000 in cash or collateral.

Futures clearing and settlement

The hedger and the speculator have entered respectively into a sale and a purchase of futures contracts. In the above example each trade has been made via a broker onto the Euronext.liffe market and will now be cleared by the exchange clearing house, LCH.Clearnet.Clearnet.

Clearing houses serving derivative exchanges are what is called central clearing counterparties. This means that at a point when the transactions that have taken place on the exchange are registered, the clearing house becomes the counterparty to the trade (Figure 4.3).

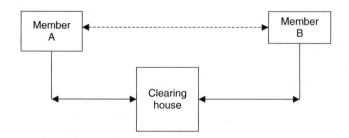

Figure 4.3   Central Counterparty

Notes: In Figure 4.3, Member A trades with Member B on the exchange (dotted line). For a time they have a direct counterparty risk. However, as the trade is registered (solid line) at the clearing house, the counterparty changes to being the clearing house and the two members no longer have a risk on each other. The process is called novation.

The clearing house will calculate the VM and initial margin (deposit) for the transactions, resulting in open positions and closed-out positions.

Variation margin

Variation margin is the revaluation by a mark to market (MTM) process of positions. The resultant value is for settlement with the clearing house.

Example

An investor purchases 1 March Long Gilt futures contract on Euronext.liffe at a price of 102.05. From the contract specification we see that the tick size and value is 0.01 and £10 respectively. That evening the contract's closing market price on the exchange is 102.10.

It has moved 5 ticks (102.10 − 102.05), so the VM will be:

$$\text{Number of contracts} \times \text{number of ticks} \times \text{tick value} = 5 \times 5 \times £5$$
$$= £125$$

The investor has purchased (gone long) the contracts and the price has risen, so the VM represents the profit the investor has made. It will be paid to the investor. Had the price gone down, the investor would have had to pay the broker. The VM will be settled the next day, T + 1, between the broker and the investor and between the clearing house and the clearing broker. Every day the position is open, this revaluation, or mark to market, process will occur and the resultant VM will be due for settlement.

Initial margin

Open positions in futures contracts are subject to a margin call that is a returnable deposit payable to the clearing house by the clearing member and by a client to their broker. The margin is referred to as either a deposit or more often the initial margin. The rate at which the margin call is made is determined by the exchange clearing house and, as it is a risk management tool employed by the clearing house, it can be changed if volatility in the market changes.

Initial margin requirements can be covered by either cash or, in most cases, collateral that is acceptable to the clearing house or broker.

Initial margin and collateral are dealt with in more detail in Chapter 8 but let us look at an example of the VM and initial margin settlement flow for some FTSE 100 Index Futures trades.

Example

Day One
Trade 1: Purchase of 250 June FTSE 100 Index Futures @ 4344
Closing Market Price: 4350

Day Two
Trade 2: Purchase of 250 June FTSE 100 Index Futures @ 4360
Closing Market Price: 4365

Day Three
Trade 3: Sale of 300 June FTSE 100 Index Futures @ 4362.5
Closing Market Price: 4357.5

Assume that the initial margin rate is £500 per contract and the sale on Day Three is a closing sale.

Tick size and value = 0.5 and £5 respectively.

What is the settlement flow?

Date	Trade B/Fwd C/Fwd	Long/ Buy	Short/ Sale	Price	Closing price	Variation margin	Initial margin
xx/xx/xxxx	Trade	250		4344.0	4350.0	15 000	125 000
yy/xx/xxxx	B/fwd	250		4350.0	4365.0	37 500	125 000
	Trade	250		4360.0	4365.0	12 500	125 000
zz/xx/xxxx	B/fwd	500		4365.0			250 000
			300	4362.5	4365.0	−7500	
	C/fwd	200		4365.0	4357.5	−15 000	
aa/xx/xxxx	B/fwd	200		4357.5			100 000

First Day: Variation margin = 15 000 receivable
Initial margin = 125 000 payable

Settlement Total Due Next Day = (a) 110 000 payable (15 000 VM
receivable − 125 000 1 M payable)
(b) 15 000 receivable plus need
to deposit collateral of atleast
125 000

Second Day: Variation margin = 37 500 plus 12 500 receivable
Initial margin = 125 000 payable

Settlement Total Due Next Day = (a) 75 000 payable
(50 000 VM receivable −125 000
1 M payable for new trade)
(b) 50 000 receivable plus need
to deposit another 125 000
collateral

Third Day: Variation margin = (7500) + (15 000)
Initial margin = 150 000 receivable

Settlement Total Due Next Day = (a) 127 500 to receive
(return of 1 M 150 000 less
22 500 VM payable)
(b) £25 500 to pay but return of
150 000 collateral

(a) = cash settlement of both variation and initial margin
(b) = cash settlement of VM and collateral deposited to cover initial
margin

Futures delivery

Futures contracts are designed to go to delivery. As we know, delivery can be either physical delivery of the underlying or by cash settlement. There can also be an Exchange For Physical (EFP) or Exchange For Swap (EFS) option on some futures.

The physically delivered futures can be commodities or financial products like bond futures or some stock futures. The exchange decides what is deliverable, i.e. the type and grade of commodity or the bond. A list of deliverable grades or bonds is then published to members. For example, Figure 4.4 shows the list of deliverable Bunds against the Eurex Bund future and Figure 4.5 gives the specification of the contract.

Expiry month Dec 2004

Deliverable Bond ISIN	Coupon Rate (%)	Maturity Date	Conversion Factor
DE0001135234	3.75	04.07.2013	0.852400
DE0001135242	4.25	04.01.2014	0.880175
DE0001135259	4.25	04.07.2014	0.874942

Expiry month Mar 2005

Deliverable Bond ISIN	Coupon Rate (%)	Maturity Date	Conversion Factor
DE0001135242	4.25	04.01.2014	0.882591
DE0001135259	4.25	04.07.2014	0.877455

Expiry month Jun 2005

Deliverable Bond ISIN	Coupon Rate (%)	Maturity Date	Conversion Factor
DE0001135242	4.25	04.01.2014	0.885049
DE0001135259	4.25	04.07.2014	0.880217

Figure 4.4   Deliverable Bond List

Eurex German Bund Future Contract Specifications (Version 03 Mar 2004)

Contract Standard
A notional long-term debt instrument issued by the German Federal Government with a term of $8\frac{1}{2}$ to $10\frac{1}{2}$ years and an interest rate of 6 per cent.

Contract Size
EUR 100,000

Settlement
A delivery obligation arising out of a short position in a Euro-BUND Futures contract may only be fulfilled by the delivery of specific debt securities – namely, German Federal Bonds (Bundesanleihen) with a remaining term upon delivery of $8\frac{1}{2}$ to $10\frac{1}{2}$ years. The debt securities must have a minimum issue amount of 2 billion euros.

Quotation
In a percentage of the par value, carried out two decimal places.

Minimum Price Movement
0.01 per cent, representing a value of EUR 10.

Delivery Day
The 10th calendar day of the respective delivery month, if this day is an exchange trading day; otherwise, the immediately following exchange trading day.

Delivery Months
The three successive months within the cycle March, June, September and December.

Notification
Clearing Members with open short positions must notify Eurex which debt instruments they will deliver, with such notification being given by the end of the Post-Trading Period on the last trading day in the delivery month of the futures contract.

Last Trading Day
Two exchange trading days prior to the delivery day of the relevant delivery month. Trading in the contract for this delivery month ceases at 12:30 CET.

Daily Settlement Price
The closing price determined within the closing auction; if no price can be determined in the closing auction or if the price so determined does not reasonably reflect the prevailing market conditions, the daily settlement price will be the volume-weighted average price of the last five trades of the day, provided that these are not older than 15 minutes; or, if more than five trades have occurred during the final minute of trading, the volume-weighted average price of all trades that occurred during that period. If such a price cannot be determined, or if the price so determined does not reasonably reflect the prevailing market conditions, Eurex will establish the official settlement price.

Final Settlement Price
The volume-weighted average price of the last ten trades, provided they are not older than 30 minutes – or, if more than ten trades have occurred during the final minute of trading, then the volume-weighted average price of all trades that occurred during that period – is used to determine the final settlement price. The final settlement price is determined at 12:30 CET on the last trading day.

Figure 4.5 Eurex German Bund Future *Source*: Eurex.

The delivery process

For financial futures, the clearing members with short positions tender for delivery of the underlying to the account of the clearing house. In turn the clearing house assigns the delivery to the holder of a long position. Delivery of shares or bonds will take place via the relevant Central Securities Depository (CSDs).

The procedures of the delivery process are determined by the clearing house and must be adhered to by the clearing members.

Most exchange-traded derivative products are designed to go to delivery, i.e. the underlying on which the derivative is based will physically move from seller to buyer. However, the delivery for some products may be a cash amount rather than the asset itself.

For example, an index futures contract is designed to provide an instrument that tracks the market or sector on which it is based. The S&P Indices, the Nikkei, the DAX, the FTSE 100, etc. are all based on a basket of stocks. To effect physical delivery for the futures contracts based on these indices by the weighted amount of all the shares in the index which would need to be delivered would be an onerous, costly and, therefore, unattractive prospect particularly as the main purpose of the contract is to enable hedging rather than necessarily taking delivery of shares for each company. Instead, on delivery, the futures and options contracts are settled by a cash payment or receipt, the final VM amount created by settlement against an exchange-established final price on expiry day.

The delivery process is different for each futures contract and varies from exchange to exchange. The UK and US government bond futures contracts have a delivery period during which delivery can be initiated on any day. Commodity contracts also have a delivery or tender period during which delivery can be initiated. The length of the tender period is variable depending on the commodity involved. Other futures contracts have a single delivery day on which delivery can be initiated.

Where physical delivery of the asset is contained in the contract specification the process can vary from product to product, typically in reflection of different cash market delivery practices. For futures contracts, it is always the holder of the short position who has the rights and can decide at what point during the delivery period that delivery will be entered into. In certain cases, like government bond futures contracts, the sellers have the right to decide what will be delivered from the list of deliverable bonds published by the exchange.

The reason for this is the nature of physical delivery. The holder of the short position is the party that has the obligation to deliver the physical asset, while the holder of the long position will be paying cash to buy the asset. It is a more involved process to move assets into the approved point. Therefore, the seller of these assets needs to have more flexibility than the party who has to pay funds into the relevant place.

Where a notional contract, such as a government bond, is being delivered, the seller has the choice because they can deliver any of the bonds which meet the acceptable criteria laid down by the exchange and are published on the Deliverable List. The seller may only have one of the bonds on the Deliverable List so they will need to deliver that particular bond. If the seller has a range of bonds on the Deliverable List, then they can choose which of the bonds is most preferable for them to deliver. There would be one bond, which is known as Cheapest to Deliver.

The delivery obligations are all laid down by the Exchange in the contract specifications, so each participant should understand the procedures involved in the delivery process. The buyers should understand that they are subject to the actions of the holders of the short positions.

It is important to remember that not all positions are taken through to delivery. In general only a small percentage of contracts go to physical delivery. The underlying value of those transactions can, however, be very high. Where a contract does not need to be held until delivery, an opposing trade can be transacted in the market, and the position can be closed out so that no further obligations are outstanding.

At delivery or expiry of each contract, the Exchange will issue the price, at a time determined in the contract specification, which will be used to calculate the settlement figure for each contract. This price is referred to as the Exchange Delivery Settlement Price (EDSP) or something similar. For government bond contracts the EDSP is used to calculate the invoicing amount; for interest rate contracts and index contracts, which are cash settled, it is used to calculate the settlement amount.

There are variations to the rules, procedures and timings governing delivery, and it is important to recognise this and check on the specific situation that applies for the market and product on a case-by-case basis. Failure to do this can result in breaches of rules caused by late or incorrect delivery with the possibility of financial penalties levied by the exchange/clearing organisation and also possible financial loss due to the erroneous delivery. Since clearing members are directly responsible to the clearing organisation, there is a risk of reputational damage where delivery procedures are not adhered to.

For delivery of a contract like the Euronext.liffe Long Gilt futures there are three very critical days in the delivery process:

First notice day

This is the first day that the holders of short positions can give notification to the exchange/clearing organisation that they wish to tender a position for delivery. A holder of a long position must have closed their position the previous trading day if they did not want the possibility of taking delivery against their position.

Last notice day

This is the final day that notification of delivery will be possible. On most exchanges all outstanding short futures contracts will be automatically delivered to open long positions.

Last trading day

This is often the day preceding the last notice day and is the final opportunity for holders of long positions to trade out of their positions and avoid delivery.

Ultimately, it is always the clearing member's responsibility to ensure that delivery of contracts is made strictly in accordance with the relevant exchange or clearing house procedures. More importantly, it is also the clearing member's responsibility to ensure that delivery does not happen unless the clearing member or its client is fully aware of the situation and consent to the delivery. Unplanned delivery can be costly and embarrassing.

It is therefore very important that all of the clearing member's staff and those of its clients are fully aware of the consequences of going to delivery in each contract. The exact procedures and timings are very important but they should always be confirmed when entering the delivery period as procedures and timings change from time to time. An easy mistake that can occur is one which relates to local times. Most exchanges quote delivery times in their local time, which in itself should not present too many problems but confusion can occur when in, for instance, the UK there is a change from Greenwich Me̶n Time to or from British Summer Time.

It is vitall᷾   ᷾tant that positions which are coming up to the delivery pe   itored by both the clearing member and the end-clien᷾   g member will need to ensure that its clients are full᷾   delivery situation and their responsibilities. Ultimately,   g member is liable if the delivery process is entered into b᷾   ke or if procedures are not followed thoroughly.

Where the delivery procedures are not followed in accordance with the rules and regulations, the exchanges have a range of penalties and fines, which may be invoked. In some cases these are quite heavy, as they are designed to be prohibitive and to ensure that the delivery procedure is both efficient and credible. This has a direct effect on the success of the exchange and the reason for participants wanting to trade on the exchange. If the delivery process were not efficient, and participants could not be sure that making or taking delivery would take place properly, then it might deter them from trading on the exchange.

For clearing members, the payment of fines and penalties is not the only issue. There is a significant element of reputational risk because the Exchange is often at liberty to publicise information relating to fines for breaches of delivery procedures. Ultimately, the clearing house and exchange could suspend the clearing member and revoke their rights to trade on the Exchange if they felt that the clearing member was not managing their business properly.

LCH.Clearnet.Clearnet delivery procedures

LCH.Clearnet sets down all its delivery rules and procedural requirements in its publication, 'General Regulations, Default Rules and

Procedures'. One of the key stipulations is that LCH.Clearnet procedures must be read in conjunction with the rules of the exchange.
The exchange rules and administrative procedures will always take
precedence in cases of conflict.

LCH.Clearnet defines its delivery procedures, some of which are
common to all contracts which LCH.Clearnet clears. These address
issues such as:

- Nomination of Transferors and Transferees.
- How tendered lots are to be allocated to receiving members.
- House and client accounts are always treated separately.
- Making the EDSP available on the Clearing Processing System (CPS).
- Margin remains held as both initial and VM on open contracts subject to delivery.
- The method of delivery of information which needs to be communicated to LCH.Clearnet.
- The delivery timetables.

The LCH.Clearnet has introduced a stand-alone computer system
specifically for electronically communicating delivery information with
its members, applicable to Euronext.liffe deliverable bond contracts
only. A product called The Deliveries Package enables all Euronext.liffe
bond deliveries to be automated in this way. All clearing members
involved in Bund and Gilt deliveries must submit and retrieve delivery
information using this system.

Users of The Deliveries Package are issued with security passwords,
which are updated at every bond delivery period.

A key factor to note is that members must always be sure to meet
delivery deadlines, notwithstanding the performance or failure of the
electronic communication system. Therefore, LCH.Clearnet stresses
that members should allow sufficient time to fulfil deadlines as laid
down in the procedures. Failure to do so would constitute late delivery for which fines and other possible disciplinary actions could be
imposed by the Exchange.

The process of delivery

The exact process involved in delivery varies from exchange to
exchange and often from contract to contract. However, the process
can be followed by looking at key stages that apply in general. The
process used at Euronext.liffe for UK Gilt contracts is given as an
illustration.

Stage One

Once a short position has been tendered for delivery, the holder advises the clearing organisation of the number of contracts, the asset to be delivered and if relevant, whether it is from the Proprietary (House) or Client Account. This may be communicated electronically using the relevant delivery system.

Stage Two

The clearing organisation allocates the short position to a corresponding long position and notifies the member which is the holder of the long position.

For Euronext.liffe contracts, this allocation is always on a random basis. The process that LCH.Clearnet employs gives each clearing member's account a sequential number according to their mnemonic sequence. The system chooses a random starting number then it begins to allocate the short positions to corresponding long positions in sequence from the starting point.

Stage Three

The clearing organisation calculates the invoice amount and advises both the short and long position holders of the amount it requires to be paid/received. This calculation takes into account the variation margin that has already occurred by incorporating the Exchange Delivery Settlement Price (EDSP) on the day of notice and a price factor.

The formula used for the calculation of the invoice amount for a delivery of a Euronext.liffe Government Bond futures contract is:

(EDSP) × (price factor) × (unit of trading) + (accrued interest)

Note: Euronext.liffe publish a list of the deliverable bonds together with their price factors and accrued interest amounts prior to the first notice day.

Stage Four

The short position holder delivers the quantity of asset to the clearing organisation and receives the invoice amount. The clearing organisation delivers the asset to the long position holder in exchange for the invoice value.

The clearing members for the long and short positions need to have accounts at the relevant depository, i.e., CREST to be able to make and take delivery from the clearing organisation account at the depository.

The Delivery Process for Government Bond Futures

Where futures markets offer a government bond futures contract, it normally relates to a notional bond rather than an actual bond which is available for trading. If the participant wishes to enter into the delivery process for a government bond contract then they need to study the contract specification carefully. For example:

Long Gilt Future

Unit of trading	£100,000 nominal value notional Gilt with 6 per cent coupon
Delivery Months	March, June, September, December
First Notice Day	Two business days prior to the first day of the delivery month
Last Notice Day	First business day after the Last Trading Day
Delivery Day	Any business day in the delivery month (at seller's choice)
Last Trading Day	11.00 hrs Two business days prior to the last business day in the delivery month
Quotation	Per £100 nominal value
Minimum Price Movement (Tick Size & Value)	0.01 (£10.00)
Trading Hours	08.00–18.00 hrs

Contract standard

Delivery may be made of any gilts on the list of deliverable gilts in respect of a delivery month as published by the Exchange on or before the tenth business day prior to the First Notice Day of such delivery month. Holders of long positions on any day within the Notice Period may be delivered against during the delivery month. All Gilt issues included on the list will have the following characteristics:

- having terms as to redemption such as provide for redemption of the entire Gilt issue in a single instalment on the maturity date falling not earlier than 8.75 years from, and not later than 13 years from, the first day of the relevant delivery month;

- having no terms permitting or requiring early redemption;
- bearing interest at a single fixed rate throughout the term of the issue payable in arrears semi-annually (except in the case of the first interest payment period which may be more or less than six months);
- being denominated and payable as to the principal and interest only in pounds and pence;
- being fully paid or, in the event that the Gilts issue is in its first period and is partly paid, being anticipated by the Board to be fully paid on or before the Last Notice Day of the relevant delivery month;
- not being convertible;
- not being in bearer form;
- having being admitted to the Official List of the London Stock Exchange;
- being anticipated by the Board to have on one or more days in the delivery month an aggregate principal amount outstanding of not less than £3bn, in the case of a Gilt issue which was first issued more than 12 months before such delivery month or £1.5bn otherwise, which by its terms and conditions, if issued in more than one tranche or tap or issue, is fungible.

Exchange Delivery Settlement Price (EDSP)
The Euronext.liffe market price at 11.00 hrs on the second business day prior to Settlement Day. The invoicing amount in respect of each Deliverable Gilt is to be calculated by the price factor system. Adjustment will be made for full coupon interest accruing as at Settlement Day.

As each Gilt issue trades in the cash market with varying coupons and final maturity dates, the exchange must find a mechanism by which these securities can be valued and traded at one unique price prevailing on the exchange. This involves the creation of an index with a value which can be uniformly applied to all of the bonds making up the list of securities which may be delivered. This list is known as the deliverable basket. A price factor system is designed to reprice each of these issues onto a uniform scale which can be used at the Exchange. These price factors are determined by a formula that calculates the price at which a specific issue would trade to yield, 6 per cent in the case of Euronext.liffe Long Gilt contracts, as of the delivery date. Euronext.liffe publishes the price factor for each Gilt in the deliverable basket as delivery approaches.

Delivery of the Euronext.liffe Long Gilt contract is physical at maturity and as in other deliverable contracts the seller has the choice of which Long Gilt is going to be delivered. However, the seller does not have a free choice. The Gilt must be selected from the List of Deliverable Gilts issued by the Exchange. This List of Deliverable Gilts with their associated price factors and accrued interest amounts is published by the Exchange ten days prior to the Last Trading Day of the relevant delivery month and distributed to its members.

Gilt deliveries must take place through the London Clearing House's account at CREST, as LCH.Clearnet is counterparty to each delivery.

As no single Gilt exists to meet the exact Euronext.liffe Long Gilt contract specification, the buyers of the Gilt in the delivery process must pay an invoice amount in settlement which takes into account the varying specifications of the Gilt which is delivered.

We have already seen that the formula for the invoicing amount is:

(exchange delivery settlement price × price factor × unit of trading) + accrued interest.

Cheapest to Deliver

As we have already noted earlier, the seller has the choice of which of the Gilts to deliver, from the deliverable list issued by the Exchange. At delivery, the buyer should expect to receive the Gilt, which will create the maximum profit or minimum loss for the seller when assessing the fair price of the futures contract. This is known as the Cheapest to Deliver Gilt.

In order to determine the Cheapest to Deliver Gilt, you need to know the price, or conversion, factors which are applicable. These price factors are issued by the Exchange. It enables the calculation of the price at which the Gilt would trade, for each 1 nominal, to yield the notional 6 per cent coupon of the Euronext.liffe Long Gilt futures contract during the delivery period. The use of the conversion factor allows higher coupon Gilts to be deliverable, when yields are below the notional 6 per cent coupon.

Source: LCH Clearnet.

The delivery process of Gilts through CREST

Delivery of the underlying Gilt stocks, in respect of Euronext.liffe Long Gilt contracts, are made through CREST usually by using the CREST book entry transfer system or possibly by using Stock Transfer Forms (STFs) accompanied by the appropriate physical certificate(s) for private clients. Matching acceptance instructions must be input by the Transferee via its CREST terminal. Payment for the delivered Gilts will be made to LCH.Clearnet from the Transferee via the CREST book entry system.

Transferors must deliver Gilts to LCH.Clearnet by the method specified on the Seller's Delivery Notice.

The Transferor must input the necessary confirmed inward delivery details via their CREST terminal. Sellers must ensure that sufficient Gilts are in their Transferor's CREST account to meet the delivery in full so that the delivery will not fail. Payment for delivered Gilts is made to the Transferor through the CREST book entry system.

Not all clearing members have direct access to CREST accounts, but often their clients will have their own accounts. If the clearing member delegates the function and allows their clients to deliver the Gilts directly to LCH.Clearnet's account in CREST, then they must ensure that the clients understand the procedures and timings exactly. Ultimately, whatever the client does or does not do, the responsibility always lies with the clearing member. In this situation, the clearing member can have very little control over what happens.

Commodity futures delivery

Commodity futures will have very different processes for delivery, depending on the type of commodity that underlies the future.

For example, the IPE Brent Crude future delivery mechanism is shown below.

IPE Brent Crude Delivery Mechanism

Unit of trading
One or more lots of 1,000 net barrels (42,000 US gallons) of Brent crude oil.

Specification
Current pipeline export quality Brent blend as supplied at Sullom Voe.

Cessation of trading

Trading shall cease at the close of business on the business day immediately preceding the 15th day prior to the first day of the delivery month, if such 15th day is a banking day in London. If the 15th day is a non-banking day in London (including Saturday), trading shall cease on the business day immediately preceding the first business day prior to the 15th day. These dates are published by the Exchange.

Delivery/settlement basis

The IPE Brent Crude futures contract is a deliverable contract based on EFP delivery with an option to cash settle against the published settlement price i.e. the IPE Brent Index price for the day following the last trading day of the futures contract.

If the contract is to be subject to the cash settlement procedure notice must be given (in accordance with LCH.Clearnet procedures) up to one hour after cessation of trading.

The IPE Brent Index

The Exchange issues, on a daily basis at 12 noon local time, the IPE Brent Index which is the weighted average of the prices of all confirmed 21 day BFO deals throughout the previous trading day for the appropriate delivery months. These prices are published by the independent price reporting services used by the oil industry.

The IPE Brent Index is calculated as an average of the following elements:

1. First month trades in the 21 day BFO market. IPE/Brent Crude Futures Contract Spec/3.
2. Second month trades in the 21 day BFO market plus or minus a straight average of the spread trades between the first and second months.
3. A straight average of all the assessments published in media reports.

Payment

Payment for contracts subject to the cash settlement procedure takes place through LCH.Clearnet within two business days of the cessation of trading.

Exchange of Futures for Physical (EFP) and Exchange of Futures for Swaps (EFS)

EFPs or EFSs may be reported to the Exchange during trading hours and registered by LCH.Clearnet up to one hour after the cessation of trading in the delivery month in which the EFP or EFS is traded. These allow more effective hedging opportunities for market participants with over-the-counter positions.

Law

The contract is governed by English law and includes provisions regarding force majeure, trade emergency and embargoes.

Source: IPE.

Physical delivery of LME contracts

The LME contracts allow producers, fabricators, merchants and consumers to insure against price risk. An important aspect of LME futures contracts is that, with the exception of the LMEX contract, they are not settled until the prompt date.

They are not cash-cleared in the way that other futures contracts are and take their characteristics from those of forward contracts. Initial margins and variation margins against risk exposure will be called during the term of a contract, but the value of a contract is not paid until delivery.

The LME lists eight metals and one index, the LMEX, comprising the six primary base metals. The LME's eight contracts are:

1. Copper grade A
2. Primary aluminium
3. Standard lead
4. Primary nickel
5. Tin
6. Special high grade zinc
7. Aluminium alloy
8. North American Special Aluminium Alloy (NASAAC).

In commodities the specified delivery date of a futures contract is referred to as the prompt date, by which time either the position must be closed or a delivery will take place. On the LME, the final trading day, the last day a position can be closed, is two days before the prompt date.

Most commodity markets are usually based on monthly prompt dates. The LME metal futures contracts run on a daily basis for a period of three months. The use of daily prompt dates is an important difference between the LME and other futures exchanges. It means the Exchange combines the convenience of settlement dates tailored to individual needs with the security of a clearing house for its clearing members.

After the three-month date, the daily prompts for forward trading are reduced to weekly and then monthly contracts out to 15, 27 or 63 months forward.

The LME also offers traded options contracts based on each of these futures contracts, together with traded average price options contracts (TAPOs) based on the monthly average settlement price (MASP) for all metals futures contracts.

All LME prices are quoted in US Dollars, but the LME permits contracts in sterling, Japanese yen and Euros and provides official exchange rates from US Dollars for each of them.

Trade is conducted in lots rather than tonnes, with each lot of aluminium, copper, lead and zinc amounting to 25 tonnes. Nickel is traded in 6-tonne lots, tin in 5-tonne lots aluminium alloy and NASAAC in 20-tonne lots.

The contract for each metal sets out the shapes, weights and methods of strapping. The contract specifications are for the quality and shape, which are most widely traded and demanded by industry.

Example Contract Specification

LME Copper Grade A Futures Contract Specification

Contract	Grade A Copper
Lot Size	Lot size 25 tonnes (with a tolerance of $+/-2\%$)
Form	Grade A cathodes conforming to BSEN 1978:1998
Weight	Each parcel of copper cathodes placed on warrant shall not exceed 4 tonnes

Delivery Dates	Daily for cash to 3 months (first prompt date two working days from cash). Then every Wednesday from 3 months to 6 months. Then every third Wednesday from 7 months out to 63 months
Quotation	US dollars per tonne
Minimum Price Movement	50 US cents per tonne
Clearable Currencies	US dollar; Japanese yen; sterling; euro

Source: LME.

Delivery against LME contracts is in the form of LME warrants, which are bearer documents of title enabling the holder to take possession of a specified parcel of metal at a specified LME-approved warehouse. Each LME warrant is for one lot of metal, the tonnage of which is dependent on the contract specification. The front of the LME warrant displays information about the parcel of metal, including its brand, the exact tonnage, the shape and the location.

Warrants are issued by the warehouse companies at the request of the owner of the metal once it is properly stored in an LME-approved warehouse and the warehouse company has ensured conformity with the LME's Special Contract Rules for that metal. These rules include, but are not limited to, the technical specification of the metal, its shape, weight and bundling. The metal must also be of a brand that is approved and listed by the LME.

The LME is very proud of its global role in providing a pricing mechanism that reflects the state of the markets it serves. For the LME, an essential factor in achieving this aim is to maintain a spread of approved warehouse locations that reflects the needs of the users of the market and to monitor those approved locations for continued compliance with the listing criteria. Such criteria include the need for locations to be in areas of net consumption or to be 'gateways' serving those areas of net consumption and also to meet the LME's strict legal, taxation and customs requirements. There are over 400 warehouses in some 32 locations covering the United States, Europe, the Middle and the Far East.

The LME is also active in assessing potential new locations as good delivery points. The location criteria are designed to ensure that metal is stored in locations close to where it is needed, rather than areas of production, thus assisting traders and industry in meeting their last resort delivery requirements as readily as possible.

In common with many financial futures only a relatively small percentage of LME contracts actually result in delivery, as the vast majority of contracts prove to be hedging contracts bought or sold back before falling due for settlement. As a result, the deliveries that do take place, either in or out of warehouse, will reflect the physical market demand and supply, and the information included in the LME's daily stock reports can play a major part in the market's assessment of the worlds metals prices.

The SWORD system

Each lot of metal, for which a warrant is issued, is held in an LME-approved warehouse. The warrant gives right of possession to the specific lot of metal against which it was issued. The warehouse companies, acting through their agents in London, issue warrants. The LME has many different warehouse locations and the delivery of warrants is at the seller's option.

In January 1999 the LME and the launched a joint initiative called SWORD that became fully operational later that year.

The SWORD is a secure electronic transfer system for LME warrants which can now be held in a central depository. All LME warrants are produced in a standard format with a barcode. Warehouse companies that are issuing these warrants ensure that the details are known to SWORD which acts as a central database, holding details of ownership and is subject to stringent security controls. The transfer of the ownership of LME warrants between SWORD members is a matter of seconds and all rent payments are automatically calculated.

The SWORD brings a number of benefits, particularly in administrative efficiency by removing the physical transfer of warrants and the manual operations that involved. It also reduces the number of times a warrant has to be passed by hand, as warrants no longer need to be physically transferred from owner to owner every time the metal is bought or sold.

Soft commodities

We can compare the various requirements associated with delivery between a soft commodity like cocoa and those of the preceding energy and metals contracts by looking at the Euronext.liffe Cocoa Futures Contract Specification.

Cocoa Futures

Unit of Trading	Ten tonnes
Origins Tenderable	Cameroon, Côte d'Ivoire, Democratic Republic of Congo (formerly known as Zaire), Equatorial Guinea, Ghana, Grenada Fine Estates, Jamaica, Nigeria, Republic of Sierra Leone, Togo, Trinidad and Tobago Plantation, Western Samoa at contract price. All other growths tenderable at set discounts
Quality	As per full contract specification (Excerpt is contained in the Appendices)
Delivery Months	March, May, July, September, December, such that ten delivery months are available for trading
Delivery Units[1]	Standard Delivery Unit – bagged cocoa with a nominal net weight of ten tonnes Large Delivery Unit – bagged cocoa with a nominal net weight of 100 tonnes Bulk Delivery Unit – loose cocoa with a nominal net weight of 1,000 tonnes[2]
Price Basis[2,3]	Pounds sterling per tonne in an Exchange Nominated Warehouse in a Delivery Area which is, in the Board's opinion, in or sufficiently close to Amsterdam, Antwerp, Bremen, Felixstowe, Hamburg, Humberside, Le Havre, Liverpool, London, Rotterdam, or Teesside
Minimum Price Movement (Tick Size & Value)	£1 per tonne (£10)
Last Trading Day	Eleven business days immediately prior to the last business day of the delivery month at 12:00
Notice Day/ Tender Day	The business day immediately following the last trading day
Trading Hours	09:30–16:50

[1] Where necessary upon tender, a seller may be instructed by the Clearing House to convert a Bulk Delivery Unit into Large and/or Standard Delivery Units, or a Large Delivery Unit into Standard Delivery Units.

[2] Bulk Delivery Units are tenderable at a discount of £20 per tonne to the contract price.

[3] Contact the Exchange to determine which Delivery Areas have Dual Capacity Warehousekeepers (i.e. those nominated for the storage of Bulk Delivery Units as well as Standard and Large Delivery Units).

Trading Platform
- LIFFE CONNECT® Trading Host for Futures and Options.
- Algorithm: Central order book applies a pro-rata algorithm, but with priority given to the first order at the best price subject to a minimum order volume and limited to a maximum volume cap.
- Wholesale Services: Against Actuals.

Contract Standard
- Delivery may be made of Cocoa meeting the contract requirements.
- Unless otherwise indicated, all times are London times.

Source: Euronext.liffe.

Once again we can see that there are specific issues related to the delivery of cocoa including the origin, types of beans, etc.

It is quite clear that the commodity derivatives sector is in general a more technical market from a delivery point of view, and whilst physical delivery might not occur for the majority of transactions there are still, nevertheless, significant amounts of a commodity subject to the delivery process in final settlement of the contract obligations and as such any settlement team whose organisation is or might become involved in commodities must have a good understanding of the peculiarities associated with each type of commodity contract.

Workflow road map

Workflow

We can use a futures transaction of a purchase of 10 Sep. FTSE 100 Index Futures @ 4500 as an example to follow the workflow associated with on-exchange futures transaction.

In the following text we describe the process from the point of view of the broker, in this case a clearing member of an exchange, and also make reference to the workflow from an institutional client's position.

Trade capture

In the case of an electronic exchange these details are automatically captured from the trader's action on the dealing screen. In the case of an open outcry market the details are either input into an electronic matching system by the trader or alternatively a deal ticket is completed, which is then passed to support staff for input to the exchange matching system.

The actual clearing and settlement processes for markets differ as do the procedures adopted internally by firms. However, the following table illustrates the kind of option trade details that are likely to be needed. These will be:

Data	Detail	Source
Future	FTSE 100 Indexes	Trade ticket/Deal system
Market	Euronext.liffe	Trade ticket/Deal system
Maturity	September	Trade ticket/Deal system
Multiplier	£10 × Index	Contract specification
Tick size	0.5 = £5	Contract specification
Buy/Sell	Buy	Trade ticket/Deal system
Counterparty	xxx	Trade ticket/Deal system
Time of trade	00/00 dd/mm/yy	Trade ticket/Deal system
Transaction reference	xxxxxx	System generated
Client/Principal trade	Client	Trade ticket/Deal system
Execution broker	N/A	Trade ticket/Deal system

The institutional client that has placed the order with their broker has in essence the same data requirements but obviously has no reference to Principal Trading.

It is important to note that high-quality static data on futures, like all products, is crucial as today most firms use systems for the processes involved from trade to settlement and beyond.

Trade validation

The transaction must be validated.

This process needs the confirmation of the trade details received from the front office against the data being received from the market.

This may be via a system link to the exchange, for instance the Trade Registration System (TRS) used on Euronext.liffe.

The TRS provides details of transactions that have taken place in the market. Each trade is shown whether the firm has transacted it, it has been 'given in' by an executing broker for the firm's account or client account or it is to be 'given up' to another clearing member. It is then accepted by the member and internally confirmed against the order details.

As the trades showing are registered to the firm's account at the clearing house and are therefore due for settlement of any obligations arising, it is important that any discrepancy between the trade details and the order details is notified to the relevant dealer/trader and resolved quickly.

Trade enrichment

To be able to process the trade internally we will need to:

1. Book the trade to the relevant client account or trading book.
2. Identify if the trade is an opening or closing transaction.
3. Perform the margin calculation (if applicable).
4. Charge the relevant commission.
5. Charge other fees (if applicable).
6. Perform the settlement of the transaction with the clearing house.
7. Effect the client settlement instructions.

Booking trade to the relevant client account or trading book

The details for this will be on the database and the posting will either be automatically generated by the dealing system to the operations system or need to be input from a trade ticket or similar document. The accurate posting of the transaction is a vital function as the trade may have been done to close out an existing obligation, and a failure to successfully post the trade and complete the close-out could cause an unwanted assignment. The next section looks at this issue.

Identify opening and closing transactions

The trades booked to a client account will be either opening transactions, i.e. creating a position, or closing transactions where there is an existing position that is offset by the trade being booked. When this occurs the two transactions are closed out to create a realised profit or loss. If a successful closeout takes place it must happen in the internal records and also in the Client Account of the Firm held at the clearing house.

If the latter does not take place then there is a risk that an action such as an assignment of the long futures open position could take place. The result could be increased settlement costs.

Principal trading accounts are usually settled net, automatically in both the internal and the clearing house accounts.

Perform margin calculation

If the transaction undertaken is creating a short position then there will be a margin requirement that needs to be calculated. In most cases this will be either Standardised Portfolio Analysis of Risk (SPAN) or Theoretical Intermarket Margin System (TIMS) depending on the exchange on which the trade has taken place. Both these margin systems are described more fully in the Appendices 9 and 10.

The margin call will be covered by collateral in the form of either cash or collateral or a combination of both. This collateral will be needed for both the initial and the variation margin call (if the net of the positions is a loss) made by the exchange clearing house to the firm and by the firm to its client.

Margin will be posted to a margin account in the ledger.

Charge the relevant commission

For client transactions, there will be a commission payable to the broker. The commission may be a rate/amount per contract or some other rate agreed by the sales desk and the client.

This rate can be charged on the opening trade, the closing trade or split so that both the opening and the closing transactions carry a commission.

The amount of commission charged on the transaction may include what is called floor brokerage. This is the fee charged by an execution broker who is giving up the trade to a clearing broker. The clearing broker will charge the client or trading book the combined floor brokerage and clearing fee and then settle the floor brokerage with the execution broker (Figure 4.6).

Commission will be posted to a commission account in the ledger and floorbrokerage to a brokerage account pending settlement with the executing brokers.

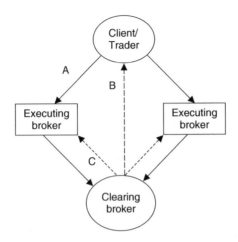

Figure 4.6 Floor Brokerage Relationships

Notes: A = Trade B = Commission (inc floorbrokerage fee) C = floorbrokerage.

Charge other fees

There are several other fees that may need to be charged on a transaction. These will include exchange fees, regulatory fees and taxes.

Although the client may be charged an all-inclusive commission, they may want to see the breakdown of commission and fees and the data will need to be posted separately in the ledgers for accounting and management information purposes.

Perform the settlement process with the clearing house

A clearing broker will need to settle the initial margin requirement and any VM with the clearing house. This will most likely be on T + 1. The amount to be settled will be included in the net settlement figure for the clearing member and will be collected or paid out by the clearing house through its normal settlement process. In many cases the settlement amount is netted across obligations by currency.

The calculation for the VM amount is:

Number of contracts × number of ticks × tick value

In our example of the purchase of 10 Sep. FTSE 100 Index Futures @ 4500, if we assume the contract closes @ 4505 this would be:

10 contracts × 10 ticks × £5 = £500

due to the clearing member and due to the clearing members client.

The transaction will need to be posted to the clearing house account with the contra entry being the client account or trading book if it was in the principal/house account.

Effect the client settlement instructions

The transaction will be posted to the relevant client account or trading book. If it is a client trade it will be booked either to their omnibus account or to a designated account. In the latter case the client will need to advise the broker of which account to book the trade to. This could be done via the sales desk or via the operations team or may be notified via both routes.

The client may maintain a monetary balance in their account(s), in which case the transaction will update the balance. Confirmation of the transaction and the revised open option position and cash balance on the account will be advised to the client.

There are several ways that this could take place.

1. Client access to accounts
2. By email
3. By fax
4. By telephone
5. Hard-copy report.

In each case the important thing is to establish that the client is aware of the settlement requirement and the impact on their open position and cash position. The process is also a fundamental control acting as an affirmation or acceptance by the client of the transaction and associated settlement. An audit trail for the trade is also established with the transaction showing in the clearing account and backed off in the client account.

Clearing account	Client account
Buy 10 FTSE 100 Index Futures @ 4500	Buy 10 FTSE 100 Index Futures @ 4500

The settlement amount of £500 as a result of the MTM process is due to the clearing member and is therefore payable to the client. It is important to remember that the firm that has the clearing account, and the broker at the clearing house is the party the clearing house deals with, irrespective of how or when the client and broker settle the obligations.

Summary

The processing of futures contracts is really about the VM and the initial margin requirements plus the ability to successfully reconcile the open positions with the clearing house, broker and client.

Part of that process is managing the posting and allocation of trades, closeouts and also deliveries, should they occur as a result of tender or assignment.

Financial futures and commodity futures have not only various similarities but also many differences. As a result, good-quality static data on margin rates, deliverable underlyings, notice days, last trading day and of course the tick size and value are all important to the operations teams.

The delivery process for physical and cash-settled products are also very different, and the deadlines and responsibilities are important to understand. The clearing member is liable to the clearing house for the settlement of contracts and if they are operating for a client it is vital to ensure that they are aware of the disciplines associated with settlement and delivery.

Futures contracts are legally binding obligations on both the buyer and the seller, so efficient position management is crucial if unwanted deliveries, and therefore cost, are to be avoided.

5

Options processing

Option contracts have different characteristics to futures. The key differences are that options are based on *calls* and *puts*. Options are traded on- and off-exchange and are usually referred to as traded options when based on a security or currency and as options on futures or futures options when the underlying is a futures contract.

A call option gives the buyer the right, but not an obligation, to take delivery of the underlying, whilst a put option confers the right but not the obligation to make delivery of the underlying.

As a result of this characteristic the risk/reward profile is very different for the buyer and the seller. The buyer cannot lose more than they pay for securing the right. This is shown in Figure 5.1.

In the Figure 5.1 the option is illustrated by the bold line. If the buyer paid 10 for the right to buy a call option then the maximum loss that can be made is 10 and we see the bold line takes a horizontal line when that amount of loss of value is reached. However, the underlying is shown as the dashed line and here the loss continues as the underlying falls in value. On the upside the underlying immediately makes a profit as the price rises but cost of securing the right must first be recovered by the rise before a profit can occur. This is shown in the Figure 5.1 by the bold line crossing the arrowed line further along the rise, i.e. after it has increased in price by 10. For the option buyer this is the breakeven point and any further increase in the value of the underlying will be a profit. Conversely, for the seller this is the point when a loss will start to occur.

The situation for the buyer of a put option is reversed as shown in Figure 5.2.

The seller of the option, called the writer, has an obligation. They receive the payment from the buyer to secure the right, often referred to as the premium, but must wait to see if the buyer exercises their right. If they do not, then the writer keeps the premium. If they do,

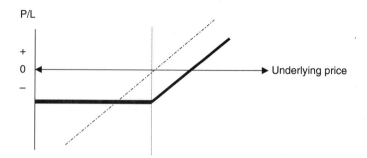

Figure 5.1   Call Option

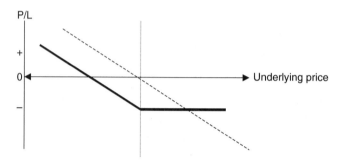

Figure 5.2   Put Option

then the writer keeps the premium but must now either make delivery of the underlying to the buyer in the case of a call option or take delivery of the underlying in the case of a put option as Figure 5.3 shows.

In the Figure 5.3 we see that there are alternative titles that can be used, for example taker, buyer and holder can all describe the purchaser of the option. We can also see that the buyer pays a premium to the writer. If the option is a call and is exercised by the buyer the underlying moves from the writer to the buyer, the opposite occurring if the buyer exercises a put.

Understanding this characteristic is important, as part of the settlement flow is based around whether the option is a call or a put.

When making an opening purchase, the buyer of an option becomes known as a position *holder* and is said to be *long* of the market.

When making an opening sale, the seller of an option becomes known as a position *writer* and is said to be *short* of the market.

Option positions can be either long or short. In special circumstances, both long and short positions can be held *gross*. Long or short option positions are normally closed out at the time of transacting the opposite position.

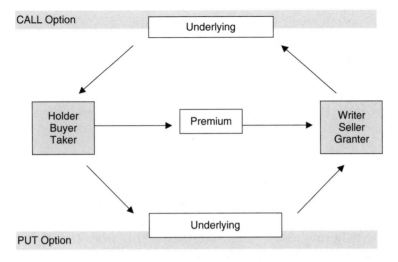

Figure 5.3 Option Obligations and Rights

Options are also traded in styles that refer to the exercising of the right by the buyer, and once again this is important in terms of the settlement profile of the option. These styles are:

- American – exercisable on any business day
- European – exercisable on expiry
- Bermudan – exercisable at preset timings
- Asian or Average – exercised against an average underlying price.

American and European style options are traded both on exchange and over-the-counter, whilst Bermudan and Asian options are predominantly traded over-the-counter.

Options have a strike price (also referred to as an exercise or a delivery price). The strike price is the price used to calculate the value of the underlying when it is delivered as a result of the buyer exercising their right.

Example

An investor purchases one BP Amoco October 330 Call option @ 20p. Their broker executes the order on the Euronext.liffe market where the contract specification states that each option contract is for 1000 ordinary shares and they are traded as American style options.

> The investor will have to pay a premium of £200, being 1000 shares × the price of 20p, to secure the right to take delivery at a day of their choice of 1000 shares at 330p until expiry in October.
>
> If the buyer exercises their right they will then pay 1000 × 330p = £3300 to take delivery of the 1000 BP shares irrespective of the price BP might be in the stock market at that time.

Workflow road map

We can use the option shown in the above example to follow the workflow associated with on-exchange option transactions.

In the following text we describe the process from the point of view of the broker, in this case a clearing member of an exchange, and also make reference to the workflow from an institutional client's position.

Trade capture

In the case of an electronic exchange these details are automatically captured from the trader's action on the dealing screen. In the case of an open outcry market the details are either input into an electronic matching system by the trader or alternatively a deal ticket is completed, which is then passed to support staff for input to the exchange matching system.

The actual clearing and settlement processes for markets differ as do the procedures adopted internally by firms. However, the following table illustrates the kind of option trade details that are likely to be needed. These will be:

Data	Detail	Source
Option	BP	Trade ticket/Deal system
Market	Euronext.liffe	Trade ticket/Deal system
Maturity	October	Trade ticket/Deal system
Strike price	330	Trade ticket/Deal system
Call or Put	Call	Trade ticket/Deal system
Shares per contract	1000	Contract specification
Buy/Sell	Buy	Trade ticket/Deal system
Counterparty	xxx	Trade ticket/Deal system
Time of trade	00/00 dd/mm/yy	Trade ticket/Deal system
Transaction reference	xxxxxx	System-generated
Client/Principal trade	Client	Trade ticket/Deal system
Execution broker	N/A	Trade ticket/Deal system

The institutional client that has placed the order with their broker has in essence the same data requirements but obviously has no reference to Principal Trading.

It is important to note that high-quality static data on options, like all products, is crucial as today most firms use systems for the processes involved from trade to settlement and beyond.

Trade validation

The transaction must be validated.

This process needs the confirmation of the trade details received from the front office against the data being received from the market. This may be via a system link to the exchange, for instance the TRS used on Euronext.liffe.

The TRS provides details of transactions that have taken place in the market. Each trade is shown whether the firm has transacted it, it has been 'given in' by an executing broker for the firm's account or client account or it is to be 'given up' to another clearing member. It is then accepted by the member and internally confirmed against the order details.

As the trades showing are registered to the firm's account at the clearing house and are therefore due for settlement of any obligations arising, it is important that any discrepancy between the trade details and the order details is notified to the relevant dealer/trader and resolved quickly.

Trade enrichment

To be able to process the trade internally we will need to:

1. Book the trade to the relevant client account or trading book.
2. Identify if the trade is an opening or closing transaction.
3. Perform the margin calculation (if applicable).
4. Charge the relevant commission.
5. Charge other fees (if applicable).
6. Perform the settlement of the transaction with the clearing house.
7. Effect the client settlement instructions.

Booking trade to the relevant client account or trading book

The details for this will be on the database and the posting will either be automatically generated by the dealing system to the operations system or need to be input from a trade ticket or similar document. The accurate posting of the transaction is a vital function as the trade may have been done to close out an existing obligation, and a failure to successfully post the trade and complete the closeout could cause an unwanted assignment. The next section looks at this issue.

Identify opening and closing transactions

The trades booked to a client account will be either opening transactions, i.e. creating a position, or closing transactions where there is an existing position that is offset by the trade being booked. When this occurs the two transactions are closed out to create a realised profit or loss. If a successful closeout takes place it must happen in the internal records and also in the Client Account of the Firm held at the clearing house.

If the latter does not take place then there is a risk that an action such as an assignment of the short side of the open position could take place. The result could be increased settlement costs.

Principal trading accounts are usually settled net, automatically in both the internal and the clearing house accounts and the same closeout rules shown in Chapter 4 on futures apply.

Perform margin calculation

If the transaction undertaken is creating a short position then there will be a margin requirement that needs to be calculated. In most cases this will be either SPAN or TIMS, depending on the exchange on which the trade has taken place. Both these margin systems are described more fully in the Appendices 9 and 10.

The margin call will be covered by collateral in the form of either cash or collateral or a combination of both. This collateral will be needed for the margin call made by the exchange clearing house to the firm and by the firm to its client.

Margin will be posted to a margin account in the ledger.

Charge the relevant commission

For client transactions, there will be a commission payable to the broker. The commission may be a rate/amount per contract or some other rate agreed by the sales desk and the client.

This rate can be charged on the opening trade, the closing trade or split so that both the opening and the closing transactions carry a commission.

The amount of commission charged on the transaction may include what is called floor brokerage. This is the fee charged by an execution

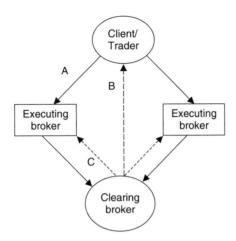

Figure 5.4 Floorbrokerage Relationships

Notes: A = Trade B = Commission (inc floorbrokerage fee) C = floorbrokerage.

broker who is giving up the trade to a clearing broker. It is described in the chapter related to futures but it is worth reminding ourselves how this works. The clearing broker will charge the client or trading book the combined floor brokerage and clearing fee and then settle the floor brokerage with the execution broker (Figure 5.4).

Commission will be posted to a commission account in the ledger and floorbrokerage to a brokerage account pending settlement with the executing brokers.

Charge other fees

There are several other fees that may need to be charged on a transaction. These will include exchange fees, regulatory fees and taxes.

Although the client may be charged an all-inclusive commission, they may want to see the breakdown of commission and fees and the data will need to be posted separately in the ledgers for accounting and management information purposes.

Perform the settlement process with the clearing house

A clearing broker will need to settle the option premium and any margin requirement with the clearing house. This will most likely be on T + 1. The amount to be settled will be included in the net settlement figure for the clearing member and will be collected by the clearing house through its normal settlement process. In many cases the option settlement amount is netted with futures obligations by currency.

The calculation for the option premium amount is:

Number of contracts $\times$ number of shares per contract $\times$ option price

In our earlier example of the purchase of one BP Oct. 330 Call option @ 20 this was:

$$1 \text{ contract} \times 1000 \text{ shares} \times 20\text{p} = £200$$

The transaction will need to be posted to the clearing house account with the contra entry being the client account or trading book if it was in the principal/house account.

Effect the client settlement instructions

The transaction will be posted to the relevant client account or trading book. If it is a client trade it will be booked either to their omnibus account or to a designated account. In the latter case the client will need to advise the broker of which account to book the trade to. This could be done via the sales desk or via the operations team or may be notified via both routes.

The client may maintain a monetary balance in their account(s), in which case the transaction will update the balance. Confirmation of the transaction and the revised open option position and cash balance on the account will be advised to the client.

There are several ways that this could take place.

1. Client access to accounts
2. By email
3. By fax
4. By telephone
5. Hard-copy report.

In each case the important thing is to establish that the client is aware of the settlement requirement and the impact on their open position and cash position. The process is also a fundamental control acting as an affirmation or acceptance by the client of the transaction and associated settlement. An audit trail for the trade is also established with the transaction showing in the clearing account and backed off in the client account.

Clearing account	Client account
Buy one BP Oct. 330 Call @ 20p	Buy one BP Oct. 330 Call @ 20p

Clearing Account	Error Account	Client Account
Buy 1 BP Oct. 330 Call @ 21p	Buy 1 BP Oct. 330 Call @ 21p	
	Sell 1 BP Oct. 330 Call @ 20p	
		Buy 1 BP Oct. 330 Call @ 20p

Figure 5.5 Account Postings

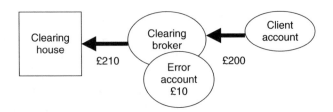

Figure 5.6 Account Postings

The settlement amount of £200 due to the clearing house is therefore receivable from the client. It is important to remember that the firm that has the clearing account, and the broker at the clearing house is liable for the settlement of £200 whether or not the client settled their obligation with the broker.

However, if there had been some kind of error with the trade, for example the price was given to the client as 20p but the actual trade in the market was 21p, then the transaction would have shown in the clearing account and backed off in the error account with a reversal out of the error account backed off to the client account (Figure 5.5).

The loss of 1p is reflected in the error account and the client account shows the transaction details as confirmed to the client. In settlement terms, the amount of £210 due to the clearing house is being met by £200 from the client and £10 from the error account (Figure 5.6).

Option exercise and assignment

The buyer of an option has purchased the right to either take delivery from call or make delivery to put the writer of the option. The underlying will be delivered unless the settlement is in cash format rather than physical.

The terms under which the buyer may exercise their right are determined by the 'style' of the option. As previously noted there are four styles of options:

1. American – exercisable on any business day
2. European – exercisable on expiry
3. Bermudan – exercisable at preset timings
4. Asian or Average – exercised against an average underlying price.

In the traded option markets, European and American options are listed. The process for exercising an option is set out in the rules and regulations of the clearing house and in the contract specification published by the exchange on which the option is traded. The clearing house establishes the method and timings for the exercise of options and the clearing members must adhere to these procedures.

The decision on whether to exercise an option depends on whether the option has any intrinsic value. Intrinsic value occurs when the strike price viewed against the current underlying asset price has a value. For example, if the underlying price is 100 and the strike price of a call option is 80 then there is an intrinsic value of 20 because the holder of the option can exercise the right to take delivery of the underlying at a cost of 80 when it is priced at 100 in the market. The option is known as an in-the-money option. However, the put option with a strike price of 80 and an underlying price of 100 is an out-of-the-money option because it has no intrinsic value as no one would want to exercise the option to sell the underlying at 80 when they could sell it in the market at 100.

*   *In-the-money* A call option where the exercise price is below the underlying asset price or a put option where the exercise price is above the underlying asset price. These options are deemed to have intrinsic value of the in-the-money difference between the exercise price and the underlying asset price.
*   *At-the-money* An option whose exercise price is equal, or closest, to the current market price of the underlying asset. This option has little or no intrinsic value as there is no in-the-money difference between the exercise price and the underlying asset price.
*   *Out-of-the-money* A call option whose exercise price is above the current underlying asset price or a put option whose exercise price is below the current underlying asset price. This option has no intrinsic value.

We can see that by knowing whether an option is in- or out-of-the-money and by knowing the option style we can determine whether or not the option position will be exercised or assigned. As a result, firms operating in options will have a report available showing the current status of the option position. The following is an example of what it would contain.

Remember, however, that although an option might be in-the-money, if the option style is European then the buyer cannot exercise the option unless it is expiry day. For this reason some investors who wish to avoid an assignment situation write only European style options and close out the position on expiry day. It should be noted that as there is a restriction as to when the holder of a European style option can exercise, the buyer will expect to pay less premium for the option than they would for an American style option.

Option Expiry and Exercise Report

Time: 08.30
Date: 16th July 2004   Stock: XYZ plc   Stock Price: 332p

Series	Status	Position	Exercise/Assignment
Jul 280 Calls	ITM	Short	Expect assignment
Jul 280 Puts	OTM	Short	No Assignment
Jul 300 Calls	ITM	Long	Exercise
Jul 300 Puts	OTM	Long	Abandon
Jul 330 Calls	ITM	Long	Possible Exercise
Jul 330 Puts	OTM	Long	Possible Exercise
Jul 360 Calls	OTM	Long	Abandon
Jul 360 Puts	ITM	Long	Exercise

Note: The 330 Calls may be exercised but the costs associated with the delivery of the shares like commission, stamp duty, etc. may make a client abandon the option if they have not closed it out in the market before the cessation of trading. A trader or market-maker paying no fees and exempt from stamp duty would probably exercise.

If the underlying is particularly volatile, the 330 Calls and Puts could oscillate between in-, at- and out-of-the-money many times in the last few days before expiry day and on the expiry day itself.

Let us look at the same positions but now at the close of trading on expiry day.

Option Expiry and Exercise Report

Time: 16.00
Date: 16th July 2004   Stock: XYZ plc   Stock Price: 330p

Series	Status	Position	Exercise/Assignment
Jul 280 Calls	ITM	Short	Expect assignment
Jul 280 Puts	OTM	Short	No Assignment
Jul 300 Calls	ITM	Long	Exercise
Jul 300 Puts	OTM	Long	Abandon
Jul 330 Calls	ATM	Long	Abandon/Possible Exercise
Jul 330 Puts	ATM	Long	Abandon
Jul 360 Calls	OTM	Long	Abandon
Jul 360 Puts	ITM	Long	Exercise

Note: With the 330 series being at-the-money it is unlikely that a client would exercise their position. The underlying is at a mid-price of 330 but if there is a spread in the underlying market so that the bid–offer is say 328–332 then it would still be advantageous for a trader/market-maker to exercise, assuming they can or have traded at the bid or offer in the stock, i.e. they sell stock at 332 and exercise their call position for delivery at 330.

In general terms, of course, most option positions are taken as parts of strategies like hedging or exposure-taking and the intention is not to go to delivery. For that reason many open options are closed out on expiry for whatever value they may have in the option market, or if they are deep out-of-the money they are abandoned. Another reason why an option position, even one with a minimal value, may be traded out on expiry is to create a realised profit or loss in the accounts. The abandonment of the option may not be accounted for in the same way as a realised profit/loss with, for instance, perhaps resultant tax issues.

Exercise and assignment procedures

Having established which options are in-the-money and therefore ready for possible exercise or assignment, the decision of the trader or client is sought (Figure 5.7). There may be standing instructions to exercise all in-the-money series but care must be taken with client positions for the reasons given above.

It is good practice to have procedures that require option exercises to be checked before submission and for an automatic daily check for any assignments. Late notification of assignment to a trader or client is not only embarrassing, but could be costly if other deals have taken place based on a wrong position.

Likewise, missing deadlines for exercise can be costly especially if, for instance, a trader was exercising on the day before a share went ex-dividend a call position to take early delivery of shares-cum-large dividend. If the exercise is missed it cannot be done the following day, as any resulting shares would be delivered without the dividend entitlement.

Operations team need to take great care in dealing with position management and must be aware of the risks associated with exercise, early exercise (i.e. before expiry in American style options), assignment, closeouts, etc.

Options on futures result in a futures position being created and again the records must be updated correctly for accounting, reporting and audit trail purposes.

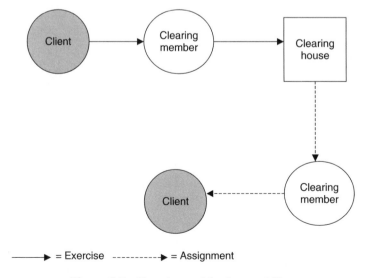

Figure 5.7 Exercise and Assignment Flow

Delivery

When an option is exercised and assigned the option position is closed out and replaced with a transaction in the underlying. So one BP 330 Call becomes 1000 BP shares @ 330p.

The internal records will need to be updated to reflect this. Clients will need to be advised of the 'result' of the exercise/assignment and they will need to amend their portfolio accordingly and arrange for delivery/payment instructions with their custodian/broker.

The settlement of that transaction will now take place under the normal market terms applicable to the underlying, for example UK equity shares would settle T + 3 via CREST.

Summary

Options present the operations team with some challenges, not least ensuring that any exercise or assignment situations are managed correctly. Good-quality data on expiry dates, strike prices and the option status, i.e. in-, at- or out-of-the-money will also prove valuable in assessing the funding and likelihood of exercise or assignment. As with futures, closeouts must be done promptly and accurately to avoid problems.

It is also a case that the impact of a corporate action on the underlying may create a change to the contract specification. This is covered in greater detail in another chapter.

6

OTC products

We have already noted elsewhere in the book that the OTC derivative market is a large and important one. In this chapter we can look at some of the popular types of OTC products.

Forward rate agreements

A forward rate agreement (FRA) is an agreement to pay or receive, on an agreed future date, the difference between a fixed interest rate at the outset and a reference interest rate prevailing at a given date for an agreed period.

The FRAs are transacted between buyers who agree to the fixed rate and sellers who agree to the floating rate or benchmark.

The benchmark rate will be, for instance, LIBOR and the settlement is calculated using a formula.

Example

Suppose a manufacturer needs to borrow £5 million in one-month time and needs the loan for a period of three months. Concerned about the raising of interest rates, the manufacturer decides to buy an a FRA that will fix the effective borrowing rate today. They do this as they have no wish to borrow the money now when it is not needed but do not want to have to pay a higher funding cost if rates rise in the next month.

The terms of the FRA are that the fixed rate is 7.25 per cent and the benchmark is LIBOR. It will start in one-month time and finish three months later and would be known as a 'one v four' FRA.

In one-month time, the calculation of the settlement of the FRA can take place. The prevailing LIBOR at 11.00 a.m. is used and let us assume this as 7.5 per cent.

Now let us consider what settlement would take place.
The formula used to calculate settlement is:

Notional Principal Amount × (Fixed Rate − LIBOR) ×
days in FRA period/days in year divided by
(1 + (LIBOR × days in FRA period/days in year))

Calculation

£5 000 000 × (0.0725 − 0.075) × 91/365 over
(1 + (0.075 × 91/365)) = £3 059.23

The LIBOR rate was higher than the fixed rate so the buyer (the
manufacturer) receives the difference from the seller, in this case a
quarter of one per cent on £5 000 000.

However, there is no exchange of the £5 million. The manufacturer will borrow the money from a lending source and the money
received from the FRA will offset the higher borrowing costs of around
7.5 per cent.

Had the LIBOR been lower than the fixed rate, the manufacturer
would have paid the difference to the seller but, of course, would
borrow the money at a lower rate.

The manufacturer 'locked' in a rate of 7.25 per cent for their
planned future borrowing.

As far as settlement is concerned, the amount due is known on the
settlement date, the date at which the FRA period starts (one-month
time) and the calculation period is known (three months).

Unlike most transactions that settle on maturity, an FRA can be
settled at the beginning of the calculation period. The amount is
present valued or discounted to reflect the interest that would
accrue if the amount paid was deposited to the end of the FRA
period.

Swaps

Swaps are products that as the title implies involve the swapping of
something. This can be, for instance, interest rates (an 'interest rate
swap' is abbreviated to IRS), currencies, equity benchmarks against
an interest rate or commodities.

> *Example*
>
> *Interest Rate Swaps*
> An IRS would be an agreement to swap or exchange, over an agreed period, two payment streams each calculated using a different type of interest rate and based on the same notional principal amount.
>   The exchange of cash flows originating from, say, a fixed rate and a floating rate would be called a 'plain vanilla' or 'vanilla' IRS.

By using swaps, a company can fix interest rates in advance for a specific period, typically from 3 to 10 years but can be any duration agreed by the two parties to the transaction.

Example:

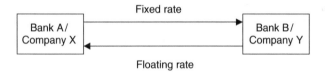

Settlement of an IRS takes place according to the agreed exchange periods. Instead of buyer and seller, in the swap market reference is made to the receiver and the payer.

For example, the receiver of the fixed rate is the payer of the floating and, conversely, the receiver of the floating is the payer of the fixed. Likewise the receiver of 3-month Floating is the payer of 6-month Floating, where the flows to be exchanged are two different floating rates, known as a *basis swap.*

During the life of the above swap (known as the *Term*) there will be an exchange of the netted payment flows at *payment date*, calculated at what is known as *reset dates*, i.e. semi-annually, annually and valued against the benchmark rate(s).

The payments cannot be netted at each reset date if the payment dates are different, i.e. the fixed is paid annually and the floating semi-annually.

The IRS will be transacted to start at a forward date and will run for the agreed period. The start date is known as the *effective date* and the end date is known as the *termination date.*

The floating rate is reset at the effective date for the next period and then at reset dates for the next period throughout the term of the swap.

Suppose a company, let us call it Company X, currently pays a float-ing rate of interest, say LIBOR + 0.4 per cent for a loan of $10 million over five years. Concerned that rates will rise, the treasurer wants to change the payment flow to a fixed rate but is unable to alter the terms of the loan.

Company X approaches Bank B and agrees a five-year IRS the terms of which are that:

Company X will pay 6.3 per cent fixed, paid annually on an actual/360 basis, and receive LIBOR, semi-annually on an actual/360 basis.

At the beginning of the swap, LIBOR is 6 per cent. At the end of the first six months the floating-rate payment is:

$$\$10\ 000\ 000 \times 6.00\% \times 181/360 = \$301\ 667$$

which is paid by Bank B to Company X.

Note: There is no netted payment against the fixed rate flow for the period as the terms state that the fixed rate settles annually.

At the beginning of the next six months LIBOR is 6.25 per cent and after the six months the payments are:

Floating
$$\$10\ 000\ 000 \times 6.25\% \times 184/360 = \$319\ 444$$
(due by Bank B to Company X)

Fixed
$$\$10\ 000\ 000 \times 6.30\% \times 365/360 = \$638\ 750$$
(due from company X to Bank B)

This time the settlement can be netted so that Company X pays $319 306 to Bank B.

In this IRS, Company X has a risk as their view on interest rates over the next five years may be wrong and rates might actually fall, not rise. By agreeing to pay a fixed rate, in this case 6.3 per cent, their cost of borrowing may be much higher than it would have been if they had not entered into the swap.

As an alternative strategy the treasurer may have entered into a *swaption*. This is an option to enter into a swap. Like all options it gives the treasurer the right, but not an obligation to enter into the swap at some stage. As this is an OTC transaction, the precise terms of the swaption and the cost of buying it will be negotiated.

> *Example*
>
> *Currency Swap*
> A currency swap is an exchange of a series of cash flows in one currency for a series of cash flows in another currency, at agreed intervals over an agreed period, and based on interest rates.
>   It is possible to have a combination of fixed and floating rates in two currencies in a currency swap.

Examples of the possible combinations are:

*   Fixed interest in one currency to floating rate in another currency.
*   Fixed interest in one currency to fixed interest in another.
*   Floating rate in one currency to floating interest in another.

In a single currency IRS as illustrated above, there is no exchange of the principal amount; however, with a currency swap there is usually an exchange of the principal amounts at the beginning and end of the Term at a rate agreed at the beginning.

Remember this is an OTC transaction so a currency swap can have an exchange of principal at the beginning or end or not at all if that is what the two parties agree.

If, say, a UK company wants to expand business in the United States by providing an influx of capital and it can borrow money cheaper in the United Kingdom where it is well known to its bankers, it can enter into a currency swap whereby: it can borrow British Pounds (GBP) on a floating rate basis from its bank and swap the GBP for dollars with the swap counterparty. It will agree to pay a fixed rate of interest on the dollars and receive a floating rate of interest on the GBP, which it uses to pay the interest on the original GBP loan from its bank.

It agrees to exchange the principal amounts at the beginning at a Foreign Exchange (FX) rate that is agreed and will therefore need to fund the repayment of the loan, which is a totally separate transaction from the swap of its own resources.

The dollars are given to the US business and the subsequent income stream pays the interest on the dollars, which is paid to the swap counterparty. As we have said the GBP interest received from the swap counterparty pays the interest on the loan.

During the Term of the swap, which will correspond to the loan duration, the payment streams will be settled on reset dates. They are not netted because they are in different currencies.

This type of swap has achieved for the company protection against foreign exchange movements during the period of the swap and protects against interest rate movement in the UK market rate during the period of its borrowing.

Example

Equity Swap

A fund manager with a portfolio that is based on but not solely invested in the FTSE 100 Index is due to receive an amount of £5 million into the portfolio. The manager is looking to hold this investment in the FTSE 100 stocks for about a year. The manager decides to look at using derivatives rather than buying the stock. After a discussion with their broker the following Equity Swap is proposed:

The fund manager will swap the interest on £5 million quarterly for one year based on LIBOR-10 basis points for the change in the value of the FTSE 100 Index quarterly for one year.

The fund manager will place the £5 million on deposit and will use the interest generated to provide one leg of the swap. The fund manager will then either receive or pay out cash flow quarterly depending on how the index moves as shown below.

Equity swap cash flow

End of quarter one

Index has moved from 4600 to 5060, an increase of 10 per cent, LIBOR is 4.5 per cent.
   The settlement amounts are therefore:

1. 5 000 000 × (4.5% − 0.10%) × day count basis
2. 5 000 000 × 10%

In this case the fund manager pays away the interest value and receives the change in index value, and will almost certainly settle this net.

End of quarter two

Index has declined from 5060 to 4807, a fall in value of 5 per cent, LIBOR is 4.5 per cent.

The settlement values are worked out as above but now, as the index has declined in value, the fund manager must pay the interest value plus the value of the fall in the index.

This has the effect of making the impact on the portfolio similar to what would have happened had the fund manager purchased the stock. In quarter one, the interest that was received on the cash was paid away; if the manager had purchased stock there would have been no interest received by the fund. The manager received the monetary value of the change in the index and so the portfolio has reflected a gain just as it would have done had the stock been purchased. A similar situation occurs each quarter.

The terms of the swap are of course negotiable between the fund manager and the broker. For instance, the value of the index change could have incorporated the dividend stream or the interest terms of LIBOR –10 basis points (bps) may have been agreed to reflect a notional dividend amount. Also the principal amount of £5 million may remain constant and any balance settled as shown in the example above.

If the terms are that the principal amount rises or falls in line with the index movement then in our example above, for the second quarter the principal amount would have been £5 million plus the net settlement and both the index value and the interest settlement would have been based on that amount.

Over-the-counter options

Over-the-counter options are often called 'exotic' because, unlike the standardised exchange-traded product, they possess additional characteristics that change the relatively simple Call and Put outcomes. As the terms are negotiated they are of course very flexible.

Common OTC options include:

- *Calls and Puts* with specific amounts and duration, for example a £1 million, two-year Call option on the FTSE 100 Index at a strike of 6005.2 (exchange-traded FTSE 100 Index options on Euronext.liffe are listed with nine-month duration and a fixed unit of trading and strike prices).
- *Interest Rate Guarantee (IRG)* is an option on a FRA.
- *Swaption* is an option on a swap.
- *European, American and Bermudan* style options which have different exercise characteristics, i.e. expiry, any time, specific timings.

- *Asian or look back, or average rate or average price, options* use a different benchmark than the price of the underlying asset on expiry to determine if they are in- or out-of-the-money, for example the average price of the underlying over the last month.
- *'Barrier options'* is a general term for a family of options, which are either cancelled or activated if the underlying price reaches a predetermined level. They are also known as *knock-out, knock-in* or *trigger* options.
- *Caps and floors* are a series of 'rollover' rates agreed whereby the difference in rates is paid, if applicable at the time of the rollover.
- *Collars* operate like ordinary options but have limits on the level at which the customer can deal at a better market rate than the underlying, in exchange for a lower premium.

We also have *Puttable* and *Callable* swaps which allow the fixed rate receiver and fixed rate payer respectively to terminate the swap early. They are traded as European, American and Bermudan styles of exercise right.

Settlement of OTC products

The settlement of OTC derivatives is determined by the terms of the product as agreed by the two counterparties. There are, however, relatively standard settlement characteristics for particular products as we have already seen.

Settlement events are triggered by such things as:

- Effective date, reset date and payment date for swaps.
- Settlement date and calculation period for FRAs.
- Premium convention, exercise date and trigger events for options.
- Maturity of all products.

We also know that most products settle at the end of a period or on maturity with the exception of FRAs and IRGs where the settlement takes place by a discounted present value.

Key to the settlement of OTC products is the terms of the transaction.

Unlike exchange-traded derivatives where the terms are stipulated by the exchange contract specification, each OTC trade is effectively a new set of terms, even though the product may be the same, i.e. a swap or an option.

The OTC derivatives have documentation that helps to ensure that the terms of the derivative trade are agreed.

In the past this was a major obstacle to the use of OTC derivatives, as each trade had a separate agreement. This had to be vetted by the legal department, and consequently delays and disputes caused considerable problems.

The International Swaps and Derivatives Association (ISDA) have greatly helped to resolve the problems by developing standard documents for use by counterparties in OTC derivatives. The BBA also developed standard documentation for FRAs.

The standard documentation, known as a Master Agreement, can be supplemented with schedules, annexes and appendices that allow specific issues to be covered.

The ISDA master documents cover provisions for numerous aspects that are relevant and may need enforcing during the term of the agreement. These include:

* Contract currency
* Multi-branch facilities
* Payment provisions
* Default procedures
* Termination events
* Warranties, covenants and representations
* Tax indemnities
* Notices
* Assignment
* Legal jurisdiction
* Waiver of immunities.

Also produced is what is known as a *confirmation.*

This is provided as a detail of the trade terms rather than the general terms under which business is being transacted between the two counterparties.

The confirm, therefore, lists key details for the operations team as well as enabling the trade details to be reconciled. Confirmations should be issued by the operations team as quickly as possible so that the trade details can be reconciled. Equally, receipt of a confirmation from the counterparty, or a signed copy of a confirmation, sent to the counterparty should be chased as the confirm cannot be legally enforced unless both parties have acknowledged the details are the same or agreed.

Typically two banks participating in a trade will send each other confirms whilst a bank and a client trade will result in a confirmation from the bank to the client, which the client will sign and return.

The role of the confirmation/documentation team in the context of OTC settlement is, therefore, vital.

The post-trade environment

There are many processes in the post-trade environment that are common to all transactions. These include:

- Trade capture and verification
- Position keeping
- Profit/loss analysis
- Confirmations and documentation
- Settlement
- Customer services
- Reconciliation
- Collateral management
- Risk management.

Trade capture and verification requires considerable details to be input to the system. From a risk and control point of view the system must be capable of handling certain key information about a trade such as:

- Title of instrument traded
- Buy or sell (FRAs, options), pay or receive (swaps)
- Currency or currencies
- Amount or number of contracts (option) notional amount (FRAs, swaps)
- Exchange rate, price, rate of premium (two rates in the case of a fixed/fixed rate currency swap)
- Floating rate basis/bases
- Exchange rate agreed for conversions of principal (currency swap)
- Strike price or rate (options)
- Trigger level (barrier option)
- Trade date and time
- Underlying asset (option, equity swap, etc.)
- Effective date
- Period (FRA)
- Settlement date(s)
- Maturity date
- Expiry date (option)

- Exercise styles and dates
- Day/year calculation bases (swaps)
- Physical/cash-settled (options)
- Special conditions, for example, for Asians options
- Trader
- Counterparty
- Deal method, for example screen, telephone.

This list is not exhaustive and certain types of products, as they may have specific terms, will need additional information. In such cases where the full details cannot be recorded in the system, adequate manual processes and checks must be employed. Certain transactions such as swaptions require both the option details and the swap underlying the option to be entered.

Details of the settlement instructions including netting if agreed will also be input to the system so too will information such as the reference sources for fixings and possibly the documentation (ISDA, FRABBA) and governing law.

It is important that all this data is in the system so that key reports and information can be supplied to operations, dealers (positions and profit/loss), risk managers, general ledgers, reconciliation systems, etc.

Event calendar

The information will also help to provide an event calendar that will enable operations to track the settlement events that will be occurring, for example resets, expiry, settlement dates.

Some events are mandatory and/or automatic. This would include those related to:

- Barrier options
- Swaps
- Caps, collars and floors
- FRAs.

Others may require an instruction and/or decision by the dealer or client and this includes:

- Option exercise; however, some options are automatically exercised on expiry if they are in-the-money.
- Termination (callable, puttable swaps).

Communication/Information

Clearly the efficient settlement of OTC products requires a high degree of skill in managing the flow of information at, and immediately after, trading and then during the term of the transaction.

Central to this is the Confirmation.

For an FRA, a confirmation will typically be sent via Society for Worldwide Interbank Financial Telecommunications (SWIFT) and would contain information such as:

Confirmation from Mega Bank	To: Interbank Inc.
Buyer: Mega Bank	
Transaction date	19 June 2004
Effective date	21 June 2004
Terms	ISDA
Currency/Amount	GBP 3 000 000
Fixing	19 September 2004
Settlement	21 September 2004
Maturity date	21 December 2004
Contract period	91 days
Contract rate	5.79% pa on a actual/360 basis

An IRS confirmation for a fixed/floating transaction would contain information such as:

Confirmation from Mega Bank	To: Interbank Inc.
Interest rate swaps	
Transaction date	19 June 2004
Effective date	21 June 2004
Maturity date	21 December 2004
Terms	ISDA
Currency/Amount	USD 5 000 000
We pay	5.76%
Frequency	Annual
Calculation basis	Actual/365
We receive	6-Month LIBOR
Frequency	Semi-annual
Calculation basis	Actual/360

There are other pieces of information that can or will be added to this, such as frequency being modified following convention.

Other settlement issues

Over-the-counter products are heavily used and the number of organisations using them increases all the time. With some of the products being quite complex in their structure and certainly different in terms of the settlement process, the relationship with counterparties and clients in particular is important.

There will be many queries related to transactions, settlement, etc. and it is important that the operations teams within the two parties to the trade work closely together to resolve any problems quickly.

Reconciliation is also a key issue and the reconciliation of the Nostro accounts in particular is important to ensure payments and receipts have been made. Any failure to receive expected payments may indicate a potential default.

It is also important to MTM OTC positions for profit/loss and to reconcile the positions against the dealers' records for exposure, limits and risk control management.

The treasury management including funding lines, cash-flow management, etc. are crucial and so too is the reconciliation.

Collateral is a key risk control and where collateral has been taken as part of the risk management process it is vital to monitor that the collateral value is sufficient to cover the exposure risk. The key to whether collateral is required at all is the credit rating of the counterparty and the type of product.

We need to be aware that with an OTC position, if a default should occur, there is no central guarantee provided by a clearing house unless the product is one of those cleared under, for instance, the LCH SwapClear facility.

As a dealer may have the fixed side of a swap 'matched' between two counterparties, for example, they are receiving fixed rate from one counterparty and paying a lower fixed rate to the other, if the first counterparty defaults the dealer faces losses as the other counterparty must still be paid and it may cost the dealer more to replace the defaulting swap with another.

The amount of collateral needed will obviously rise or fall during the duration of the product. Making calls and returns is part of the operations role, as is the calculation of any interest due on cash collateral.

Collateral helps to offset its replacement cost and, therefore reconciling its value and managing the process generally is vitally important.

As well as the event calendar there are other key static data issues to focus on including the standing settlement instructions, client and product profiles, records of fixings, which need to be maintained in case of queries or for subsequent calculations.

Accounting and regulatory issues

Products like an IRS are shown as off-balance sheet items as there is an exchange of flows but no actual loan or deposit is made between the two counterparties.

As far as profit-and-loss treatment is concerned the profit and loss on trading should be realised immediately. The profit or loss on a hedge should take place simultaneously with the profit or loss on the item being hedged.

There are various accountancy standards around the world that require banks to disclose information on interest rate risk, currency, liquidity, maturity, information on fair values and the effects of hedge accounting as described above.

The FSA has reporting requirements related to transactions including options, and the European Union (EU) and Bank for International Settlements have established guideline limits on risks, which each bank may take. In turn the local regulator such as the FSA in the United Kingdom will enforce these limits and may even make them stronger.

SwapClear

The introduction of a central clearing counterparty facility for OTC products including derivatives greatly helps to reduce the capital adequacy requirements associated with OTC transactions. The LCH launched SwapClear in September 1999 so that existing members that meet the membership criteria for SwapClear can have their OTC transaction cleared under the same principles used for exchange-traded derivatives, i.e. variation margin, initial margin.

By having the OTC transaction cleared by LCH.Clearnet, an independent third party, the requirement to put up capital to cover counterparty risk is removed.

SwapClear went live in September 1999, initially clearing vanilla swaps in G-4 currencies for up to 10 years' maturity and in June 2002 extended the service to clear trades in G-4 currencies to a 30-year maximum maturity as well as introducing the clearing of Swiss Franc trades with a 10-year maximum maturity. In February 2003 the service was extended once again to provide clearing facilities for compounding and plain vanilla IRS with the following tenors:

* USD, EUR, JPY and GBP up to 30 years
* CHF, AUD, DKK, CAD and SEK up to 10 years
* HKD, NOK and NZD up to 5 years.

In the process of clearing swaps, the clearing house becomes the central counterparty to, and has responsibility for, the corresponding trade obligations arising from each half of the original bilaterally negotiated trade. This principle is known as registration and is the same role that was explained earlier in respect of the clearing of exchange-traded derivatives.

SwapClear offers the interbank swap market a facility that aims to free up credit lines, reduce risk and use of capital, thus increasing return on investment and trading opportunities.

The extent of these benefits will depend on the individual bank, but are likely to include:

- Lower counterparty risk
- Lower operational risk
- Reduced credit line utilisation
- Reduced regulatory capital requirements
- More secure and standardised collateral handling procedures
- Standardised processing of swaps, simplifying documentation and operations, enabling back offices to handle higher volumes at lower cost
- Fewer payments.

Benefits of netting

The major benefit provided to banks by SwapClear is the ability to net several counterparty swap books multilaterally into a single account with the clearing house, which becomes the counterparty to every trade registered with SwapClear. As a result, current bilateral netting arrangements are replaced with more efficient multilateral netting. It has been estimated that the effect of multilateral netting can reduce exposures by up to 90 per cent when compared to bilateral netting.

Multilateral netting is at the heart of central clearing and delivers the greatest benefit in terms of reduced credit risk, significantly beyond that available from bilateral netting and collateralisation.

In addition, credit risk is reduced through the use of VM. Daily margining effectively reduces the risk horizon to a single trading day, with the result that banks are no longer concerned with the probability of default over the life of a swap book, but only over the next business day. Portfolio analysis has indicated that SwapClear reduces 60–80 per cent of current exposures for mixed swap portfolios, i.e. where a proportion of swaps are non-clearable.

Improved return on capital

The combination of multilateral netting and margining effectively eliminates credit risk for those transactions cleared through SwapClear.

Freeing credit lines

As a result of the clearing house becoming the counterparty to trades after SwapClear registration, original bilateral credit lines are freed for other purposes. The need for the current market practice of assigning or 'tearing up' swaps to free up credit lines is removed. As original counterparties are replaced by the clearing house there is no need to assign trades to manage credit lines. Trades required to adjust market risk positions may be carried out with any SwapClear Dealer.

Reduced regulatory capital requirements

Many European regulators have recognised the reduced risk inherent in cleared OTC transactions by adopting the risk treatment set out in amendments made in 1998 to the EU Capital Adequacy Directive (CAD II).

The CAD II allows national regulators to exempt banks from calculating counterparty risk in respect of cleared OTC trades if they meet the margin requirements of the clearing house with debt securities issued by Organisation for Economic Cooperation Developments (OECD) governments.

Operational savings

SwapClear provides an automated facility once the matched trades have been received. The service marks-to-market swaps and collateral used to meet initial margin requirements, determines reset amounts, and nets payments into a single payment or receipt per currency. These operations should:

- Reduce users' operational overheads
- Permit efficient utilisation of collateral
- Reduce settlement costs
- Reduce costs associated with collateralisation under bilateral agreements.

Operational risk reduction

The BIS issued a paper in June 1999 proposing that regulatory capital charges be extended to include operational risk.

It is recognised that it is as important to control operational risk as it is to control market and credit risk, but operational risk can be more difficult to assess and quantify. SwapClear clearly reduces operational risk by introducing standard contract terms, by simplifying the settlement of swaps and by the removal of ambiguity in confirmations. This serves to reduce both the bilateral negotiations and the operational issues caused by the handling of exceptions.

Collateralisation introduces operational and legal risk associated with the processes of securities movements or settlements, and through the lack of legal certainty surrounding perfection of title. Central clearing, by providing uniformity of collateral handling procedures, within the same rules applied to exchange clearing, significantly reduces those risks. Day-to-day cash flows, floating rate resets, and transaction valuation are all performed centrally by the clearing house, thus further minimising operational risk and reducing banks' operational requirements.

This centralised, straight-through-processing (STP) delivers a quick and effective reduction in risk management complexity and operational interfaces.

The above contains excerpts from the LCH.Clearnet SwapClear brochure, a full copy of which can be downloaded from their website (see appendices).

Today LCH.Clearnet also provide the same type of facility for other products through RepoClear and EquityClear.

SwapsWire

SwapsWire is an electronic dealing system designed for the electronic platform designed to promote efficiencies for the OTC derivatives market.

Its objectives are to provide

- Lower transaction costs.
- Fast transfer of deal information in a standard format.
- The facilitation of STP in OTC transactions.

One significant advantage is that SwapsWire provides the evidence of the deal and thereby removes the need for a confirmation to be sent. This will dramatically reduce the paperwork and process currently undertaken by OTC operations teams.

SwapsWire supports Interest Rate Swaps (IRS), Forward Rate Agreements (FRAs), Overnight Index Swaps (OIS), Interest Rate Caps and Floors, Interest Rate Swaptions, and Credit Default Swaps (CDS) in nine currencies (CAD, CHF, DKK, EUR, GBP, JPY, NOK, SEK and USD) with additional currencies to be added. The system is available globally and is currently being used by clients in Asia, Europe and North America.

All parties to the trade affirm a single copy of trade data, and this record becomes the legal confirmation. This single copy remains in a central repository, and is available to the parties to feed their STP process. It also greatly facilitates the process of amending, terminating or assigning trades, since everyone starts from the same place. The repository can also be used for reconciliation purposes.

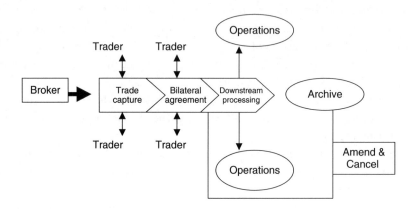

Source: SwapsWire.

Summary

Over-the-counter derivatives have characteristics very different from exchange-traded products, and in particular the clearing and settlement processes can be quite different. In the appendices you will find 'workflow road maps' for some of the OTC products and it is important to note the way in which the trade to settlement flow works and where there are similarities and differences between on- and off-exchange products.

7

Using derivatives in investment management

Introduction

There are numerous ways in which derivative products are used in investment decisions. The fund mandate, regulatory requirements, investment objectives and relevance to the market conditions determine strategies and product selection.

Other key issues include liquidity and market risk, counterparty risk, and the operational risk environment.

In this chapter we shall look at some basic examples of different ways of using derivatives in the fund and investment management process.

Basic illustration of derivatives use in asset allocation

A fund manager has a portfolio made up of equity shares in the United States and United Kingdom, Gilt stocks and cash. The current ratio is 40 per cent of the fund invested in US equities, 20 per cent in UK equities, 20 per cent in Gilt stock, 10 per cent in Japanese stock and 10 per cent cash.

The fund manager believes that the US equity market is due a fall and that Japan will rise. They expect this to occur in the next six to eight weeks.

The fund manager can adjust the balance of the portfolio by selling US shares and purchasing stocks in Japanese-based companies.

They will need to research the markets then undertake several transactions and therefore it may take some time to achieve. Commission fees will be incurred for each transaction.

Alternatively the fund manager can use derivatives, in this case index futures, to gain and reduce exposure to the respective markets.

They will sell S&P Index futures contracts and purchase Nikkei Index futures.

If they are correct in their assumptions the sale of the S&P futures will offset the fall in price of the US stocks they hold whilst the Nikkei futures will rise enabling the fund to participate in the increase.

There are several advantages for the fund manager.

- The futures transactions are very quick to effect and there is less commission. Typically it might be 2 per cent for equities against say 0.2 per cent for futures.
- Exposure adjustment is immediate, reducing the risk of loss because of the market moving before shares can be sold/bought.
- The futures transactions can be quickly reversed if the assumptions are wrong.
- The fund manager can effect the actual sale/purchase of shares when ready.

There are, however, some important points to be aware of.

The portfolio must have congruence with the index product to be used, otherwise the exposure will be incorrect and may result in gearing of the fund. This could breach internal/external regulations. The fund manager can avoid problems like that by working out the beta of the fund and adjusting the number of futures accordingly.

There is also the need to calculate the value of the proposed allocation in the underlying currency of the index futures and then considering any foreign exchange issues that arise.

From a clearing and settlement point of view, the futures positions will of course generate both initial and VM requirements, and the funding of the VM and what collateral to use for the initial margin call will need to be decided. Incorporating the funding requirements into the portfolio's overall funding is vital but so too is ensuring that the positions are recorded and accounted for, otherwise the fund's performance may be incorrectly reported to investors.

Income enhancement

A fund manager buys or holds significant amounts of equity stock. They are happy to sell some of these holdings at certain levels and would like to increase income over and above the dividend if possible. They look to the traded options market.

They have purchased 500 000 BP shares at 400p and will be happy to sell half of the holding if the stock rises by more than 10 per cent.

They note that the 440 Call options expiring in two months can be sold for 25p. They sell 250 contracts (1000 shares per contract) at 25p.

The fund manager has given the right to someone to call the 250 000 shares at 440p anytime in the next two months in return for £62 500 (250 × 1000 × 25p) of premium paid to them immediately.

If the stock rises above 440p they will, unless they close out the position, have to deliver the stock at 440p. If it does not rise above 440p they will not have to deliver the stock.

In the first scenario they have effectively sold the stock for 465p (440 + 25), which meets their criteria of selling on a 10% + share rise, i.e. 440. Note: their profit is restricted to the difference between 400p and 465p, no matter to what price the stock rises.

In the second scenario they still have the stock but have received income of £62 500 or looked at another way they have reduced the purchase price to 375p. This means they are protected against a fall to this level to half of their holding.

In all probability the fund manager will, if the position is not assigned or is closed out, continue to write new series on expiry/closeout of existing positions, moving up or down strike prices in relation to movement in the stock price.

Remember the manager or for that matter private client can close out the short position and therefore the obligation at any time. So if, for instance, after a couple of weeks the share price had fallen and as a result the option price had halved, the fund manager or investor could buy back the option, remove the risk of losing the stock and will have generated an additional amount for the portfolio.

Remember also that option styles are important. The writer of a European style option will only be assigned if the position is open and in-the-money after trading ceases on expiry day. The writer of an American style option on the other hand could face early exercise at any time.

As far as settlement is concerned, collateral in respect of the margin on the short option position will be needed. Also the option premium received will need to be accounted for correctly in the port-folio. It must be ascertained whether it is treated as income or part of the profit or loss of the transaction. Also there is the issue of valuing the shares that are covering the written call position because, as we have seen, the effect of writing the option against the stock is to 'cap' the possible profit at the combination of the difference in strike price plus the option premium.

For example, if we buy shares at 100 and write the 150 calls for 10, the maximum profit possible (unless the option is closed out) is 60.

The shares rise to 190. In our portfolio we are showing a profit of 90 on the stock. However, the option price has risen to 50 so we are also showing a loss of 40 on the option position. The net result is that we are showing a profit of 50 so that is OK. However, if we failed to reflect the loss on the option revaluation we would be overstating the portfolio's performance by 90.

Then the option position is assigned and we deliver the shares at 150 realising a profit of 50 and though yesterday we showed a profit of 90 the share price has not moved! If the option premium of 10 has been 'lost' elsewhere in the records as income then not only is the performance measurement unrealistic but the valuation of the funds assets is wrong, the published price of the fund is wrong and reports to the investors may be wrong. It will take some explaining to the investors.

More importantly it will take some explaining to the auditors, the trustee and the regulator and will hardly fill them with confidence that the fund is using derivatives safely and properly.

Hedging

The fund manager is reviewing the portfolio and is concerned that the UK stock market may fall in the short term. However, they does not wish to change the weighting in the portfolio. They, therefore, are not looking at an asset allocation or to sell stock. They look at two possibilities. First, they can sell FTSE Futures Contracts which will provide them with a profit as the market falls thereby offsetting the fall in value of the stocks. Secondly, they could buy a three-month FTSE Put option.

With the futures contracts the fund manager risks incurring a loss if the market should rise until they decide to close the position. With the put option they can determine how much the 'insurance' against a fall in the market will cost and has the comfort that if the market should rise they will never pay more than the original cost of the option.

Index stands at 6960 on January 3rd

The March Futures contract is trading at 6975.
The FTSE Feb 6950 Put is quoted at 50p.

Scenario one

Fund manager sells 2 FTSE futures contracts @ 6975.

Market RISES to 7010 by mid-Feb and fund manager decides the market will not fall and buys 2 contracts at 7050 to close the position.

Outcome – The hedge has cost the fund manager 2 × 75 points or 150 ticks, (7050 – 6975) × £5 = £1500.

Scenario two

Fund manager buys 2 Feb. 6950 Puts @ 50p.

Market rises to 7010 by mid-Feb.

The 6950 Puts are priced at 10p.

Outcome – The hedge has cost the fund manager £1000 in option premium paid to open the position. If they close the position by selling the put option they receive £200.

Therefore, there is a net cost of £800 excluding dealing fees.

Both strategies gave protection against a fall in the market. The put option restricted the cost of the hedge against a rise in the market.

However, bear in mind that whilst there is a loss occurring on the futures position as the index rises, the value of the stock has increased to compensate.

With the option, the rise in the stock prices accrues to the portfolio once the £1000 outlay has been compensated for.

The settlement issues are that once again the use of the derivative, whether it is futures or options must be properly recorded in the portfolio so that both the hedged item and the hedging item are valued and included in the overall value of the portfolio.

Additionally the sale of the futures would create margin calls, which need funding and reflecting in the accounts. It is important that the operations teams and fund managers are aware that an imbalance in funding can occur.

For example in the above scenario if the market was to rise, from a profit-and-loss perspective the portfolio is flat, i.e. the rise in the shares is offset by the loss on the future's. However, that is not the case in terms of the cash flow.

The loss on the futures will generate daily VM that must be settled. The profit on the shares does not create a cash flow, it is merely a revalued position.

There also needs to be a careful reconciliation of positions to make sure that one leg of a derivative strategy like hedging has not been closed out while the other remains open, i.e. the shares have been sold out of the portfolio but the futures being used as a hedge are open. Those futures are now creating a straight exposure to the market for the portfolio.

These are very simplistic examples, and the decision on whether to use futures or options to hedge a portfolio or stock will be made taking into account many factors. In both cases the position could be quickly closed out if desired.

In the above examples we have seen how the fund manager wants to disperse or minimise the impact of risk on their portfolio. But an investor or indeed a fund manager or a hedge fund manager may wish to take advantage of an anticipated market situation.

Speculation and exposure taking

Buying options

A speculator believes that BP stock price, which is currently at 400p, will rise in the next few weeks. They have approximately £60 000 to invest.

They could purchase 15 000 shares at 400p or, in the traded option market they could buy 250 of the 440p Call option contracts for 25p or £62 500.

The call options give them an exposure to 250 000 shares so if BP stock price rises as they expect it to, their potential profit far exceeds the amount they would make buying 15 000 shares yet they have made the same outlay.

If the stock price goes to 500p, the 440p Call options would be worth at least 60p so they would sell them for £150 000 for a profit of £87 500. Had they bought the 15 000 shares they would sell them for £75 000 for a profit of £15 000.

The characteristic of derivatives that enables a far greater reward for the same, or much smaller, initial outlay is often called *gearing*.

The option return was well over 100 per cent, yet on the shares it was 25 per cent.

However, if the stock price fails to rise or indeed falls, they would risk losing all their £62 500 if they buy the options.

Example

If the stock falls to 375p by the expiry of the options, the 440p Call options are worth nothing. However, if they had taken a conservative view and only bought the 15 000 BP stock, although it is showing a loss, it is still worth £56 250. The speculator, therefore, wants to assume risk for potentially much higher rewards.

The reason why the fund manager might buy options, or futures, is to gain an immediate exposure to the market. Having achieved this the fund manager can now actually take the exposure in the relevant stock or bonds or currencies by buying the underlying and then simultaneously closing out the derivatives. The big advantage is participation in any immediate market move, but also if the anticipated move does not happen the fund manager can easily and quickly close out the derivative positions and whilst a loss may occur, the fund had not had the expense associated with buying and then selling the underlying.

Looking at the settlement issues, they are once again about funding and recording, valuing and accounting for the derivatives in the portfolio so the overall value of the portfolio is complete.

Use of OTC derivatives

Until fairly recently most funds have been restricted in their use of OTC derivatives, many only being able to use currency forwards to manage currency exposures. That has changed with the latest European Directive (see appendices) and greater use of IRS, equity and total return swaps and credit derivatives is not being made where the fund's mandate allows.

From a settlement point of view, the key issues are to understand the product, how to account for these products and the need to manage negotiated terms and conditions rather than a standardised product. A key issue here can be the valuation of the OTC position as no exchange or public price may be available.

In this case the fund management must determine a fair and consistent valuation approach that may include using other parties to verify internal pricing methodology and or that of the counterparty bank.

Given the bespoke nature of OTC products it is not easy to set out standard procedures; however, many common OTC products like IRS do have fairly standard settlement procedures as we have seen earlier.

The OTC settlement is usually, but not always, under the terms of the documentation provided by ISDA and these can be obtained from the ISDA website (see appendices).

Regulation and compliance

Derivatives are not always the best instrument to use for investment strategies. Sometimes derivatives create what is known as contingent liabilities, a situation where there is an ongoing actual or potential settlement process. In other words, there is more than one settlement amount that might create funding issues, for example VM.

Other kind of contingent liabilities relate to issues like the ability to simultaneously close out one derivative position and open another or to trade two opening transactions together. If this is not achieved then there is likely to be some funding or exposure issues created.

The characteristics of derivative products may also create situations that are beneficial to some kinds of investors but not to others. For instance, gearing favours hedge fund strategies and speculators but is less advantageous in risk-averse investment funds and strategies.

The nature of the derivative product is one that means regulators and those charged with protecting other parties' interests like trustees will often restrict, and in some cases prohibit, the use of derivatives in funds or the marketing of some of the products to 'unsuitable' private investors.

On the other hand, the regulators and trustees see the sense in allowing investors and fund managers to hedge against risks.

Not surprisingly breaches of rules, regulations and mandates, etc. are not viewed lightly by the aforementioned, and a manager could find themselves not only suffering some kind of fine but also being barred from using the products again.

In the United Kingdom the regulator, the FSA, requires a Derivatives Risk Warning to be provided to certain categories of customers. The FSA also has regulations governing the use of derivatives by investment schemes limiting things like exposures, ensuring the use meets 'efficient portfolio management' criteria, and the type of derivative product that can be used.

In the wider context there are the European Directives that permit the use of derivatives in various ways and the use of various products, and these have recently allowed a greater use of OTC derivatives by funds.

There are specific regulations related to US markets and investors and of course every jurisdiction has its own regulatory requirements over exchanges, clearing houses, brokers, investment managers and usually foreign investors.

Mutual fund mandates and unit trust's trust deeds will make it clear whether derivatives are permitted for use, which derivatives can be used, which markets are acceptable and sometimes how the products can be used?

Some funds like hedge funds are registered offshore and so may be exempt from some regulation that applies to onshore funds thereby allowing much greater and unrestricted use of derivatives.

Needless to say, some rules are based on Conduct of Business Rules (can be found at www.fsa.gov.uk) and refer to the protection of clients' assets, type and accuracy of communication, etc; and in fact to most of the issues we have highlighted in this chapter and the rest of the book.

Summary

The growth in the use of derivatives and the use of OTC derivatives is certainly a challenge for operations teams in fund management companies and custodians.

In general terms it is the issues surrounding margin verification, collateral, OTC position valuation, sometimes accounting and exercise/assignment that cause the major problems.

As the growth in the use of derivatives will undoubtedly continue and as the products used will become greater in terms of volume and maybe complexity, fund management companies, fund administrators and custodians need to have greater product knowledge and technology resource.

8

Margin and collateral

For exchange-traded products the risk that the clearing house faces is that the contracts it clears represent a far greater value than has actually been settled. To manage this risk the clearing house utilises several risk management techniques including the use of margin.

By applying an initial margin or deposit and requiring the valuation amount or obligation associated with open positions in futures and options to be settled daily, the clearing house is able to monitor and manage the risk of open positions and closeout trades.

Initial margin

The deposit which the clearing house calls to cover margin requirements is called *initial margin* and is returnable to the clearing member once the position is closed.

The amount for each product will vary as it is geared to the current volatility of the particular product. The margin will be sufficient to cover an approximate 3–5 per cent movement in the price of the contract on a day but can and often is changed to reflect the current situation. If this occurs during the day it is called *intra-day margin*. This will only occur when there is a very large movement up or down in the price of the contract.

When you buy or sell a futures contract you do not pay the full value of the contract, only the margin requirement. This initial margin or deposit is held by the clearing house throughout the time that the position is maintained. The clearing house must have some kind of insurance that any settlement or delivery obligations could be fulfilled.

By settling with clearing members on a daily basis the clearing house restricts the level of risk itself and the other market members are exposed to.

Options on futures positions are margined in the same way as futures contracts with initial and VM requirements.

Long premium paid or traded option positions are not charged initial margin because once the premium has been paid for the option, on T + 1, then there is no further risk to the clearing house. The worst that can happen is that the option can expire at zero.

If a long option is exercised then the clearing house will call margin to cover the delivery obligations.

Short option positions are margined, as there is a risk of the writer being unable financially to fulfil their delivery obligations. This margin requirement is typically calculated using SPAN or a similar exchange margin method such as TIMS. Detailed explanation of both SPAN and TIMS is given in the appendices.

Most clearing houses pay interest to members on cash deposited to cover their initial margin requirements. At LCH.Clearnet interest is paid on cash balances using rates that are actually set by the clearing house. These rates are known as the London Deposit Rates (LDR) and they are derived from bid rates for overnight funds quoted by selected money brokers and major banks for each currency. The highest and lowest rates are discounted to calculate the average. Many brokerage houses use the LDR rates plus 1 per cent or minus $1/_2$ per cent as a basis of rates charged or paid to their clients.

An explanation of delta

When it comes to margin calculation the process is sometimes very straightforward and sometimes more complex. For example, a futures position can be margined on a rate-per-contract basis whilst option positions, because they have strike prices and Calls and Puts, present more of a challenge in determining a fair but realistic margin rate. The price of different option series can move at different rates and by different values. One measure of the amount that an option series should change by a given change to the underlying is called delta.

The delta of an option can be described as the amount by which an option's premium moves, with respect to the changes in the underlying security price. Gamma measures the speed of change and as time value, the theta, decreases, this also affects the price or value of an option. A deep in-the-money option has a delta of 1, a far out-of-the-money option a delta of 0 and an at-the-money option a delta of 0.5.

The SPAN uses the delta value of options to convert them to equivalent futures when calculating the inter-month spread charge because gains in one month may not exactly offset losses in another and there is a risk for the clearing house.

Intra-day margin

As we have already said, in times of very large movements up or down in the price of a contract, the clearing house or exchange will recalculate the initial margin requirement. An additional amount may be required per contract for all contracts open, which are affected. It is unlikely that all contracts are affected because the news that caused the volatility may concern for example, a foreign economy, which has a knock-on effect for domestic bonds.

If the clearing house believes that the situation is only temporary and that conditions will quickly return to a more stable environment, then they will leave the initial margin requirement at its original level for the next day, only calling the intra-day margin as a one-off payment. More likely however, the initial margin level will be changed as a result of volatile conditions.

The intra-day margin call is made to cover the increased risk since the original initial margin was paid in the morning, and then the new increased initial margin rate is called from the next day onwards.

Intra-day margins can be called from the clearing members by the clearing house up to any time as determined in their rules. The clearing members must pay the required amount to the clearing house; however, depending on the time of day that the call is made, it may be difficult for the clearing member to receive the funds from their clients. In some cases the clearing house only calls intra-day margin from one side; for example, if the underlying has risen sharply then the short positions are losing money. It is the holders of the short positions that represent the risk to the clearing house because they will have obligations to settle the next day. The holder of the long positions are making a profit so will not owe anything to the clearing house.

Brokers must endeavour to receive the funds or additional collateral from their clients difficult as this may be and at the very least must contact the client and let them know that additional funds are due. In this respect, it is necessary that the clearing member is able to re-calculate margin requirements during the day on their own systems so that they may see accurately which clients are affected and reconcile the amounts that are due.

Spot month margin

This is an additional rate of margin which is charged by the clearing house to cover the risk that they incur between the last trading day of a contract and its ultimate delivery. It covers the risk of a default during the delivery process.

There are no offsets allowed for spread positions. The clearing house on settlement day +1 releases initial and spot month margins, once they are satisfied that delivery has been effected correctly.

Margin methods

The method for calculating margin also varies from clearing house to clearing house. It may be different for futures and traded options. However, in 1988 the CME devised a method known as *SPAN*. This risk-based margining system is now used by many exchanges for the calculation of the initial margin on futures and options. Most exchanges that have adopted SPAN have 'tweaked' it for their own particular use and therefore there are different versions in use. For example, Euronext.liffe use London SPAN.

The SPAN looks at a set of 16 possible changes in market conditions within the boundaries of the risk parameters set by the clearing house which is known as the risk array. The profit or loss for one long position in each futures and options contract is worked out under each scenario, for valuing positions. By combining all of the individual arrays, London SPAN determines the scanning risk, which is the worst possible loss for the portfolio.

Each position in the member's portfolio is calculated and totalled across the same underlying contract. The final result is the largest potential loss for the portfolio, which is charged as initial margin.

London SPAN uses pricing models to calculate the option prices. The Binomial model is used for equity and index options but the Black-76 model is used for options which are priced off the future.

The parameters are set using both the historic and the implied volatility of the contract, and in agreement with the exchange.

A detailed example of SPAN is given in the appendices.

Margin offsets

Where investors in a market employ particular trading strategies the clearing house may allow certain reductions in the margin require-ments to reflect the reduced risk of the position.

In the US markets, for example, a 'hedge' rate of initial margin is quoted which can be applied to positions that are a hedge. This is a position where the opposite side reduces the risk of one side of the position.

Movements in the market would have a negative impact on one side but a positive impact on the other side. This would be a significantly lower initial margin rate than a 'spec' rate, which carries the full risk of the position, as there is no balancing side to offset any of the risks.

London SPAN calculates an inter-month spread charge to compensate for the basis risk incurred because futures prices do not correlate exactly across contract months. This is calculated for futures and using the delta value for options to convert them to equivalent futures. Where a spread exists but does not have equal and opposite sides the spread margin is only charged on the number of contracts that are equal. The remaining contracts are charged margin at the full rate.

The inter-month spread charge calculation is:

Number of spreads × inter-month spread charge rate

Additionally certain different contracts can be offset across portfolios, where the clearing house can justify it on risk grounds.

Delta spreads are used in the calculation:

Weighted futures price risk × spread credit rate × number of spreads × delta spread ratio

In order to calculate the total initial margin requirement, the following rule is applied:

Scanning risk + Inter-month spread charge + Spot month charge − Inter-commodity charge

Note: 'Delta' is also a term used in options where it is the rate of change of price of the option in response to a change in the price of the underlying asset (see Appendix 9: SPAN).

Variation margin

We know that for most types of futures contracts, the clearing organisation pays and collects the profit or loss that is accruing on the open futures positions as the price moves up or down each day. This movement generates pay-and-receive situations for the members with the open positions. The clearing organisation will call in and pay out this net amount to each clearing member daily. This amount is known as VM.

)r other types of futures contracts, usually known as forwards, the VM is calculated each day but any profits accrued are not paid out until the settlement date of the contract.

This applies even if the position is closed out in the exchange early on in its life. The profit will stay with the clearing house until the settlement (delivery) date.

Any profit that is accrued can be used to offset initial margin requirements but it does not attract interest, as it is unrealised.

All losses that occur must be settled on a daily basis. This is true of contracts traded on the LME and the Swedish markets.

An example of the calculation of VM over a period of time follows:

The client buys 1 Sep. Long Gilt Future at 109.13 on June 1st.
The client sells the position at 109.42 on June 8th.

The contract size is £100 000 nominal value with a minimum price fluctuation of one pence per £100 nominal or 0.01. This gives a tick size of £10.

The initial margin rate is £500 per contract.

The table below shows the VM over a period.

Date	Trade price	Net position	Closing price	Daily movement	Price	Sett. date	Daily settlement
1/06	109.13	+1	109.09	−4 ticks		2/06	£40 Loss
2/06		+1	109.28	+19 ticks		3/06	£190 Profit
3/06		+1	109.28	No change		4/06	No Movement
4/06		+1	109.35	+7 ticks		5/06	£70 Profit
5/06		+1	109.40	+5 ticks		8/06	£50 Profit
8/06	109.42	0		+2 ticks		9/06	£20 Profit
Total				+29 ticks			£290 Profit

The profit on the trade was 29 ticks or points, which is the difference between the buying and selling price.

Each tick = £10 therefore 29 × £10 = £290

The initial margin of £500 per contract would be called by the clearing house on 2/6 and held until 9/6 when it would be returned.

It must be remembered that VM must always be settled in cash.

This is because the broker must always settle with the clearing organisation in the currency of the contract. Clients without cash in place to cover VM may incur harsh debit interest penalties.

Tick size

The point was made earlier in the book that the tick size of a contract is not always the same and there are therefore different ways that they are arrived at.

Examples

Chicago Mercantile Exchange Standard & Poor's 500 Index Future
- The contract size or trading unit is S&P Index X $250.
- The price is quoted in index points and the minimum price fluctuation is 0.10 index points. This gives a tick size of $25 ($250 divided by 10).

Euronext.liffe Short Sterling Interest Rate Contract
- The tick size is the value of a one-point movement in the contract price. This price is arrived at by multiplying the notional contract size by the length of time of the notional time deposit underlying the contract in years multiplied by the minimum tick size movement of 0.01 per cent.

$$£500\ 000 \times 3/12 \times 0.01 \text{ per cent} = £12.50$$

The tick size of the Short Sterling Future therefore = £12.50

Option margin

The writers or holders of short positions in either calls or puts are required to put up margin. The rationale behind this is that the writer has an obligation and must either be able to buy back the option position or be able to make or take delivery upon assignment. However, there is a difference between the situation regarding calls and puts.

The writer of a call option, if you recall, is required to deliver to the buyer the underlying at the strike price of the option if the buyer exercises their right. This means that the writer will either already have possession of the underlying, i.e. they are a covered writer or will need to purchase the underlying for onward delivery, i.e. they are a naked writer.

The writer of a put option, on the other hand, is required to take delivery of the underlying at the strike price of the option if the buyer exercises their right. In this case the writer needs to have sufficient capital to meet the purchase cost of the underlying.

The risk of course is that the writer cannot or does not meet their obligation.

Option margin is often calculated by exchange clearing houses using the previously mentioned TIMS. For example the OCC, Eurex AG as well as, amongst many others, the Australian Clearing House all use TIMS but it must be remembered that TIMS is not just about calculating option margin anymore than SPAN is about futures margin; both calculate margins on 'groups' of products.

Methodology

The TIMS uses advanced pricing models to project the liquidation value of each portfolio, given changes in the price of each underlying product. These models generate a set of theoretical values based on various factors including current prices, historical prices and market volatility. Based on flexible criteria established by a clearinghouse, statistically significant hedges receive appropriate margin offsets. TIMS also is used to predict a member's potential intra-day risk under varying sets of assumptions regarding market changes.

TIMS organises all classes of options and futures relating to the same underlying asset into class groups and all class groups whose underlying assets exhibit close price correlation into product groups. The daily margin requirement for a clearing member is calculated based on its entire position within a class group and various product groups. The margin requirement consists of two components, a MTM component and an additional margin component.

Premium margin

The MTM component takes the form of a premium margin calculation that provides margin debits or requirements for net short positions and margin credits for net long positions. The margin debits and credits are netted to determine the total premium margin requirement or credit for each class group. The premium margin component represents the cost to liquidate the portfolio at current prices by selling the net long positions and buying back the net short positions.

Additional margin

The additional margin component, the portion of the margin requirement that covers market risk, is calculated using price theory in conjunction with class group margin intervals. TIMS projects the theoretical cost of liquidating a portfolio of positions in the event of an assumed worst case change in the price of the underlying asset. Theoretical values are used to determine what a position will be worth when the underlying asset value changes. Given a set of input parameters (i.e., option contract specifics, interest rates, dividends and volatility), the pricing model will predict what the position should theoretically be worth at a specified price for the underlying instrument.

The class group margin interval determines the maximum one-day increase in the value of the underlying asset (upside) and the maximum one-day decrease in the value of the underlying asset (downside), which can be expected as a result of historical volatility.

The methodology used to determine class group margin intervals and product groups can be specified by each clearing institution.

Settlement of option margin

Operations teams need to be a bit careful in terms of what margin is called and what is acceptable as collateral.

First, a clearing broker's systems must be able to run the margin system utilised by the exchange clearing houses of which they are members. Huge problems in reconciliation and risk control will occur if the margin calls cannot be agreed. In the same way an institutional client needs to be able to reconcile their broker's margin call.

Let us look at the case of a call option. If the trader or client has a short position in, say, 20 BP Mar. 390 Call options with each option contract being for 1000 shares and if the client has 20 000 BP shares then they are fully covered in the event of assignment. They could pledge those shares as good collateral over the full liability.

If BP share price, however, was only 360, a trader would be pretty loathed to have to buy or hold 20 000 shares on their book as the likelihood of the 390 calls being exercised is extremely low at this point. This is where the concept of deltas mentioned earlier comes in, and why systems like SPAN and TIMS which take into account the out-of-the-money element of the risk are so good.

What about the writer of the puts?

It is clear here that the margin must reflect the cost of acquiring the underlying. Therefore if the client wanted to put up say 20 000 BP shares as collateral against 20 BP 390 Put options it cannot be fully covered if the option is in-the-money.

The reason is simple enough to understand. BP shares are, say, currently 360p. Therefore 20 000 shares are worth £72 000; however, if the option was assigned the writer would have to find 20 000 × 390 = £78 000.

To be covered, either there would have to be more shares deposited as collateral or the collateral would have to be 'topped' up with something additional like cash. Also the value of the collateral must be monitored very carefully as the value could change quickly and leave the margin call under-collateralised. For this reason most brokers will agree with their client that the client should leave a buffer in terms of collateral to avoid constant deposits and withdrawals.

The broker may also propose something else to the client. If the client wishes to deposit collateral in a form other than cash, the broker will probably charge some kind of administration fee. However, this may be waived if the client agrees to rehypothecation. That is, the client agrees to the transfer of the collateral to the broker to be used however the broker wishes.

For some clients this is not a problem but for others it may be, and operations teams within the client must understand the terms of any collateral agreements they may have with their brokers.

Collateral

Initial margin obligations for futures and options positions at the clearing house can be covered in various ways. Collateral in the form of cash in the currencies of the contracts traded is most commonly used. In addition, Bank Guarantees, Government Treasury Bonds and Bills, Certificates of Deposits and certain Equities are accepted at the London Clearing House for example. Each clearing house or exchange will publish the collateral that they accept. LCH.Clearnet has quite a wide range but some markets only accept cash in their domestic currency.

It is possible to use a combination of cash and physical collateral in some markets. For 10-Year Japanese Government Bond Futures in the Tokyo Stock Exchange, however, only a maximum of 2 per cent of the margin requirement may be covered using collateral and the remaining 1 per cent must be cash.

The collateral that the broker will accept from a client is usually negotiable. There may however be restrictions about where it must be held and also an arrangement fee. In some cases, the client may have to check with their trustees about whether they have any additional restrictions.

By physically transferring the collateral into the name of the clearing member or clearing house, the client loses 'beneficial ownership' of the collateral. Therefore, there is a credit risk with the clearing member or wherever the collateral is held, as it is shown as their asset and may be seized in the event of a default by the organisation, even though the client is not involved in the default situation.

Acceptable collateral

Most of the clearing houses for exchanges publish lists of acceptable collateral. Below is an example list of the types of collateral accepted by LCH.Clearnet. It is for illustrative purposes only and clearing houses can and do vary in the types of collateral they will accept. Operations teams would need to check with the relevant clearing house for the current list of acceptable collateral.

LCH.Clearnet Limited Acceptable Collateral

Collateral	Acceptable types (Bloomberg Description & Code)	Valuation & Haircut	Prices TRS Code
Cash			
	Sterling	Nominal Nil	
	Euros		
	US Dollars		
	Swiss Francs		
	Japanese Yen		
	Swedish Krona		
	Danish Krone		
	Norwegian Kroner		
Bank Guarantees			
	Limited range of acceptable issuers	Nominal Nil to termination date	
Government Securities			
UK	United Kingdom GBP Treasury Bill (UKTB)	Nominal 5%	
	United Kingdom Gilt Bond (UKT)	Market 3% 10 calendar days–3 years 4% 3–7 years 6% 7–11 years 12% 11+ years	$Gil

Continued

LCH.Clearnet Limited Acceptable Collateral—cont'd

Collateral	Acceptable types (Bloomberg Description & Code)	Valuation & Haircut		Prices TRS Code
US	US Treasury Bill (B)	Nominal	4%	
	US Treasury Note/Bond (T)	Market	3% 2 working days–3 years	$Bon
	Current US Treasury Note/Bond (CT)		4% 3–7 years 6% 7–11 years 7% 11+ years	
Italian	Buoni Ordinari del Tesoro (BOTS)	Nominal	3%	
	Buoni del Tesoro Poliennali (BTPS)	Market	5% 3 working days–3 years	$Bun
	Certificati di Credito del Tesoro (CCTS/ICTZ)		8% 3+ years	
Spanish	Spanish Letras del Tesoro (SGLT)	Nominal	3%	
	Spanish Government Bond (SPGB)	Market	4% 2 working days–7 years	$Bun
			6% 7–11 years 9% 11+ years	
German		Nominal	3%	
	German Treasury Bill (BUBILL)	Market	3% 2 working days–3 years	$Bun
			4% 3–7 years	
	Bundesobligationen (OBL)		6% 7–11 years	
	Bundesschatzanweisungen (BKO)		9% 11+ years	
	Deutsche Bundesbahn (DBB)			
	Deutsche Bundesrepublik (DBR)			
	Treuhandanstalt (THA)			
French	Bons du Tresor a Taux Fixe et Interet Precompte (BTF)	Nominal	3%	
	Bons du Tresor a Taux Fixe et Interet Annuel (BTNS)	Market	3% 4 working days–3 years	$Bun
	Obligations Assimilables de Tresor (FRTR)		4% 3–7 years 6% 7–11 years 8% 11+ years	

LCH.Clearnet Limited Acceptable Collateral—cont'd

Collateral	Acceptable types (Bloomberg Description & Code)	Valuation & Haircut		Prices TRS Code
Dutch	Dutch Treasury Certificate (DTB)	Nominal 3%		
	Dutch Government Bond (NETHER)	Market	3% 10 working days–3 years 4% 3–7 years 5% 7–11 years 8% 11+ years	$Bun
Austrian	Austrian Treasury Bill (RATB)	Nominal 5%		
	Austrian Government Bond (RAGB)	Market	3% 4 working days–3 years 4% 3–7 years 6% 7–11 years 14% 11+ years	$Bun
Belgian	Belgian Treasury Bill (BGTB)	Nominal 3%		
	Belgian Government Bond (BGB)	Market	3% 4 working days–3 years 5% 3–7 years 6% 7–11 years 8% 11+ years	$Bun
Canadian	Canadian Treasury Bill (CTB)	Nominal 3%		
	Canadian Government Bond (CAN)	Market	4% 10 calendar days–3 years 5% 3–7 years 6% 7–11 years 7% 11+ years	$Bon
Swedish	Swedish Treasury Bill (SWTB)	Nominal 3%		
	Swedish Government Bond (SWED)	Market	3% 4 working days–3 years 5% 3–7 years 6% 7–11 years 8% 11+ years	$Bun
Australian	Australian Government Bond (ACGB)	Market	3% 13 calendar days–3 years 5% 3–7 years 6% 7+ years	$Bon
Finnish	Finnish Treasury Bill (RFTB)	Nominal 3%		
	Finnish Government Bonds (RFGB)	Market	3% 4 working days–3 years 6% 3–7 years	$Bun

Continued

LCH.Clearnet Limited Acceptable Collateral—cont'd

Collateral	Acceptable types (Bloomberg Description & Code)	Valuation & Haircut	Prices TRS Code
Denmark	Danish Treasury Bill (DGTB) Danish Government Bond (DGB)	Nominal 3% Market 3% 5 working days–3 years 5% 3–7 years	$Bun
Other Securities			
Sterling CDs	Limited range of acceptable issuers, under 1 year to maturity	Nominal 5%	
US Dollar CDs	Limited range of acceptable issuers	Nominal 5%	
UK Equities	FT-SE 100 & stocks underlying equity options SET 1 SET 2	Market 35% Market 50%	$Equ

Notes:

1. Members should refer to LCH.Clearnet Limited's General Regulations, Default Rules and Procedures, or telephone LCH.Clearnet Limited Treasury Operations on +44 (0)20 7426 7124 for information relating to the acceptance of collateral.

2. Before any securities are accepted, members must complete a legal form of charge, for further information telephone LCH.Clearnet Limited Membership on +44 (0)20 7426 7627.

3. LCH.Clearnet Limited imposes overall limits on CDs, bank guarantees and equities.

4. Certain taxation restrictions and requirements may apply to securities.

5. Any collateral may be used to cover any margin liability with the following restrictions:
   (i) US Dollar securities held in New York may not cover equity options (including index options) margins, and EquityClear margins;
   (ii) Equities may only cover equity-related margins.

6. To be acceptable, government securities must be issued in the home country of the issuing government and be denominated in its domestic currency (a definition which, for Euroland countries, includes both their legacy currencies and the euro).

7. SET3 Equities will not be accepted as collateral.

8. The list refers to collateral acceptable to LCH.Clearnet Limited as margin cover for all business cleared. Certain European regulators have agreed that OTC instruments registered with LCH.Clearnet Limited should be exempt (following Directive 2000/12/EC of 20 March 2000) from credit equivalent amount add-on. Any such exemption applies to LCH.Clearnet Limited members only where initial margin requirements are met with Cash or the Government Securities acceptable by LCH.Clearnet Limited. Members are responsible for ensuring that they comply fully with regulatory requirements in this respect.

9. Charge and Credits
   (i) Cash – Interest is paid on cash at the London Deposit Rate (LDR). This is accrued daily and paid on a monthly basis to your PPS account. LDR can be viewed daily on TRS at $BRT.

(ii) Bank Guarantees – LCH charges 10 basis points (annualised) for utilisation. This is accrued daily and charged on a monthly basis to your PPS account.

(iii) Government Securities, CDs and equities – LCH charges 10 basis points for utilisation. This is accrued daily and charged on a monthly basis to your PPS account.

Source: LCH.Clearnet.

It must be understood that these are lists of collateral accepted from the clearing member. The clearing member may or may not be prepared to accept the same collateral from a client. Even where it does agree, it may levy additional charges to cover the administration costs, just like the clearing house does as we see above.

Margining to a client

It is relatively easy to understand the concept of VM. It is possible for the client to calculate the amounts themselves, in order to verify what their clearing broker is charging or paying them. Depending on the complexity of the position, it would be easily possible for the clients to work it out for themselves using a pen, paper and a calculator, so long as they know the necessary variables such as the tick size and value.

Initial margin is much harder to explain. For futures contracts where an initial margin rate is published by the clearing house, it can be easily calculated and verified by clients, but only if the position is very simple and no offsets have been given under a portfolio margining system.

The biggest problem can occur if the client wants to trade a particular strategy and needs to know how much the initial margin will be approximately, so that they can work out the financing costs.

It may be possible for some clearing brokers to run test accounts for clients where such positions could be input and the margining run using the last available arrays. This would give the approximate cost but can be very time-consuming for the broker's staff to accomplish and would not necessarily be part of a regular service to the client.

Although risk-based margining systems are very efficient and result in the client paying a lower overall initial margin, clients can find it very difficult to understand and generally have to take the clearing broker's word for it that the amount required is correct. In order for the client to accurately verify the initial margin required, they need to be able to receive the risk arrays from the clearing house or exchange and then have a system, which is able to correctly compute this. Some clearing houses publish their risk arrays openly and clients are able to obtain the information easily. A charge is usually made for this service though. Other exchanges do not openly publish the arrays except to their clearing members. Additional problems occur for clients who have a portfolio of global market positions, so it becomes almost impossible for clients to perform margining themselves.

For larger volume clients, a solution may be for them to use a recognised futures system for their own processing and accounting. Systems such as Sungard and Rolfe & Nolan may be available on a bureau basis so that clients only pay for the use that they make of the system. These systems should have all of the margining capabilities already established.

Single currency margining and settlement

For clients trading in various different markets around the world and having numerous currencies to move, the settlement process can be quite cumbersome. Therefore, many clearing brokers offer a service known as single currency margining.

This involves the deposit of one currency, which is equal to or more than the total amount of currencies due.

In order to calculate this, each currency is notionally converted to the base currency chosen by the client as the preferred settlement currency. Interest would normally be received on the currency deposited and would be charged on the currencies, which are in debit. Both the clearing broker and the client, as the amount due in the settlement currency is only calculated once overnight, using the end-of-day FX rates incur an intra-day FX risk. Therefore, if this service is offered to many clients it needs careful control by Operations management to ensure that FX risks are properly managed. Even major currencies need to be monitored so that the Management Team is aware of exposure to each currency. Additional problems can be incurred with some of the minor global currencies, as these are not always readily available for use. It may be useful for the clearing broker to have an agreement for single currency margining which stipulates which currencies are included under normal use and what should happen for the exceptional currencies.

Although no formal charge is made for this service, clearing brokers recoup their expenses through the interest rates that are paid and received. They need to be relatively competitive in order to make the service viable but they are designed to cover at least all of the financing costs that the broker incurs on behalf of the client. From the client's point of view it makes the settlement process much more efficient and in particular reduces bank charges and administration for foreign transactions.

Margining OTC positions

The OTC positions can give rise to a situation where one or other party is winning and one losing. An obvious answer is to margin the losing position, but given that it is a negotiated rather than a standardised product that is easier said than done.

Collateral management of OTC exposures and risks is a complicated business governed by various issues like credit ratings of the two parties, suitable and agreeable margin system or basis and acceptable collateral. However, given the counterparty risk that exists it is still hugely important to negotiate and agree any applicable margin terms at the time of the trade.

Summary

Margin and collateral are not only core elements of undertaking derivative activity, but also fundamental risk control tools.

Efficient use of collateral, i.e. does a fund manager use cash or assets to cover margin calls, what are the relevant charges and funding costs, what can/does a broker want to use or take as collateral etc. are all key business issues and will impact in terms of profitability and returns on derivatives activity.

9

Impact of corporate actions

Introduction

Many derivatives are affected by corporate actions that occur on the underlying. This is particularly the case with equity, where there may be a change to the capital structure of a firm and bond derivatives where the deliverable list of bonds may change because of some event on a bond in that basket. However, there are events that occur with derivative products that we might refer to as being similar to corporate actions. These might be maturity and tender, exercise/assignment actions and changes to the number of shares or the amount of underlying decided by the exchange in response to a significant change in the price of the underlying. For example, if a share price rises to say £30 per share the exchange might change the contract size from 1000 shares to 100 shares. If the price then fell to £3 the exchange may change the contract size back to 1000 shares.

The key thing is that a firm or investor risks financial loss if they fail to deal with changes to contract specifications, which could occur when there is a corporate action on an underlying, or fail to deal with an action or event related to the derivative itself.

It is therefore crucially important that as part of the derivatives clearing and settlement process there is good-quality data management including static data covering:

- Expiry dates
- Delivery periods
- First and Last notice days
- Deliverable baskets
- Last trading dates

- Exercise triggers
- ITM/ATM/OTM data
- Corporate actions on underlyings.

Exchanges publish data on the contracts listed by them including maturity and expiry dates, notice days and last trading days (see Appendix: IPE Expiry Dates). The deliverable baskets and various delivery options are also provided by the exchange. These will include whether the contract is physical, cash, EFP or EFS and what delivery processes there may be.

When it comes to a corporate action on an underlying, the exchange will also publish what action it proposes to take. This may be a change to the contract specification and therefore has great importance.

To illustrate this we can loom at the following notice related to a corporate action issued by the CBOE and also one issued by Euronext.liffe

---

Research Circular #RS04-559
October 26, 2004

Devon Energy Corporation (DVN/YQ/VVH) 2-for-1 Stock Split Ex-Distribution Date: November 16, 2004

Devon Energy Corporation ('DVN/YQ/VVH') has announced a 2-;for-;1 common stock split, with a payable date of November 15, 2004, to shareholders of record October 29, 2004. The ex-date for the stock split is Tuesday, November 16, 2004.

Contract Adjustment
Pursuant to OCC rules (Article VI, Section 11), all outstanding DVN/YQ/VVH option series will be adjusted to reflect this 2-;for-1 stock split on Tuesday, November 16, 2004, at 8:30 A.M. Chicago time. The OCC will issue one additional contract for each open contract on the ex-date. Also on the ex-date, each DVN/YQ/VVH series will have an adjusted exercise price equal to one-half of the exercise price rounded to the nearest 1/8 of a point for each DVN/YQ/VVH series existing on the business day immediately prior to the ex-date. The option symbols will remain the same. Adjusted exercise prices are shown below. [Any FLEX series that may exist will be adjusted in a similar manner to the standardized option.]

The option adjustment will appear in the Daily Position Report of the clearing member firms on the ex-date. After 8:30 A.M. Tuesday, November 16, 2004, all trades, corrections, and exercises must be submitted to the CBOE and OCC on an adjusted basis.

Adjusted Exercise Prices

On Tuesday, November 16, 2004, the ex-distribution date, trading in DVN/YQ/VVH series will be on an adjusted basis. At 8:30 A.M., Chicago time, an opening rotation will be effected with the following adjustments:

	EXISTING SERIES (100 Shares)				ADJUSTED SERIES* (100 Shares)		
MONTH/	STRIKE	CALLS	PUTS	MONTH/	STRIKE	CALLS	PUTS
Nov	60	DVNKL	DVNWL	Nov	30	DVNKF	DVNWF
Nov	65	DVNKM	DVNWM	Nov	32 1/2	DVNKZ	DVNWZ
Nov	70	DVNKN	DVNWN	Nov	35	DVNKG	DVNWG
Nov	75	DVNKO	DVNWO	Nov	37 1/2	DVNKU	DVNWU
Nov	80	DVNKP	DVNWP	Nov	40	DVNKH	DVNWH
Dec	60	DVNLL	DVNXL	Dec	30	DVNLF	DVNXF
Dec	65	DVNLM	DVNXM	Dec	32 1/2	DVNLZ	DVNXZ
Dec	70	DVNLN	DVNXN	Dec	35	DVNLG	DVNXG
Dec	75	DVNLO	DVNXO	Dec	37 1/2	DVNLU	DVNXU
Dec	80	DVNLP	DVNXP	Dec	40	DVNLH	DVNXH
Dec	85	DVNLQ	DVNXQ	Dec	42 1/2	DVNLV	DVNXV
Jan	40	DVNAH	DVNMH	Jan	20	DVNAD	DVNMD
Jan	45	DVNAI	DVNMI	Jan	22 1/2	DVNAX	DVNMX
Jan	50	DVNAJ	DVNMJ	Jan	25	DVNAE	DVNME
Jan	55	DVNAK	DVNMK	Jan	27 1/2	DVNAY	DVNMY
Jan	60	DVNAL	DVNML	Jan	30	DVNAF	DVNMF
Jan	65	DVNAM	DVNMM	Jan	32 1/2	DVNAZ	DVNMZ
Jan	70	DVNAN	DVNMN	Jan	35	DVNAG	DVNMG
Jan	75	DVNAO	DVNMO	Jan	37 1/2	DVNAU	DVNMU
Jan	80	DVNAP	DVNMP	Jan	40	DVNAH	DVNMH
Jan	85	DVNAQ	DVNMQ	Jan	42 1/2	DVNAV	DVNMV
Jan	90	DVNAR	DVNMR	Jan	45	DVNAI	DVNMI
Jan	95	DVNAS	DVNMS	Jan	47 1/2	DVNAW	DVNMW
Apr	55	DVNDK	DVNPK	Apr	27 1/2	DVNDY	DVNPY
Apr	60	DVNDL	DVNPL	Apr	30	DVNDF	DVNPF
Apr	65	DVNDM	DVNPM	Apr	32 1/2	DVNDZ	DVNPZ
Apr	70	DVNDN	DVNPN	Apr	35	DVNDG	DVNPG
Apr	75	DVNDO	DVNPO	Apr	37 1/2	DVNDU	DVNPU
Apr	80	DVNDP	DVNPP	Apr	40	DVNDH	DVNPH
2006 LEAPS							
Jan	40	YQAH	YQMH	Jan	20	YQAD	YQMD
Jan	45	YQAI	YQMI	Jan	22 1/2	YQAX	YQMX

Continued

EXISTING SERIES (100 Shares)				ADJUSTED SERIES* (100 Shares)			
Jan	50	YQAJ	YQMJ	Jan	25	YQAE	YQME
Jan	55	YQAK	YQMK	Jan	27 1/2	YQAY	YQMY
Jan	60	YQAL	YQML	Jan	30	YQAF	YQMF
Jan	65	YQAM	YQMM	Jan	32 1/2	YQAZ	YQMZ
Jan	70	YQAN	YQMN	Jan	35	YQAG	YQMG
Jan	75	YQAO	YQMO	Jan	37 1/2	YQAU	YQMU
Jan	80	YQAP	YQMP	Jan	40	YQAH	YQMH
2007 LEAPS							
Jan	40	VVHAH	VVHMH	Jan	20	VVHAD	VVHMD
Jan	45	VVHAI	VVHMI	Jan	22 1/2	VVHAX	VVHMX
Jan	50	VVHAJ	VVHMJ	Jan	25	VVHAE	VVHME
Jan	55	VVHAK	VVHMK	Jan	27 1/2	VVHAY	VVHMY
Jan	60	VVHAL	VVHML	Jan	30	VVHAF	VVHMF
Jan	65	VVHAM	VVHMM	Jan	32 1/2	VVHAZ	VVHMZ
Jan	70	VVHAN	VVHMN	Jan	35	VVHAG	VVHMG
Jan	75	VVHAO	VVHMO	Jan	37 1/2	VVHAU	VVHMU
Jan	80	VVHAP	VVHMP	Jan	40	VVHAH	VVHMH

Any additional DVN/YQ/VVH series that are added prior to the ex-date will also be adjusted in the manner described above.

The following series have non-standard strikes and price symbols with respect to the OPRA exercise price symbol format:

Y (27–1/2)   Z (32–1/2)   U (37–1/2)   V (42–1/2)   W (47–1/2)

IMPORTANT Order Entry After Adjustment
Please note that at the time of the adjustment, the strike prices of all DVN/YQ/VVH options will be reduced by one-half, and OCC will issue one additional contract for each open contract on the ex-date. At 8:30 A.M., Chicago time, on Tuesday, November 16, 2004, all outstanding DVN 40 options will become 20 options, and DVN 80 options will become 40 options. Any DVN 40 positions opened prior to the ex-date that are closed out on or after the ex-date must be closed out as 20 options. Negligence in this matter could lead customers to establish new positions in the 40 options rather than closing out then-existing positions in the 20 options.

Strikes that will be affected by the adjustment in the manner described above are included in the table below. Members should be aware of the potential for confusion respecting any of the related pairs of strikes shown below, and should be cautious in this regard.

Existing	Adjusted	&	Existing	Adjusted
40	20		80	40
45	22 1/2		90	45

GTC Order Conversion
On Monday, November 15, 2004, immediately after the CBOE close, the system will convert or cancel all resting orders in the DVN/YQ/VVH order books. If your firm has requested, all EBook orders (phone, wire, and electronic) and all ORS orders residing outside the book (booth or crowd routed) will be converted reflecting the adjustments. If your firm has requested, all EBook orders and ORS orders residing outside of the book will be canceled. If your firm receives EBook CXL drops, the CXL confirms will print at your booth at 3:15 p.m. ORS CXLs will also be transmitted electronically to your branches.

Immediately after the close, the book staff will return a final written report listing the orders that are converted or canceled to all firms. If converted, this list will also show how the new orders will be adjusted. This report will be available on request anytime during the day prior to the night of the adjustment.

Position and Exercise Limits
The CBOE Department of Market Regulation has determined that: 'The position and exercise limits following this stock split will be any combination of DVN, YQ and VVH on the same side of the market not to exceed 150,000 contracts (15,000,000 shares) through January 20, 2007. Following the January 2007 expiration, the position and exercise limits will revert to the standard limit of 75,000 contracts (7,500,000 shares) of DVN.'

Source: CBOE.

We can see from the above how important it is to be aware of the changes that the exchange has made as a result of this corporate action related to a stock split and to ensure that the internal systems and records are changed accordingly.

Any incorrect data held in systems will cause untold problems in performing calculations related to delivery, etc. Clients must also be made aware of the change so that they maintain the correct records in their portfolios, particularly writers of options who have the delivery obligation.

Now look at the following notice published by the Euronext.liffe market in respect of a Special Cash Dividend and Consolidation of Share Capital:

Mitchells & Butlers plc

Special Cash Dividend and Consolidation of Share Capital
Mitchells & Butlers plc ('M&B') has announced its intention to pay a special cash dividend of 68 pence per M&B Ordinary 5 pence share.

In addition, existing holdings in M&B Ordinary 5 pence shares will be consolidated on the basis of twelve new M&B Ordinary 71/12 pence shares for every seventeen M&B Ordinary 5 pence shares currently held.

The proposed special dividend and consolidation of share capital are subject to shareholder approval at the M&B Extraordinary General Meeting to be held on Monday 1 December 2003.

Dealings in the new M&B ex event shares are expected to commence on Tuesday 2 December 2003.

Option Contract Adjustments
The Corporate Events Policy, www.liffe.com/trade/specs/ corpevents.pdf, detailed the methods for contract adjustments to be employed by the Exchange to cater for Corporate Events. Consistent with this policy, the Exchange has resolved that the ratio approach be used in order to determine option contract adjustments in M&B equity options.

The adjustment ratio will be based on the official closing price of M&B Ordinary shares on Monday 1 December 2003 and will be calculated as follows:

$$\text{Ratio} = \frac{(17 \times \text{cum event share price}) - 1{,}156 \text{ pence}}{12 \times \text{cum event share price}}$$

Exercise prices will be adjusted by being multiplied by this ratio. The lot size will be adjusted by being multiplied by the inverse of this ratio.

The M&B official closing share price on Monday 1 December 2003 was 235.5 pence and, as a consequence, the ratio used to determine contract adjustments is 1.0076.

With effect from Tuesday 2 December 2003 exercise prices will be adjusted as follows:

Mitchells & Butlers plc Exercise Prices: 1 December 2003	Mitchells & Butlers plc Exercise Prices: 2 December 2003
140	141
160	161
180	181
200	202
220	222
240	242
260	262
280	282
300	302
330	333

Exercise Notices submitted in respect of M&B equity options on and from Tuesday 2 December 2003 will result in Delivery Contracts for 992 M&B Ordinary 71/12 pence shares, ex event, at the adjusted exercise prices.

New Series
Additional equity option series introduced for trading on M&B Ordinary shares on and from Tuesday 2 December 2003 will be at standard exercise prices and will have a standard contract size of 1,000 shares per lot.

Source: Euronext.liffe.

We can again see how the exchange has had to alter the contract specifications and once again it is clear that the operations teams within firms, the customer service teams and the client must be aware of the changes.

The use of, access to and sharing of data in the organisation, for instance between securities settlements teams and derivative settlement teams, is fundamental to the safe handling of corporate action events across the business. Likewise, good communication of data between the two areas that is related to the delivery process of derivatives, such as an option exercise or assignment resulting in a stock bargain, is again vital for efficient and safe processing.

The kind of outcome associated with a corporate action is not always identical and so it is important to ascertain exactly how an exchange is dealing with each and every event that occurs.

We have already seen that Exchanges publish notices related to corporate actions, trading calendars, etc. They also make other information available; for instance, Euronext.liffe publish their Corporate Actions Policy. This explains the Exchange's policy on corporate action events and a copy is included in Appendix 8.

It is, as we have said, important to know what contract specification changes will take place and then to know when and for how long the change applies. Euronext.liffe published a list of 'Unusual Contract Sizes', an example of which is shown below:

Company	LIFFE TRS Code	Expiry month	Strike prices	Unusual contract size
AstraZeneca plc	AZA	Dec 04	All	100
		Jun 05	All	100
Centrica plc	CTR	Dec 04	119–298	1,006
		Mar 05	119–298	1,006
		Jun 05	199–298	1,006
International Power plc	IPR	Dec 04	80–178	1,123
		Mar 05	80–178	1,123
London Stock Exchange plc	LSE	Dec 04	259–458	1,004
		Mar 05	299–458	1,004
Prudential plc	PRU	Nov 04	346–577	1,040
		Dec 04	231–625	1,040
		Jan 05	375–529	1,040
		Mar 05	346–577	1,040
		Jun 05	250–625	1,040
		Sep 05	375–577	1,040
		Dec 05	288–625	1,040
		Jun 06	346–625	1,040
		Dec 06	346–577	1,040
Sainsbury (J) plc – Return of Capital & Share Consolidation	SAN	Dec 04	159–387	1,008
		Mar 05	198–387	1,008

As at October 25th 2004
Source: Euronext.liffe.

The contract changes are made to series only for the duration of the series; for instance, Euronext.liffe's standard contract size is 1000 shares and following a corporate action, new series and expiry months are introduced with the standard contract size.

If any of these option series were still showing as 1000 shares in the systems, the premium amounts calculated on trades will be wrong and so too will the bargain be booked in the underlying, in the event of an exercise or assignment.

For corporate actions like scrip issues, rights issues, etc. the contract specification is altered; however, for other types of actions there may be a change not to the strike price, number of shares or amount of underlying but to the underlying itself.

An example of this would be a merger or takeover. Again the easiest way to illustrate this is to look at an example of what an exchange does and below is such an example.

RECOMMENDED OFFER BY WM MORRISON SUPERMARKETS

Introduction

Wm Morrison Supermarkets plc ('Morrisons') and Safeway plc have announced the terms of a recommended offer by Morrisons for Safeway plc (the 'Offer'). The Offer will be effected by means of a Scheme of Arrangement. This General Notice describes the adjustments to be made in respect of Safeway plc Equity Option Contracts subject to the Offer becoming effective.

Details of the Offer

Under the terms of the Offer, shareholders in Safeway plc will have their holdings replaced on the basis of one new Morrisons Ordinary 10 pence share and 60 pence in cash for each Safeway plc Ordinary 25 pence share held. The Offer is expected to become effective on Monday 8 March 2004. The Offer is conditional on the sanction of the Court being obtained at hearings on 1 March and 4 March 2004. The suspension of listing and dealings in Safeway plc Ordinary 25 pence shares is expected to occur at the close of business on Friday 5 March 2004. Dealings in the new Morrisons Ordinary 10 pence shares are expected to commence on Monday 8 March 2004. Further details are available in the formal Offer document.

Contract Adjustments The Exchange's Corporate Events Policy, issued under cover of General Notice No. 2125 on 25 November 2002, detailed the methods for contract adjustments to be employed by the Exchange to cater for Corporate Events. Consistent with this policy, the Exchange has resolved that the package approach be used in order to determine contract adjustments in Safeway plc Equity Option Contracts.

Should the Offer become effective, on and from Monday 8 March 2004 Safeway plc Equity Option Contracts will become options on a package of 1,000 Morrisons Ordinary 10 pence shares and £600 in cash per lot. No changes will be made to exercise prices or lot size (contract multiplier). The TRS code will remain unchanged as 'AYL' and the Contracts will be referred to by LIFFE as 'Safeway plc ex event' Equity Options until they are delisted in September 2004.

Prior to the Offer becoming effective, contracts in respect of equity shares created under Exchange Contract No. 211 (Equity Shares Contract (Denominated in Sterling)) as part of a Stock Contingent Trade will continue to reflect the delivery of Safeway plc Ordinary 10 pence shares. Should the Offer become effective, on and from Monday 8 March 2004 Safeway plc Ordinary 10 pence shares will cease to be available under Exchange Contract No. 211 and Stock Contingent Trades will thus no longer be made available in respect of Safeway plc Equity Options.

In respect of Safeway plc Equity Options, exercise notices submitted:

(a) by 17.20 hours on Friday 5 March 2004 will be satisfied by the delivery of 1,000 Safeway plc Ordinary 25 pence shares per lot;

(b) on and from Monday 8 March 2004 will be satisfied by the delivery of a package of 1,000 Morrisons Ordinary 10 pence shares and £600 in cash per lot as described in paragraph 3.6, for a consideration of 1,000 multiplied by the relevant exercise price. The Exchange will publish prices at which each element of the package shall be entered into CREST.

In respect of Safeway plc Equity Options, members should note that:

(a) Delivery Contracts arising as a result of exercise of Safeway plc Equity Options prior to Friday 5 March 2004 should continue to result in the delivery through CREST of 1,000 Safeway Ordinary 25 pence shares per lot, in exchange for the settlement amount; and

(b) Delivery Contracts arising as a result of exercise of Safeway plc Equity Options on and from Monday 8 March 2004 should result in the transfer through CREST of a package of

1,000 Morrisons Ordinary 10 pence shares and £600 in cash per lot, in the following line:

Security	ISIN Code
Morrisons Ordinary 10 pence shares	GB0006043169

(c) It is anticipated that Delivery Bargains held within CREST which have not settled by Monday 8 March 2004 will be automatically transferred into bargains for 1,000 Morrisons Ordinary 10 pence shares and £600 in cash per lot. The consideration for such bargains will remain unchanged.

(d) Members are requested by LCH.Clearnet to enter their delivery instructions as per LCH.Clearnet's alleged transactions within CREST. The consideration of the alleged delivery instructions entered by LCH.Clearnet will reflect the £600 cash adjustment within the offer.

No additional series will be introduced in respect of Safeway plc Equity Options and no further expiry months will be listed.

Source: Euronext.liffe.

As can be seen in the above example there is no change to the contract strike price but there is a change to the underlying that will be delivered, in this case a combination of new shares and cash.

Once again it is crucially important that this change is updated internally and also that clients holding positions, either long or short, are aware of the change to the option and to the delivery obligation. Note the situation regarding the delivery instructions and the treatment of bargains in CREST.

Naturally the Safeway series of options will not see any new series introduced.

OTC derivatives

With OTC derivatives the terms are negotiated and this will include what will happen in the event of a corporate action on the underlying occurring. This may be anything from the termination of the position to a choice of decision by either the issuer or the holder of the position.

It is vitally important that on the announcement of a corporate action, the terms of any OTC transactions that are based on the underlying on which the action is taking place are reviewed and that there are procedures set down to deal with the event.

Bear in mind that there may be no requirement for a counterparty to notify the other counterparty about an action or what options there are for settlement.

Summary

Corporate actions can cause all sorts of problems for operations teams and can result in financial and, not to mention, reputation loss. Procedures must be devised and maintained, with operations teams aware of both the impact and how to deal with an event should it occur. A 'checklist' for corporate actions can prove invaluable.

An example of the 'checklist' we can draw up for corporate actions is as follows:

Event Capture	Source of data on the corporate action
Characteristics of Event	What are the terms of the event Exchange policy Situation in respect of OTC derivative positions
Awareness of Key Timings and Changes	Deadlines for decisions and changes Reconciliation of positions affected Alterations to contract terms Start of changed specifications Updating of systems and static data Reconciliation of positions after data changes
Information Distribution	Notification to traders, fund managers and clients Notification of revised positions (where applicable) Reconciliation that any compliance requirements related to exchange and clearing house rules, clients etc have been met
Corporate Action Procedure Manual	Reconciliation that the event has been dealt with in accordance with the procedures set out For funds, ensuring that the event and the managers decision (where applicable) has been recorded and that the corporate action has been accounted for and reported correctly
Log	Maintenance of a log of actions and any errors etc that might have occurred

Source: thedsc.portfolio.

The above list is only an example, and each organisation would have its own list relevant to its structure, processing and procedures, but it is certainly an important aid to the successful managing of what could be a difficult process.

It is also important to bear in mind that other kinds of events can that affect derivatives and therefore that adequate procedures must be in place for them as well. This will include things like the trading calendars, expiry dates, holidays, list of deliverable bonds, price/ conversion factors, trigger events for OTC derivatives, etc.

In short, the more data and control we have on and over corporate actions and other events, the more efficient and risk-managed the clearing and settlement process will be.

10

Operational risk

When looking at risk in relation to any activities in the financial markets it is usually broken down into three high-level definitions covering market, credit and operational risk.

Market risk can be simply defined as the risk of financial loss due to trading errors, liquidity issues, adverse market movements or breaches of market rules and regulations.

Credit risk can be simply defined as the risk of financial loss due to the failure of a counterparty. This loss can be failure to receive either cash or assets, or both, and the cost of replacement.

Not surprisingly market and credit risk are high on the agenda of regulators and risk managers.

Establishing the extent of the market risk associated with trading is not simple, but it is possible to measure the exposure, given various scenarios, and to allocate capital to cover the possible worst-case outcome. Value at Risk (VaR), Monte Carlo Simulation, etc. are common approaches.

Operational risk is defined by the Basel Committee on Banking Supervision as being the risk of loss resulting from inadequate or failed internal processes, people and systems or from external events.

Given that derivatives have certain characteristics that not only make them risk management tools but also generate certain types of risk if they are not managed and settled properly, we need to look at operational risk in some detail.

Identifying and managing specific risks

Within the derivatives operations environment, the use of systems and technology is extensive. Everything from SPAN and TIMS margin calculations to value-added services to clients are run on in-house and/or external systems. Important interfaces exist for processes such as trade registration and clearing with the clearing house, as well as in some cases the process for submitting exercise and tender notices between client and broker and broker and clearing house.

It is therefore important to understand the operational risk that exists in the form of system or technology risk.

System/Technology risk

This risk can include the following:

*   Inadequate controls over the input and management of static data in the systems. This will cover critical data such as:
    –   Contract size
    –   Tick size and value
    –   Expiry/maturity dates
    –   Option styles.
*   Inability of systems to handle specific types of derivative products:
    –   Margin method
    –   Settlement and/or MTM calculation (VM, option premium).
*   Lack of knowledge of the systems capabilities by staff and management.
*   Inability to provide vital risk management information. This will include:
    –   Exception reports;
    –   Client money calculations;
    –   Margin reconciliation;
    –   Exercise and assignment data including positions that are in-the-money and are likely to be exercised or assigned;
    –   Expiry calendars and times.

With so much reliance on systems to provide not only vital internal functions but also client services such as single currency settlement, average pricing and direct client access to data via intranets, etc. any system failure, corruption of data in the system, unauthorised access or delay in setting up a new client or product on the system is a significant risk to the business.

The use of systems must be accompanied by strict controls and segregation of certain functions like static data, trade input, client account set-up, accounting and treasury functions.

Positions in derivatives represent exposures and the positions must be reconciled to those held by the clearing house or agent broker or, in the case of a client, their broker. As some products like futures are not only marked to market each day but that MTM amount is also settled; any incorrect position will result in problems agreeing the settlement amount. We must also remember that some products go to physical delivery and positions that remain open at the clearing house can become subject to the delivery process. Therefore, maintaining the correct net and gross positions through correct closeout of longs and shorts is vital. So too is managing the tender, exercise and assignment process as these will alter the open position which must be amended accordingly.

We noted earlier in the book that if an option position is assigned but the dealers are not informed and/or the position in our records is not amended, the dealer is trading on an incorrect position and this could cause a severe financial loss.

It is important to assign responsibility to people to manage the processes of:

- position agreement to clearing house/broker and internal records;
- tendering and exercising for delivery and amending positions;
- checking for assignments (remember some options could be exercised early) and notifying dealers as well as amending positions;
- reconciling settlement figures (premium, variations and initial margin) to internal records. This will highlight any position/price error.

The systems in the derivatives operations area will also provide key regulatory reports and reporting information, either directly to the regulator or to the compliance department; and therefore any lack of control over the quality and timeliness of the data used could lead to a potential breach of regulations.

Mapping operational risk in a derivatives operations environment

What qualifies as operational risk?

One reason for the delay in recognising operational risk as a separate category of risk is probably the difficulty in determining exactly what operational risk is.

Some would argue that it is everything that affects a business, which is not market or credit risk. Others argue that it is everything and anything to do with the post-transaction clearing and settlement process.

Another key factor in this lack of recognition is that the subject of risk is viewed primarily in terms of potential financial loss. As such operational risk is frequently considered to be unlikely to cause a severe financial loss, at least not in one hit. The logic here is that an inappropriate or incorrect deal can result in substantial loss, whereas a settlement problem with the transaction, whilst it may incur costs, is not likely to generate a significant loss.

History would tend to suggest that the headline-making 'disasters' in the financial services industry are all mainly related to market and/or credit risk, in the sense that they involve significant positions in derivatives where the obligations could not be met.

However, delve a little deeper and it may be that associated operations issues contributed to the problem. The contribution may not have been 'physical' in the sense of an error in processing transactions but rather a failure to carry out the risk management role that the operations team undoubtedly have.

Understanding the risk sources and the impact of that risk is called *risk mapping*. This involves the analysis of the workflow and the critical tasks through the clearing and settlement process. It is also prudent to consider any risk sources that could occur prior to clearing and settlement. These would include pre-trade checks on:

- Authorised products
- Deal limits
- Position and exposure limits
- Counterparty limits
- Liquidity limits.

In addition we can include product knowledge and static data in the list.

Some other areas in the organisation like the Credit Team and Compliance will monitor some of these.

However, the operations area is involved in some of this risk management process as the information produced on positions, for example, is critical to an accurate risk management process.

Key functions such as reconciliation and error resolution must be effective; otherwise the dealing function is hampered, or the organisation may be put at risk by 'hidden' positions, unauthorised exposures, etc. As these present not only an unacceptable risk but also a breach of regulations, the consequences are clear.

Specific operational risks

The use of derivatives creates some specific risks associated with key functions. These are listed below and anyone working in a derivatives team must understand them.

Trade input

Source of trade data (i.e., manual or automated);

- Deal ticket processing
  - Confirmations (OTC)
- Format considerations in terms of clarity of information
- Volume fluctuation
- Peaks and troughs, influenced by issues like economic announcements, etc.
- Timely and accurate allocation of trade or account bookings.

Valuation

- Sources of prices
- Input method-manual/automatic
- Validation of prices
- Generation of profit/loss figures
- Valuing collateral.

Reconciliation

- Positions
- Confirmations (OTC)
- Intra-day
- End of Day
- Trade day + 1
- Initial margin
- Variation margin
- Option premium
- Cash position/ledger balance
- Value-dated payments and receipts
- Nostro/bank reconciliations
- Profit/loss account
- Collateral.

Client settlement

- Production of settlement information
- Automatic/overnight-associated reconciliation timing
- Trigger payment instructions
- Collateral requests
- Instructions
- Value date of payments and internal control in the interim, i.e. cash margin.

Funding

- Deadlines
- Allocation of collateral
- Source of funding
- Exceptions
- Instructions
- Payments/receipts
- Borrowing stock to ensure timely delivery of futures or options.

Management information

- Expiries and delivery periods
- Credit exposure–intra-day
- Profit/loss versus settlement requirements
- Justification of payments
- Breaches of controls.

Recognising, measuring and managing operational risk

Operational risk can and does manifest itself in many ways. Sometimes the operational risk will not be easily or immediately identifiable. In most cases, an error on a transaction can and should be identified quickly and adjusted, so that the loss is quantified. With operations, a problem may occur only occasionally and yet have an unseen, dramatic and damaging effect. For instance, a client could be inconvenienced and, as a result, lose confidence in their broker/bank as their counterparty.

In such a situation it is not inconceivable that the client may gradually move their business elsewhere and the counterparty may never be aware that it is the operations team's performance that is to blame.

Operational risk is difficult to measure and hard to quantify in terms of likely financial loss. It is therefore difficult to allocate capital to cover such a risk turning into an actual loss. Nevertheless, progress is being made on operational risk models, as more and more organisations seek to quantify the operational risk of their business. It is therefore important that managers begin the process of measuring risk by developing risk measurement models suitable for in-house use.

On a day-to-day basis, when we look at quantifying and measuring operational risk we need to first consider what it consists of.

At the highest level, operational risk can be said to comprise:

- Settlement risk
- System risk
- Personnel risk
- Infrastructure risk
- Counterparty risk
- Regulatory risk
- Legal risk
- Reputational risk.

However within these headings are many subsets of risk that can (and often do) combine to generate risk situations that go across one or more categories. The combination of risks makes measuring and managing operational risk a complex exercise, and it can also result in a situation where the cost of managing the risk is prohibitive.

As with all types of risk, there is operational risk that is acceptable as part of the business, provided that the risk is known and understood. There is a danger that the subject of operational risk can be so diverse and so large that managing it becomes an administrative and costly nightmare. It is therefore important for any organisation, and any individual person with responsibility for operational risk (this includes everyone working in a derivative operations team), to establish exactly what the objectives are when trying to measure and manage operational risk.

One way to do this is to perform a workflow analysis that demonstrates:

- The processes and their duration
- The complexity, ranking (in terms of primary, secondary) and the extent of automation of these processes
- The deadlines associated with the processes
- The level of resource available for the process

- The level of management needed
- The scope to absorb additional workload and/or delays to the processing.

From the above, it can be seen that some kind of operational risk measurement is possible; and that it should be continuous. We can choose not to measure, even crudely, the risk on the basis that it may never create a major problem but then you could leave your house unlocked all day and never get burgled!

Summary

Operational risk is highly relevant to derivatives, and derivatives clearing and settlement. Sources of risk must be identified and in conjunction with the firm's overall risk management structure they must be managed. Operational risk sources can be diverse as the following list shows:

- Lack of product knowledge
- Poor system reliability
- Inadequate levels of staffing
- Inefficient counterparties
- Diverse and unpredictable business levels
- Overseas clients
- Lack of critical skill sets including product knowledge
- Fraud and criminal activity
- Poor communication and poor internal relationships.

Each of these sources is very different, and so are the types of risk and the frequency with which they might occur.

Lack of product knowledge could be put down to:

- Turnover of staff
- Loss of experienced personnel
- New products being traded
- Non availability of information
- Lack of training.

It may be a major problem, or it may only be relevant if and when a particular type of product is traded. Bear in mind also that other risks may become associated with it such as regulatory risk and reputational risk.

For example, a clearing member will usually have to demonstrate to the clearing house the competency of its staff, systems and processes.

If problems occur with the member because of the introduction of a new type of product the clearing house may feel that the member is failing to meet the standards required. Any prolonged problem or subsequent repetition may result in clearing status being withdrawn.

Errors could be caused by not being alert to a corporate action, expiry date or by being unaware of settlement problems in the jurisdiction where the product was traded.

Individually, the problem might be easily identified and managed; but a combination of risk problems might create a far more difficult situation to manage.

Operational risk in a derivatives operation needs to be fully understood by all personnel. A failure to handle routine functions that we have covered elsewhere in this book (like margin, delivery, closeouts, etc.) may lead to severe financial and reputation loss and breaches of regulation.

Issues like money laundering and systems risk have significant implications in derivatives operations and this must also be recognised and suitable controls and procedures, including BCP and disaster recovery, must be in place.

Glossary of derivatives terms

Accrued Interest Interest due on a bond or other fixed income security that must be paid by the buyer of a security to its seller. Usual compensation: coupon rate of interest times elapsed days from prior interest payment date (i.e. Coupon date) up to but not including settlement date. Is used in the calculation of the invoice amount for bond futures being delivered.

Actuals An actual physical commodity someone is buying or selling, for example, soybeans, corn, gold, silver, Treasury bonds, etc.

Against Actuals A transaction generally used by two hedgers who want to exchange futures for cash positions. Also referred to as 'versus cash'.

AEX Amsterdam Exchanges now part of EURONEXT.

Agent Bank A commercial bank that provides services as per their client's instructions.

Agent One who executes orders for or otherwise acts on behalf of another (the principal) and is subject to its control and authority. The agent takes no financial risk and may receive a fee or commission.

All or None (AON) Instruction to buy or sell the entire order in a single transaction, i.e. not to execute a partial transaction. The AON restricts the size but not necessarily the time of the transaction.

Allocation (Give Up) The process of moving the trade from the executing broker to the clearing broker in exchange-traded derivatives.

American Style Option	The holder of the long position can choose to exercise the position into the underlying instrument until the expiry day.
Arbitrage	The simultaneous buying and selling of two different derivatives, or a derivative and its underlying where the fair value prices are different. The arbitrageur has a risk-less trade as the exposure is flat and the profit is the difference between the two prices traded.
Asian Option	See average rate option.
Asset Allocation	The use of derivatives by a fund manager to immediately gain or reduce exposure to different markets or asset classes.
Assignment	The process by which the holder of a short option position is matched against a holder of a similar long option position who has exercised his right.
ASX	Australian Stock Exchange.
At-the-Money	An option whose exercise price is equal, or very close, to the current market price of the underlying share. This option has no intrinsic value when the strike and the underlying price are equal.
ATM	See At-the-money.
At-the-Money (currency option)	An option where the strike is the same as the current spot or forward market rate.
Authorised Unit Trust	Unit trust that meets the requirements of the Financial Services Authority to allow it to be freely marketable. Permitted to use derivatives for some strategies subject to Trustee's approval.
Average Rate Option	An option where the settlement is based on the difference between the strike and the average price of the underlying over a predetermined period. Also known as Asian option.
Average Strike Option	An option that pays the difference between the average rate of the underlying over the life of the option and the rate at expiry.
Bargain	Another word for a transaction or deal. It does not imply that a particularly favourable price was obtained.
Base Currency	Currency chosen for reporting purposes.
Base Rate	The rate of interest set by the banks as a basis for the rate on loans and deposits. Can be used as a reference value for certain derivatives.

Basis (Gross)	The difference between the relevant cash instrument price and the futures price. Often used in the context of hedging the cash instrument.
Basis (Value or Net)	The difference between the gross basis and the carry.
Basis Point (B.P.)	A change in the interest rate of one hundredth of one per cent (0.01 per cent). One basis point is written as 0.01 when 1.0 represents 1 per cent.
Basis Risk	The risk that the price or rate of one instrument or position might not move exactly in line with the price or rate of another instrument or position which is being used to hedge it.
Basis Trade	A trade simultaneously of a future and the underlying; a facility offered by some exchanges.
Bear	Investor who believes prices will fall.
Bear Market	A market in which prices are falling, and sellers are more predominant than buyers. Usually refers to equity markets.
Benchmark Bond	The most recently issued and most liquid government bond.
Bermudan Option	An option where the holder can choose to exercise on any of a series of predetermined dates between the purchase of the option and expiry. See American option, European option.
Best Execution	The requirement for a broker to obtain the best market price when buying or selling a marketable investment on behalf of the client.
Bid	(a) The price or yield at which a purchaser is willing to buy a given security.
	(b) To quote a price or yield at which a purchaser is able to buy a given security.
	(c) The investor's selling price of units in a unit-linked policy.
BIFFEX	The Baltic International Freight Futures Exchange.
Bilateral Netting	A netting system in which all trades executed on the same date in the same security between the same counterparties are grouped and netted to one final delivery versus payment.
Block Trade	A purchase or sale of a large number of futures or options normally much larger than what constitutes a 'normal' size trade in the market in question. Not all exchanges permit block trades.

Bond	A certificate of debt, generally long term, under the terms of which an issuer contracts, inter alia, to pay the holder a fixed principal amount on a stated future date and, usually, a series of interest payments during its life.
Bonus Issue	A free issue of shares to a company's existing shareholders. No money changes hands and the share price falls pro rata. It is a cosmetic exercise to make the shares more marketable. Also known as a capitalisation or scrip issue. Affects the specification of derivatives based on the underlying share.
Bretton Woods Agreement	An agreement that set a system of exchange rate stability after the Second World War, with all member currencies having a par value pegged to the US$, allowing a 1 per cent variance. This was agreed by major economists from 44 countries. The International Monetary Fund and the World Bank were set up at this conference. The dismantling of the Agreement led to the launch of the first financial futures contracts in 1975.
Brokers	Agents, often members of a stock exchange firm or exchange members themselves, who act as an intermediary between buyer and seller. A commission is charged for this service.
Broker/Dealer	Firm that operates in dual capacity in the securities marketplace: as principal trading for its own account and as broker representing clients on the market.
Broking	The activity of representing a client as agent and charging commission for doing so.
Building Societies	Institutions that provide a safe haven for investor's deposits and who charge interest on long-term mortgages and loans on property. Since the 1986 Building Societies Act, the services societies are able to provide have widened to include those traditionally offered by banks and insurance companies. Many have indeed converted into banks as a result.
Bull	Investor who believes prices will rise.
Bull Market	A market in which prices are rising, and buyers are more predominant than sellers. Usually refers to equity markets.

CAC 40	French Equity Index on which futures and options are traded on Euronext.
Calendar Spread	The simultaneous purchase (or sale) of a futures or an option contract for one date and the sale (or purchase) of a similar futures contract for a different date. See spread.
Call Option	An option that gives the seller the right, but not the obligation, to buy a specified quantity of the underlying asset at a fixed price on or before a specified date. The buyer of a call option has the obligation (because they have bought the right) to make delivery of the underlying asset if the option is exercised by the seller.
Call Spread	The purchase of a call option coupled with the sale of another call option at a different strike, expecting a limited rise or fall in the value of the underlying. The sale reduces the cost of the purchase.
Capital Markets	A term used to describe the means by which large amounts of money (capital) are raised by companies, governments and other organisations for long-term use and the subsequent trading of the instruments issued in recognition of such capital.
Cash Market	Traditionally, this term has been used to denote the market in which commodities were traded for immediate delivery against cash. Since the inception of futures markets for T-bills and other debt securities, a distinction has been made between the cash markets in which these securities trade for immediate delivery and the futures markets in which they trade for future delivery.
Cash Settlement	The settlement in cash rather than a physical asset of a derivative, for example index and interest rate futures and options.
CBOE	Abbreviation for the Chicago Board Options Exchange.
CBOT	Abbreviation for the Chicago Board of Trade. Term 'Board' is also used.
Central Securities Depository (CSD)	An organisation that holds securities in either immobilised or dematerialised form thereby enabling transactions to be processed by book entry transfer. Also provides securities administration services.
Certificate	Paper form of shares (or bonds), representing ownership of a company (or its debt).
Certificate of Deposit	A money market instrument in bearer form issued by a bank certifying a deposit made at the bank. Usually acceptable as collateral against margin calls.

CFD See contract for difference.

CFMA Commodity Futures Modernization Act introduced in the United States to change the regulatory environment in derivatives markets.

CFTC The Commodities and Futures Trading Commission, a US regulatory organisation.

CGO The Central Gilts Office – formerly responsible for the settlement of UK Government securities prior to transactions being taken over by CREST through which UK Bond futures settle on delivery.

Cheapest to Deliver The cash security that provides the lowest cost (largest profit) to the arbitrage trader; the Cheapest to Deliver instrument is used to price the futures contract and is the most likely to be delivered against the future.

Clean Price The total price of a bond less accrued interest.

Clearing The centralised process whereby transacted business is recorded and positions are maintained.

Clearing Agent An institution that settles transaction for a large number of counterparties.

Clearing Broker Is the clearing agent for the trading broker in the market where the trade will settle. It is usually the party with which the sub-custodian will actually settle the trade.

Clearing Fee Fee charged by the Clearing House or Clearing Broker usually per trade or contract/lot.

Clearing House Company that acts as central counterparty for the settlement of on-exchange transactions (also some OTC transactions, i.e. SwapClear). The clearing organisation acts as the guarantor of the performance and settlement of contracts.

Clearing Corporation Formerly the Board of Trade Clearing Corporation, will clear the business of the new Eurex USA exchange starting in 2004.

Clearing Organisation Another name for a clearing house.

Clearing System System established to clear transactions.

Clearnet The clearing house for Euronext now merged with LCH.

Clearstream The CSD and clearing house based in Luxembourg and Frankfurt and linked into Deutsche Borse.

Closing Trade	A bought or sold trade which is used to partly offset an open position, to reduce it or to fully offset it and close the position out.
CME	Abbreviation for the Chicago Mercantile Exchange. Term 'Merc' is also used.
Collateral	An acceptable asset used to cover a margin requirement.
Commission	Charge levied by a firm for agency broking.
Commodities	The raw materials traded on specialist markets (see also Soft and Hard Commodities).
Commodity Futures	These comprise five main categories: agriculturals, for example wheat and potatoes; softs, for example coffee and cocoa; precious metals, for example gold and silver; non-ferrous metals, for example copper and lead; and energies, for example oil and gas.
Common Stock	US term for securities that represent ownership in a corporation. The two most important common stockholder rights are the voting right and the dividend right. Common stockholder's claims on corporate assets are subordinate to those of bondholders, preferred stockholders and general creditors.
Common Clearing Link	The linking of the clearing of the CME and CBOT transactions under one clearing house.
Commodity Swap	A swap involving either two commodities or a commodity and a floating rate.
Compliance Officer	Person appointed within an authorised firm to be responsible for ensuring compliance with the rules.
Conduct of Business Rules	Rules introduced by the Financial Services Authority to dictate how firms conduct their business. They deal mainly with the relationship between firm and client.
Conflicts of Interest	Circumstances that arise where a firm has an investment which could encourage it not to treat its clients favourably. The more areas in which a firm is involved the greater the number of potential conflicts.

Confirm   An agreement for each individual OTC transaction which has specific terms.

Consideration   The value of a transaction calculated as the price per share multiplied by the quantity being transferred.

Contract   The standard unit of trading for futures and options. It is also commonly referred to as a 'lot'.

Contract for Difference Contract designed to make a profit or avoid a loss by reference to movements in the price of an item. The underlying item cannot change hands.

Contract Note   Legal documentation sent by brokers/banks to clients providing details of a transaction completed on their behalf.

Contract Specification A derivative exchange designs its own products and publishes a contract specification setting out the details of the derivative contract. This will include the size or unit of trading and the underlying, maturity months, quotation and minimum price movement and value (see also tick) together with trading times, methods and delivery conditions (see appendix, for example contract specification).

Convergence   The movement of the cash asset price towards the futures price as the expiration date of the futures contract approaches. On expiry they will both have the same value, as time or volatility is no longer affecting the derivatives price.

Corporate Action   One of many possible capital restructuring changes or similar actions taken by the company, which may have an impact on the market price of its securities, and which may require the shareholders to make certain decisions.

Correlation   Refers to the degree to which fluctuations of one variable are similar to those of another.

Cost of Carry   The net running cost of holding a position (which may be negative), for example, the cost of borrowing cash to buy a bond less the coupon earned on the bond while holding it.

Counterparty   A trade can take place between two or more counterparties. Usually one party to a trade refers to its trading partners as counterparties.

Coupon	Generally, the nominal annual rate of interest is expressed as a percentage of the principal value. The interest is paid to the holder of a fixed income security by the borrower. The coupon is generally paid annually, semi-annually or, in some cases, quarterly, depending on the type of security.
Covered Option	An option bought or sold offsetting an existing underlying position.
Covered Writing	The sale of call options but the seller owns the underlying which, would be required to cover the delivery, if the position is assigned.
Credit Default Swap	A swap where one side is a default event that results in the payment of the related loss and the other is the payment of a premium to secure the protection. If no event occurs then the seller of the protection keeps the premium.
Credit Derivatives	Credit derivatives have as the underlying asset some kind of credit default. As with all derivatives, the credit derivative is designed to enable the risk related to a credit issue, such as non-payment of an interest coupon on a corporate or sovereign bond, or the non-repayment of a loan, to be transferred.
Credit Risk	The risk that a borrower, or counterparty to a deal, or the issuer of a security, will default on repayment or not deliver its side of the deal. Also known as counterparty risk.
CREST/Euroclear Crest	The organisation in the United Kingdom that holds UK and Irish company shares in dematerialised form and clears and settles trades in UK and Irish company shares. Now merged with Euroclear.
Cross Currency Interest Rate Swap	An IRS where the interest payments are in two different currencies and the exchange rate, for the final settlement, is agreed at the outset of the transaction.
Cum-dividend	A security that is traded with the current dividend right.
Cum-rights	A term applied to a stock trading in the marketplace 'with subscription rights attached' which is reflected in the price of that security.

Cumulative Dividend

Dividend that is due but not yet paid on cumulative preferred shares. These must be paid before any ordinary dividends are paid.

Currency Exposure

Currency exposure exists if assets are held, or income earned, in one currency while liabilities are denominated in another currency. The position is exposed to changes in the relative values of the two currencies such that the cost of the liabilities may be increased or the value of the assets or earning decreased.

Currency Futures

Contracts calling for delivery of a specific amount of a foreign currency at a specified future date in return for a given amount of say US Dollars.

Custodian

Institution holding securities in safekeeping for a client. A custodian also offers different services to its clients like settlement, portfolio services, etc. and this can include services related to derivatives where the custodian settles margin calls, etc. on trades with the client's broker.

Customer-non-Private

Customer who is assumed to understand the workings of the investment world and, therefore, receives little protection from the Conduct of Business Rules.

Customer – Private

Customer who is assumed to be financially unsophisticated and, therefore, receives more protection from the Conduct of Business Rules.

Dealer

Individual or firm that acts as principal in all transactions, buying for his own account.

Default

Failure to perform on a derivatives contract or trade either cash settlement or physical settlement or to be in default of other exchange or clearing house rules.

Deliverable Basket or Deliverable List

The list of securities that meets the delivery standards of futures contracts, for example the list of deliverable bonds against a bond future published by the exchange.

Delivery

The physical movement of the underlying asset on which the derivative is based from seller to buyer.

Delivery versus Payment

Settlement where transfer of the security and payment for that security occur simultaneously. Also known as DVP.

Delta	The sensitivity of an option price to changes in the price of the underlying product. Also used to determine the amount of underlying needed to hedge a derivative position and vice versa.
Dematerialised (form)	Circumstances where securities are held in a book entry transfer system with no certificates.
Department of Trade and Industry	Department of government responsible for some commercial matters including monopolies and prosecution of insider dealing. Also issues some guidelines on use of derivatives.
Derivative	A financial instrument whose value is dependent upon the value of an underlying asset.
Derivative Instruments or Derivative Securities	Instruments that are based on other underlying instruments. Examples would be options on shares or futures on bonds or forwards on commodities or swaps on interest rates.
Direct Market Participant	A broker, broker/dealer or any direct member of an exchange.
Dirty Price	The total price of a bond including accrued interest.
Discount	The amount by which a future is priced below its theoretical price or fair value. If the fair value of an index future is 3000 and it is trading at 2990 it is described as trading at a discount of 10 points to its fair value.
Discount Factor	The number by which a future cash flow must be multiplied in order to calculate its present value.
Discount Rate	The rate of interest charged by the Federal Reserve in the United States to banks to whom money has been lent. Is also a term used by other central banks for the same purpose. Some derivatives reference sources are based on it.
Discount Securities	Non-interest-bearing short-term securities that are issued at discount and redeemed at maturity for full face value.
Deutsche Börse	The German Stock and Derivatives Exchange Group that includes Eurex.

Dividend   Distribution of profits made by a company to its share-holders if it chooses to do so.

Diversification   Investment strategy of spreading risk by investing the total available in a range of investments. Derivatives are sometimes used to achieve this (see also asset allocation).

Domestic Bond   Bond issued in the country of the issuer, in its country and according to the regulations of that country.

Dow Jones Index   A share index used in the USA which is the underlying for futures and options contracts.

DTC   Depository Trust Company – CSD for shares in the USA.

Due Diligence   The carrying out of duties with care and perseverance. Due diligence is generally referred to in connection with the investigations of a company, carried out by accountants to ascertain the value of that company and also applies from a regulatory point of view that firms and key personnel should carry out their duties with due diligence to the regulatory environment.

Duration   A measure of the relative volatility of a bond; it is an approximation for the price change of a bond for a given change in the interest rate. Duration is measured in units of time. It includes the effects of time until maturity, cash flows and the yield to maturity. Bond futures are used to manage duration.

ECB   European Central Bank.

EFP   Exchange of futures for physical. Common in the energy markets. A physical deal priced on the futures markets, with the derivative transacted off-exchange but recognised by the exchange for clearing.

EUREX   German-Swiss derivatives exchange created by the merger of the German (DTB) and Swiss (SOFFEX) exchanges; part of Deutsche Börse.

EURONEXT   A pan-European securities and derivatives exchange listing Dutch, French, Portuguese and Belgium securities and derivatives plus the derivative products traded on LIFFE.

Emerging Market   Often a non-industrialised country with
- Low or middle per capita income, as published annually by the World Bank,
- Undeveloped capital market (i.e. the market represents only a small portion of their GDP).

Investors sometimes prefer to use derivatives that give an exposure to shares, commodities, interest rates or currencies on the emerging market but which are traded on established derivative markets or off-exchange with banks.

Equity
A common term to describe stocks or shares.

Equity/Stock Options
Contracts based on individual equities or shares. On exercise of the option the specified amount of shares are exchanged between the buyer and the seller through the clearing organisation.

ETD
This is the common term which is used to describe Exchange-Traded Derivatives which are the standardised products. It also differentiates products which are listed on an exchange as opposed to those offered over-the-counter.

ETF/Exchange-Traded Funds
Passively managed basket of stocks that mirrors a particular index and that can be traded like ordinary shares. They trade intra-day on stock exchanges, like securities, at market-determined prices. In essence, ETFs are index funds that trade like stocks.

Ethical Investments
The investment in specific sectors through either personal conviction or the view that such companies have a higher potential, for example investment in funds or companies supporting 'green' issues, or the avoidance of the so-called 'unethical' areas such as animal experimentation, pollution, etc.

EURIBOR
A measure of the average cost of funds over the whole euro-area based on a panel of 57 banks. Is the underlying for the highly successful LIFFE interest rate futures and options.

Euro
The name of the single European currency.

Eurobond
An interest-bearing security issued across national borders, usually issued in a currency other than that of the issuer's home country. Because there is no regulatory protection, only governments and top-rated multinational corporations can issue Eurobonds that the market will accept.

Euroclear
A book-entry clearing facility for most Euro-currency and foreign securities. Linked to Euronext through the acquisition of SICOVAM and recently announced a merger with CREST.

European Style Option	An option which can only be exercised on the expiry day.
Execution and Clearing Agreement	An agreement signed between the client and the clearing broker. This agreement sets out the terms by which the clearing broker will conduct business with the client including how trades to be received from other execution brokers will be advised to the clearing broker.
Exchange	Marketplace for trading futures and options, the derivative exchange develops (see contract specification), markets and lists its own products as well as setting out the membership criteria, rules and regulations for trading.
Exchange Delivery Settlement Price (EDSP)	The price determined by the exchange for the closing out of the futures position and the calculation of the final value for the cash or physical delivery of the underlying instrument or cash settlement.
Exchange-Owned Clearing Organisation	Exchange- or member-owned clearing organisations are structured so that the clearing members guarantee each other with the use of a member's default fund and additional funding like insurance, with no independent guarantee.
Exchange Rate	The rate at which one currency can be exchanged for another.
Execute and Eliminate Order	The amount that can be tracked immediately against displayed orders is completed, with the remainder being rejected.
Execution	The action of trading in the markets.
Execution and Clearing Agreement	An agreement signed between the client and the clearing broker. This agreement sets out the terms by which the clearing broker will conduct business with the client.
Execution Only or Give-Up Agreement	Tripartite agreements that are signed by the executing broker, the clearing broker and the client. This agreement sets out the terms by which the clearing broker will accept business on behalf of the client.
Exercise	The process by which the holder of an option may take up their right to buy or sell the underlying asset.

Exercise Price (or Strike Price)	The fixed price, per share or unit, at which an option conveys the right to call (purchase) or put (sell) the underlying shares or units.
Exotic Options	New generation of option derivatives, including look-backs, barriers, baskets, ladders, etc. They have different terms to standardised traded call and put options.
Expiry Date	The last date on which an option holder can exercise their right. After this date an option is deemed to lapse or be abandoned.
Face Value	The value of a bond, note, mortgage or other security that appears on the face of the issue, unless the value is otherwise specified by the issuing company. Face value is ordinarily the amount the issuing company promises to pay at maturity. Face value is also referred to as par value or nominal value. For instance, a bond future that has a unit of trading of £100 000 would require a bond(s) with a face value of £100 000 to be delivered if tendered.
Fair Value	For futures, it is the true price not the market price, allowing for the cost of carry. For options, it is the true price not the market price, as calculated using an option pricing model.
Fill or Kill Order	Type of order input into SETS. It is either completed in full against displayed orders or rejected in full.
Final Settlement	The completion of a transaction when the delivery of all components of a trade is performed. In the case of delivery of a derivative it can be the final amount due on closeout, maturity or delivery. At final settlement any collateral covering margin calls is returned.
Financial Futures/ Options Contracts	Financial futures and options is a term used to describe futures or options contracts based on financial instruments like currencies, debt instruments, interest rates and financial indices.
Financial Services and Markets Act 2000	The legislation that created the single UK Regulator, the Financial Services Authority.
Financial Services Authority (FSA)	The agency designated by the Treasury to regulate investment business as required by FSA, 1986. It is the main regulator of the financial sector and was formerly called the Securities and Investments Board (SIB). It assumed its full power on 1st December 2001.

First Notice Day — The first day as listed in the contract specification that the holders of short positions can give notification to the exchange/clearing house that they wish to effect delivery.

Fit and Proper — Under Financial Services Act, everyone conducting investment business must be a 'fit and proper person'. The Act does not define the term, a function which is left to the regulators such as FSA.

Fixed Income — Interest on a security that is calculated as a constant specified percentage of the principal amount and paid at the end of specified interest periods, usually annually or semi-annually, until maturity.

Fixed Rate — (i) A borrowing or investment where the interest or coupon paid is fixed throughout the arrangement.
(ii) In an FRA or coupon swap, the fixed rate is the fixed interest rate paid by one party to the other in return for a floating-rate receipt (i.e., an interest rate that is to be re-fixed at some future time or times).

Flat Position — A position which not only is equal in terms of long and short amounts or value but has been fully closed out so that no liability to make or take delivery exists, i.e. no exposure.

Flex Options — Newly introduced contracts which are a cross between OTCs and exchange-traded products. The advantage of flex options is that participants can choose various parts of the contract specification such as the expiry date and exercise price.

Floor — A package of interest rate options whereby, at each of a series of future fixing dates, if an agreed reference rate such as LIBOR is lower than the strike rate, the option buyer received the difference between them, calculated on an agreed notional principal amount for the period until the next fixing date. See also cap, collar.

Floorbrokerage — The process of delegating the execution of futures and options to another counterparty who then charges a floorbrokerage fee for doing the trade. The floorbroker then 'gives up' or allocates the trade to the broker concerned or if a client trade to the clearing broker of the clients choice who deals with the clearing and settlement.

Foreign Exchange — Exchange of one currency for another one.

Forex — Abbreviation for foreign exchange (currency trading).

Forward Market	Where a price is agreed now for delivery of goods in the future. Used in currency, securities and commodities markets, often in conjunction with dealing in immediate delivery (see Spot Market) as a safety net.
Forward Delivery	Transactions that involve a delivery date in the future.
Forwards	These are very similar to futures contracts but they are not mainly traded on an exchange. Often they are not marked to market daily but settled only on the delivery date. However, for some forward contracts there is a mark to market process and any loss occurring during the life of the contract is paid to the clearing house and profits are held by the clearing house until settlement on maturity with interest being paid on the amount held.
Friendly Society	Societies formed initially to benefit members in return for regular contributions against sickness, poverty and bereavement. Now generally provide various insurance covers (life, medical, etc.) as well as savings vehicles.
Front Running	The illicit utilising by brokers and market-makers of advance warning or information for personal or corporate profit. Illegal on derivative exchanges.
FSA	Financial Services Authority (UK), also Financial Services Agency (Japan).
FT Index	The Financial Times Ordinary Share Index consists of 30 large companies across a broad field and gives an indication of share price trends. The larger Index, the FT-SE 100 (Footsie) provides a wider indication of 100 leading companies on the Stock Market. All stock markets have an index, for example The Dow Jones in the US, the DAX in Germany or the Nikkei in Japan.
FT-SE 100 Index	Main UK share index based on 100 leading shares.
FT-SE Mid 250	UK share index based on the 250 shares immediately below the top 100.
Fund Manager	Individuals or specialists companies responsible for investing the assets of a fund in such a way as to maximise its value. They do this by following a strategy to buy and sell equities and other financial instruments.
Fungible Contract	A futures contract with identical administration in more than one financial centre. Trades in various geographical locations can be offset (e.g. bought on the IPE and sold on the SIMEX).

Futures	An agreement to buy or sell an asset at a certain time in the future for a certain price.
Future Value	The amount of money which can be achieved at a given date in the future by investing (or borrowing) a given sum of money now at a given interest rate, assuming compound re-investment (or re-funding) of any interest payments received (or paid) before the end.
Futures and Options Fund (FOF)	Type of authorised unit trust that can invest in derivatives to a greater degree than other authorised unit trusts but still within certain parameters.
Gamma	The rate at which the delta of an option changes.
Geared Futures and Options Fund (GFOF)	Type of authorised unit trust that can invest in derivatives to a greater extent than other unit trusts including FOFs but still only within certain parameters.
Gearing	The characteristic of derivatives which enables a far greater reward for the same, or much smaller, initial outlay. It is the ratio of exposure to investment outlay, and is also known as leverage.
General Principles	Eleven fundamental principles of behaviour written by FSA to apply all investment businesses.
Gilt	Domestic sterling-denominated long-term bond backed by the full faith and credit of the United Kingdom and issued by the Treasury.
Gilt Edged Security	UK government borrowing through the issue of bonds that is considered a very 'safe' investment in terms of the likelihood of default.
Give-Up	The process of giving a trade to a third party who will undertake the clearing and settlement of the trade.
Global Clearing	The channelling of the settlement of all futures and options trades through a single counterparty or through a number of counterparties geographically located.
Global Custodian	Institution that safekeeps, settles and performs processing of income collection, tax reclaim, multi-currency reporting, cash management, foreign exchange, corporate action and proxy monitoring, etc. for clients' securities in all required market-places.
Global Depository Receipt (GDR)	A security representing shares held in custody in the country of issue.

GLOBEX	The overnight trading system operated by Reuters and the Chicago Mercantile Exchange (CME).
Gold	Widely used commodity and regarded as a safe haven in times of uncertainty.
Granter	Another term for a person who has sold an option position to a buyer.
'Greeks'	A collective term for delta, gamma, theta and vega which relate to the movement in price of an option as a result of the movement in the underlying price, the rate of that movement and time erosion.
Gross	A position which is held with both the bought and the sold trades kept open rather than being netted out.
GSCC	Government Securities Clearing Corporation – clearing organisation for US Treasury securities.
Haircut	Amount by which collateral put-up against margin is discounted.
Hard Commodities	Commodities such as tin or zinc. Futures and options on them are traded on specialist derivative exchanges like the London Metal Exchange.
Hedge Ratio	Determining the ratio of the futures to the cash position so as to reduce price risk. Also the proportion of the underlying asset needed to delta hedge an option.
Hedging	A trading method which is designed to reduce or mitigate risk. Reducing the risk of a cash position in the futures instrument to offset the price movement of the cash asset. A broader definition of hedging includes using futures as a temporary substitute for the cash position.
HKE/HKEx	The holding company of the Hong Kong Futures Exchange, The Stock Exchange of Hong Kong Ltd and The Hong Kong Securities Clearing Company Ltd Exchange is collectively called HKEx (Hong Kong Exchanges).
Holder	A term describing a person who has bought a derivatives contract that creates an open long position.
Home State Regulation	Under the ISD, an investment business is authorised in the place of its head office and registered office. This home state authorisation entitles it to conduct business in any member state of the European Union.
Host State Regulation	Any European investment business operating outside its home basis is regulated by its host for its Conduct of business.

In-the-Money	A call option where the exercise price is below the underlying share price, or a put option where the exercise price is above the underlying share price.
Income Enhancement	Strategy that uses written call options to generate premium against underlying assets held.
Independent Clearing Organisation	A clearing house or organisation that is quite separate from the actual members of the exchange, and will guarantee to each member the performance of the contracts by having them registered in the organisation's name.
Index Funds	Unit trusts or mutual funds which invest in the constituent parts of an index.
Indirect Market Participation	Non-broker/dealers, such as institutional investors, who are active investors/traders.
Initial Margin	The deposit that the clearing house calls as protection against a default of a contract. It is returnable to the clearing member once the position is closed. The level is subject to changes in line with market conditions.
Inside Information	Information relating to a security which is not publicly known and which would affect the price of the security if it was public.
Insider	Directors, employees, shareholders and other persons having inside information.
Insider Dealing	The criminal offence whereby those with unpublished price sensitive information deal, advise others to deal or pass the information on. Maximum penalty is seven-year jail and an unlimited fine. Where sudden severe movements in a share price occur, the regulatory authority will check dealings in derivatives on the share as well as share trades to establish if any insider dealing has possibly occured.
Institutional Investor	An institution that is usually investing money on behalf of others. Examples are mutual funds and pension funds.
Integration	The third stage of money laundering, in which the money is finally integrated into the legitimate economy. See placement, layering.
Interest Rate Futures	Based on a debt instrument such as a Government Bond or a Treasury Bill as the underlying product and require the delivery of a bond or bill to fulfil the contract.

International Equity	An equity of a company based outside the UK but traded internationally.
International Petroleum Exchange (IPE)	London market for derivatives of energy contracts like those based on gas, electricity and oil products. It is now part of the Intercontinental Exchange.
International Securities Exchange (ISE)	A US electronic option exchange that has quickly established significant volumes in traded options.
International Securities Identification (ISIN)	A coding system developed by the ISO for identifying securities. The ISINs are designated to create one unique worldwide number for any security. It is a 12-digit alpha/numeric code.
In-the-Money	An option whose strike is more advantageous to the option buyer than the current market rate. See at-the-money, out-of-the-money.
Intra-Day Margin	An extra margin call which the clearing organisation can call during the day when there is a very large movement up or down in the price of the contract.
Intrinsic Value	The amount by which an option is in-the-money.
Investment Banks	A bank that has multiple activities, i.e. banking, principal trading, asset management, etc.
Investment Services Directive (ISD)	European Union Directive imposing common standards on investment business. The most recent Directive has opened up the greater use of derivatives, particularly off-exchange, by funds.
Investment Trust Company	Company whose sole business consists of buying selling and holding shares. The difference with unit trusts is that investors in unit trusts do not receive a part of the profits of the company managing the trust.
Investment Business	Dealing, advising or managing investments. Those doing so need to be authorised.
Investments	Items defined in the FSA 86 to be regulated by it, includes shares, bonds, options, futures, life assurance and pensions.
Investment Grade	A grading level that is used by certain types of funds for determining assets that are suitable for investment by the fund.

Initial Margin or Deposit   A returnable deposit required by a clearing house and clearing broker for open positions, the exception being some long option positions where the maximum possible loss (the premium) has already been paid by the buyer.

Invoice Amount   The amount calculated under the formula specified by the futures exchange, which will be paid in settlement of the delivery of the underlying asset.

Know Your Customer   The conduct of business rule requiring investment advisers to take steps, before giving investment advice, to determine the financial position and investment objectives of the client.

Last Notice Day   The final day that notification of delivery of a futures contract will be possible. On most exchanges all outstanding short futures contracts will be automatically delivered to open long positions.

Last Trading Day   Often the day preceding last notice day which is the final opportunity for holders of long positions to trade out of their positions and avoid ultimate delivery.

Layering   The second stage of money laundering, in which the money is passed through a series of transaction to obscure its origin. See placement, integration.

LCH/LCH.Clearnet   London Clearing House now merged with Clearnet to create LCH.Clearnet.

Leverage   The magnification of gains and losses by paying only for part of the underlying value of the instrument or asset; the smaller the amount of funds invested, the greater the leverage. It is also known as gearing.

LIBID   The London interbank bid rate. The rate at which one bank will lend to another.

LIBOR   The London interbank offered rate. It is the rate used when one bank borrows from another bank. It is the benchmark used to price many capital market and derivative transactions.

LIFFE   London International Financial Futures and Options Exchange.

LIFFE Connect   LIFFE electronic dealing system.

Limit Order	(i) Type of order input into SETS. If not completed immediately the balance is displayed on the screen and forms the Order Book. (ii) An order in which a customer sets the maximum price he is willing to pay as a buyer or the minimum price he is willing to accept as a seller.
Liquidation	Term used to describe the closing of open positions.
Liquidity	A liquid asset is one that can be converted easily and rapidly into cash without a substantial loss of value. In the money market, a security is said to be liquid if the spread between bid and asked price is narrow and reasonable size can be done at those quotes.
Liquidity Risk	The risk that a bank may not be able to close out a position because the market is illiquid.
Local	An individual member of an exchange who trades solely for their own account.
Local Currency	Currency of the country of settlement.
Lombard Rate	The rate of interest at which the German Bundesbank lends to commercial banks when the loans are against Treasury Bills or bills of exchange.
London Interbank Offer Rate (LIBOR)	Rate at which banks lend to each other which is often used as the benchmark for floating rate loans (FRNs).
London International Financial Futures and Options Exchange (LIFFE)	Market for trading in bond, interest rate and index futures and options, plus equity stock options and universal share futures plus soft commodity derivatives, now part of Euronext.
London Metal Exchange (LME)	Market for trading in derivatives of metals such as copper, tin, zinc, etc.
London Stock Exchange (LSE)	Market for trading in securities. Formerly known as the International Stock Exchange of the United Kingdom and Republic of Ireland or ISE.
Long	A term to describe a market view or a bought position in a derivative, which is held open. Thus a fund manager or a trader may be bullish of the equity market and is contemplating going 'long' of say 50 index futures. If purchased they have a long position (see below).

Long Position   Refers to an investor or trader's account in which he has purchased and is holding open a bought position. The position may be created as a result of the combination of several trades and therefore can increase of decrease. If the position is sold off in its entirety then the position would become flat.

Lot   A common term used to describe the standard unit of trading for futures and options but equally it is also often referred to as a 'contract'.

Managed Fund   A unit-linked policy where the managers decide on the allocation of premiums to different unitised funds.

Mandatory Event   A corporate action that affects the securities without giving any choice to the security holder. Likely to affect the contract specification of any related derivative.

Margin
    (i)   *Initial* margin is collateral placed by one party with a counterparty or clearing house at the time of a deal, against the possibility that the market price will move against the first party, thereby leaving the counterparty with a credit risk.
    (ii)   *Variation* margin is a payment made, or collateral transferred, from one party to the other because the market price of the transaction of collateral has changed. Variation margin payment is either in effect a settlement of profit/loss (for example, in the case of a futures contract) or the reduction of credit exposure.
    (iii)   In a loan, margin is the extra interest above a benchmark such as LIBOR required by a lender to compensate for the credit risk of that particular borrower.
    (iv)   Money or assets that must be deposited by participants in securities lending, repo's or OTC derivatives markets as a guarantee that they will be able to meet their commitments at the due date.

Mark-to-Market   The process of revaluing an OTC or exchange-traded product each day. It is the difference between the closing price on the previous day against the current closing price. For exchange-traded products this is referred to as variation margin.

Market   Description of any organisation or facility through which items are traded. All exchanges are markets.

Market Counterparty	A person dealing as agent or principal with the broker and involved in the same nature of investment business as the broker. This also includes fellow members of the SFA or trading members of an investment exchange, for those products only where they are members.
Market Forces	Supply and demand allowing buyers and sellers to fix the price without external interference.
Market Maker	A trader who works for an organisation such as an investment bank. They quote bids and offers in the market and are normally under an obligation to make a price in a certain number of contracts. They create liquidity in the contract by offering to buy or sell.
Market Price	In the case of a security, the market price is usually considered as the last reported price at which the stock or bond has been sold. In derivatives it can be the current price showing hence the term trade 'at market'.
Market Risk	Also position risk. The risk that the market value of a position falls.
Market Value	The price at which a security is trading and could presumably be purchased or sold.
MATIF	Former French derivatives exchange now part of EURONEXT.
Maturity	The date on which the derivative ceases.
Model Risk	The risk that the computer model used by a bank for valuation or risk assessment is incorrect or mis-interpreted.
MONEP	Former French options exchange now part of EURONEXT.
Money Laundering	The process where criminals attempt to conceal the true origin and ownership of the proceeds of their criminal activities and to legitimise these proceeds by introducing them into the mainstream of financial activities.
Money Market	The market for the purchase and sale of short-term financial instruments. Short term is usually defined as less than one year.
Mutual Fund	Fund operated by an investment company that raises money from shareholders and invests it in stocks, bonds or other instruments (unit trust, investment fund, SICAV – BEVEK).

Naked Option   An option bought or sold for speculation, with no offsetting of existing position behind it.

Naked Writing   Where the seller does not own the stock corresponding to the call option which he has sold and would be forced to pay the prevailing market price for the stock to meet delivery obligations, if called.

NASDAQ   National Association of Securities Dealers Automated Quotation system.

National Association of Pension Funds (NAPF)   Trade association of pension funds through which they can voice their opinions collectively.

Netting   Trading partners offset their positions, thereby reducing the number of positions for settlement. Netting can be either *bilateral, multilateral* or *continuous net settlement.*

Nikkei Dow Index   Main share index in Japan. Futures and options are listed on this index.

Nikkei Futures   Futures contracts traded on the Tokyo Stock Exchange, SGX and OSAKA exchange.

Nominal Amount   Value stated on the face of a security (principal value, par value). Securities processing: number of securities to deliver/receive.

Non Clearing Member   A member of an exchange who does not undertake to settle their derivatives business. This type of member must appoint a clearing member to register all their trades at the clearing organisation.

Non-Private Customer A person who is not a Private Customer or who has requested to be treated as a Non-Private Customer.

Notional   Most derivatives and contracts for differences require a notional principal amount on which strategies and settlement can be calculated.

Novation   The process where registered trades are cancelled with the clearing members and substituted by two new ones – one between the clearing house and the clearing member seller, the other between the clearing house and the clearing member buyer.

NYMEX   New York Mercantile Exchange; the largest energy derivative exchange.

Offer Price	The price at which a trader or market maker is willing to sell a contract.
Omnibus Account	Account containing the holdings of more than one client.
Open Ended	Type of investment such as Unit Trusts or OEICs which can expand without limit.
Open Ended Investment Company (OEIC)	Corporate structure introduced in 1997. It is a form of collective investment vehicle.
Open Order	A purchase or sale order at a stated price that is good until cancelled or executed.
Open Outcry	The style of trading whereby traders face each other in a designated area such as a pit and shout or call their respective bids and offers. Hand signals are also used to communicate. It is governed by exchange rules.
Opening Trade	A bought or sold trade that is held open to create a position.
Open Interest	The number of contracts both bought and sold which remain open for delivery on an exchange. Important indicator for liquidity.
Open Position	The number of contracts which have not been offset at the clearing organisation by the close of business.
Operational risk	The risk of losses resulting from inadequate systems and control, human errors or management failings.
Option	An option is in the case of the *buyer*, the right, but not the obligation, to take (call) or make (put) for delivery of the underlying product and in the case of the *seller*, the obligation to make or take delivery of the underlying product.
Option Premium	The sum of money paid by the buyer, for acquiring the right of the option. It is the sum of money received by the seller for incurring the obligation, having sold the rights, of the option. It is the sum of the intrinsic value and the time value.
Options on Futures	These have the same characteristics as an option, the difference being that the underlying product is either a long or a short futures contract. Premium is not exchanged as the contracts are marked to market each day.

Order Driven Market   A stock market where brokers acting on behalf of clients match trades with each other either on the trading floor of the exchange or through a central computer system.

Ordinary Shares   Known as common stock in the United States and equities in the United Kingdom. Shareholders are the owners of a company and are protected so the maximum loss is the value of their shares and not the full debt of the company. Ordinary shares are divided into Preferred and Deferred ordinaries.

Out-of-the-Money   A call option whose exercise price is above the current underlying share price or a put option whose exercise price is below the current underlying share price. This option has no intrinsic value.

Out-Trade   A trade which has been incorrectly matched on the floor of an exchange.

Over-the-Counter (OTC)   A one-to-one agreement between two counterparties where the specifications of the product are completely flexible and non-standardised. A negotiated trade where counterparty risk is potentially an issue.

Par Value   See *Nominal Value.*

Pension Fund   Fund set up by a corporation, labour union, governmental entity or other organisation to pay the pension benefits of retired workers. Pension funds invest billions annually in the securities markets and are therefore major market players who also use derivatives markets.

Physical Delivery   A derivative contract that on delivery will result in the asset being delivered, for example bond futures, stock options, commodities.

Pit   The designated area on the market floor where a particular contract is traded. It may have an alternative name in some markets, for example on the LME trading takes place in the 'ring'.

Placement   The first stage of money laundering, in which the money is passed placed in the banking system. See layering, integration.

Portfolio   List of investments held by an individual or company, or list of loans made by a bank or financial institution. Can also be the derivatives positions held by a trader/dealer.

Premium	An option premium is the amount paid up-front by the purchaser of the option to the writer.
Present Value	The amount of money which needs to be invested (or borrowed) now at a given interest rate in order to achieve exactly a given cashflow in the future, assuming compound re-investment (or re-funding) of any interest payments received (or paid) before the end. See future value.
Pre-settlement	Checks and procedures undertaken immediately after execution of a trade prior to settlement.
Price (Conversion) Factor	The price at which a bond would trade, per 1 nominal, to yield the notional coupon of the futures contract on the delivery day (or the first day in the deliverable month if this applies).
Principal Trading	When a firm uses its own money for trading (also called proprietary trading).
Principal-to-Principal Market	A market where the clearing house only recognises the clearing member as one entity, and not the underlying clients of the clearing member.
Principal Value	That amount inscribed on the face of a security and exclusive of interest or premium. The amount is the one used in the computation of interest due on such a security.
Private Customer	An individual person who is not acting in the course of carrying on investment business.
Project A	The after-hours trading system used by the CBOT.
Proprietary Trader	A trader who deals for an organisation such as an investment bank taking advantage of short-term price movements as well as taking long-term views on whether the market will move up or down.
Put Option	An option that gives the buyer the right, but not the obligation, to sell a specified quantity of the underlying asset at a fixed price, on or before a specified date. The seller of a put option has the obligation (because they have sold the right) to take delivery of the underlying asset if the option is exercised by the buyer.
RCH	Recognised Clearing House under the Financial Services Act.
Realised Profit	Profit which has arisen from a real sale.

Reconciliation   The comparison of a person's records of cash and securities position with records held by another party and the investigation and resolution of any discrepancies between the two sets of records. Crucially important in derivatives business to reduce operational risk.

Reputational Risk   The risk that an organisation's reputation will be damaged by being in breach of regulations, poor service or by having inadequate controls over risk and performance.

RIE   A Recognised Investment Exchange designated by a regulatory authority.

Rights Issue   Offer of shares made to existing shareholders. As a corporate action it may change the strike price and number of shares on which an option or share future is based.

Right of Offset   Where positions and cash held by the Clearing Organisation in different accounts for a member are allowed to be netted.

Risk Warning   In the United Kingdom a document that must be despatched and signed by private customers before they deal in traded options.

Rollover   A rollover can be when the next leg of a swap is calculated or when a futures position in an expiring month is 'rolled' to the next maturity. For example, the position in the March expiry is closed out and reopened in the next available maturity, say the June expiry.

Securities   Can mean any instrument in the markets but generally refers to bonds and equities.

Securities House   General term covering any type of organisation involved in securities although usually reserved for the larger firms.

**Securities and Exchange   The overall investment regulatory body in the
Commission (SEC)**   United States.

Segregated Account   Account in which there is only the holdings of one client.

Segregation of Funds   Where the client assets are held separately from those assets belonging to the member firm.

Serious Fraud Office   Specialist unit established to tackle large-scale fraud.

Settlement	The fulfilment of the contractual commitments of transacted business.
Settlement Date	The date on which a trade is cleared by delivery of securities against funds (actual settlement date, contractual settlement date).
Share Futures	Based on individual shares. Delivery is fulfilled by the payment or receipt of cash against the exchange-calculated delivery settlement price. Also called stock futures and universal stock futures.
Share Option	A right sold to an investor conferring the option to buy or sell shares of a particular company at a predetermined price and within a specified time limit.
Short	A term used to describe a market view that if traded would create a sold position in a derivative that is held open. For instance, a fund manager believes the equity market might fall and so contemplates going short by selling index futures to hedge the portfolio of shares held. Opposite of long.
Short Position	The selling of securities, commodities, etc. that are not already owned, which creates a position.
SGX	The merged central Stock Exchange of Singapore & the derivative exchange SIMEX.
Soft Commodities	Description given to commodities such as sugar, coffee and cocoa, traded through LIFFE since its incorporation of the former London Commodity Exchange (LCE).
SPAN	Standardised Portfolio Analysis of Risk. A form of margin calculation which is used by various clearing organisations.
Speculation	A deal undertaken because the dealer expects prices to move in his favour and thereby realise a profit.
Speculator	The speculator is a trader who wants to assume risk for potentially much higher rewards.
Spot Delivery	A delivery or settlement of currencies on the value date, two business days later.
Spot Market	Market for immediate as opposed to future delivery. In the spot market for foreign exchange, settlement is in two business days ahead.
Spot Month	The first month for which futures contracts are available.
Spot Rate	The price prevailing in the spot market.

Spread	(i) 1. The difference between bid and asked price on a security or derivative
	2. Difference between yield on or prices of two securities of different types or maturities
	3. In underwriting, difference between price realised by an issuer and price paid by the investor
	4. Difference between two prices or two rates. What commodities traders would refer to as the basis.
	(ii) A trading strategy in which a trader buys one instrument and sells another, related instrument with a view to profiting from a change in the price difference between the two. A futures spread is the purchase of one futures contract and the sale of another; an option spread is the purchase of one call (or put) and the sale of another.
	(iii) The difference between one price or rate and another, for example, the extent to which a swap fixed-rate is higher than a benchmark Treasury bond yield, or the extent to which the floating-rate in a swap is above or below LIBOR.
Standard Settlement Instructions	Instructions for settlement with a particular counterparty which are always followed for a particular kind of deal and, once in place, are therefore not repeated at the time of each transaction.
Standing Instruction	Default instruction, for example, provided to an agent processing payments or clearing securities trades; provided by shareholder on how to vote shares (for example, vote for all management-recommended candidates).
Standard & Poors	US indices on which futures and options contracts are based CME introduced S&P 500 Index Futures as the first index-based derivative.
Stock	In some countries (e.g. United States), the term applies to ordinary share capital of a company. In other countries (e.g. United Kingdom), stock may mean share capital that is issued in variable amount instead of fixed specified amounts, or it can describe government loans.
Stock Dividend	Dividends paid by a company in stock instead of cash. As a corporate action it does not usually change the contract specification.

Stockmarket	Term used to describe where securities are/have been traded, i.e. 'today on the stockmarket shares closed higher'.
Stock Index Futures/Options	Based on the value of an underlying stock index like the FTSE 100 in the UK, the S&P 500 Index in the United States and the Nikkei 225 and 300 in Japan. Delivery is fulfilled by the payment or receipt of cash against the exchange-calculated delivery settlement price. These are referred to as either indices or indexes.
Stop (Order)	An owner of a physical security that has been mutilated, lost or stolen will request the issuer to place a stop (transfer) on the security and to cancel and replace the security.
Straddle	The purchase or sale of a call combined with the purchase or sale of a put at the same strike (generally purchased with both at-the-money).
Straight-through Processing	Computer transmission of the details of a trade, without manual intervention, from their original input by the trader to all other relevant areas – position keeping, risk control, accounts, settlement, reconciliation.
Strike Price	The fixed price, per share or unit, at which an option conveys the right to call (purchase) or put (sell) the underlying shares or units.
Strike Price/Rate	Also exercise price. The price or rate at which the holder of an option can insist on the underlying transaction being fulfilled.
SWIFT	Society for Worldwide Interbank Financial Telecommunications – secure electronic communications network between banks.
Tender	Futures positions that are depending on the market short on or before expiry are tendered for delivery.
Theoretical Value	Another term for fair value of a futures or options contract.
Theta	A term used to describe the rate of decline of time value in an option price.
Tick Size	The value of a one-point movement in the contract price.
Time Value	The amount by which an option's premium exceeds its intrinsic value. Where an option has no intrinsic value the premium consists entirely of time value.
TIMS	Theoretical Intermarket Margin System, margin system used on some exchanges.

Traded Option	An option which is traded on an exchange.
Trader	An individual who buys and sells securities with the objective of making short-term gains.
Trading Permits	These are issued by exchanges and give the holder the right to have one trader at any one time trading in the contract(s) to which the permit relates.
Treasury Bill	Money market instrument issued with a life of less than one year issued by the US and the UK governments. Good collateral against margin calls.
Treasury Bonds (US)	US government bond issued with a 30-year maturity. Underlying of the CBOT Treasury Bond future.
Treasury Note	A government obligation with maturities of one–ten years, carrying a fixed rate of interest.
Treasury Notes (US)	US government bond issued with 2-, 3-, 5- and 7-year maturity. Underlying for futures traded on CBOT.
Triple A – Rating	The highest credit rating for a bond or company – the risk of default (or non-payment) is negligible.
Underlying Asset or Underlying	The asset or product from which the future or option's price is derived and which may be deliverable.
Unit Trust	A system whereby money from a number of investors is pooled together and invested collectively on their behalf. Each owns a unit (or number of them) the value of which depends on the value of those items owned by the trust. Unit trusts can use derivatives subject to regulatory directives and trust mandates.
Unrealised Profit	Profit that has not arisen from a sale – an increase in value of an asset.
Value at Risk (VaR)	The maximum amount which a bank expects to lose, with a given confidence level, over a given time period.
Variation Margin	The process of revaluing an exchange-traded product each day. It is the difference between the closing price on the previous day against the current closing price. It is physically paid or received each day by the clearing organisation. It is often referred to as the mark-to-market.
Vega	Another part of the 'Greeks' and is a measure of the rate of change in an option's price caused by changes in volatility.

Volatility	The range or scatter of the price of an underlying or a derivative around a mean. Volatility is a crucial part of option pricing and therefore option price models as the price of the option is affected by both the volatility of the underlying and the specific option series. Option strategies like straddles are based on the expected volatility of the underlying through to maturity.
Warrants	An option which can be listed on an exchange, with a life-time of generally more than one year.
Warrant Agent	A bank appointed by the issuer as an intermediary between the issuing company and the (physical) warrant holders, interacting when the latter want to exercise the warrants.
Writer	A person who has sold an open derivatives contract and is obliged to deliver or take delivery upon notification of exercise from the buyer.
XETRA	Dealing system of the Deutsche Börse.

The contents of this glossary of terms and appendices have been compiled from reliable sources and are believed to be correct; however, Derivatives Management Services Ltd and Computer Based Learning Limited can take no responsibility whatsoever for any loss, claim or damages caused in whatever manner as a result of the reader using information taken from this work.

© *Computer Based Learning Ltd/DMS Ltd October 2004*

No part of this document may be copied or stored in any format without prior permission from: Computer Based Learning Ltd, 1 Talbot Yard, London Bridge, London, SE1 1YP.

Appendix 1

Euronext.liffe equity index future contract specification

EXCHANGE CONTRACT NO. 29

FTSE 100 INDEX CONTRACT

CONTRACT TERMS – Issue Date: 5 December 1997
ADMINISTRATIVE PROCEDURES – Issue Date: 12 February 1998
Delivery months: June 1998 onwards

FTSE 100 INDEX CONTRACT

THE LONDON INTERNATIONAL FINANCIAL FUTURES AND OPTIONS EXCHANGE

Terms of Exchange Contract No. 29

1. Interpretation

1.01 Save as otherwise specified herein, words and phrases defined in the Rules shall have the same meanings in these terms and in the Administrative Procedures.

1.02 In these terms and in the Administrative Procedures: 'Administrative Procedures' means all procedures from time to time implemented by the Board pursuant to the Rules for the purposes of this Exchange Contract.

'business day' means a day on which the market and the Stock Exchange are open for business.

'Contract' means a contract made expressly or impliedly in the terms of this Exchange Contract for the sale and purchase of one or more lots, and 'registered Contract' means a Contract registered by the Clearing House.

'Conversion Date' means the date on which pursuant to Economic and Monetary Union in the European Union the conversion rate for Sterling against a Single Currency which is on such date 'a currency in its own right' is 'irrevocably fixed' in accordance with Article 109_ of the EC treaty.

'delivery month' means each month specified as such by the Board pursuant to the Rules.

'EC Treaty' means the treaty establishing the European Community. 'EDSP' means the Exchange Delivery Settlement Price and has the meaning attributed to it in term 5.

'FTSE International' means FTSE International Limited.

'Index' means the index of stock prices calculated by FTSE International and known as 'The FTSE 100 Index'.

'Last Trading Day' means in respect of any delivery month the third Friday in that month provided that if it is not a business day then the Last Trading Day shall be the last business day preceding the third Friday (subject in all cases to term 7).

'Market day' means a day on which the market, the Clearing House and banks in London are open for business.

'£' denotes the lawful currency of the United Kingdom, known, at the date of issues of these contract terms, as 'Sterling'.

'Regulations' means the General Regulations and Default Rules from time to time in force of the Clearing House.

'Settlement Day' means in respect of a delivery month the first market day after the Last Trading Day.

'Single Currency' means a lawful currency introduced in the United Kingdom pursuant to its participation in Economic and Monetary Union in the European Union.

'Stock Exchange' means The London Stock Exchange Limited.

'Weighting' means the factor which, when multiplied by the price of a constituent stock expressed in Sterling, determines the contribution to the Index figure made of that constituent stock.

1.03 In these terms references to 'lawful currency' shall be construed to include units of value of a Single Currency which may be used validly to discharge payment obligations pursuant to the law of the United Kingdom upon introduction of such Single Currency and notwithstanding that such units of value of such Single Currency may not at all material times follow-ing the Conversion Date constitute legal tender in the United Kingdom.

1.04 Reference to a 'term' refers to a term hereof and reference to a 'Rule' refers to a rule of the Exchange's Rules. Save where the context otherwise requires references herein to the singular include the plural, and vice versa.

2. Contract Specification

2.01 These terms shall apply to all Contracts.

2.02 Each Contract shall be for one or more lots for the delivery month specified.

3. Price

3.01 Bids and offers shall be quoted in 'Value Points' and prices shall be a whole number multiple of the minimum price fluctuation, as specified in the Administrative Procedures.

3.02 One Value Point shall be 0.1 and shall have a value of £1.00 per lot.

4. Last Trading Day

4.01 On the Last Trading Day:
(a) trading in Contracts for the relevant delivery month shall cease at such time as may be specified in the Administrative Procedures; and
(b) the Exchange will calculate the EDSP in accordance with term 5.

5. Exchange Delivery Settlement Price ('EDSP')

5.01 The EDSP for Contracts for a particular delivery month shall, subject as provided in term 6, be calculated by exchange officials as the average of such Index figures (but subject to any corrections in accordance with term 6), on the Last Trading Day as are specified for this purpose in the Administrative Procedures, rounded to the nearest 0.5 or, where such average is an exact uneven multiple of 0.25, to the nearest higher 0.5.

5.02 The Exchange shall publish a provisional EDSP and the final EDSP at or by such times as may be specified in the Administrative Procedures. The final EDSP shall be final and binding for all purposes.

5.03 This term 5.03 shall apply to Contracts for delivery months from September 1997 onwards. The Board may from time to time amend the method for and timing of the calculation of the EDSP for any reason determined by the Board and any such changes shall have such effect with regard to existing and/or new Contracts as the Board may determine.

6. Errors in Index

6.01 If, not later than the time on the Last Trading Day specified for that pur-pose in the Administrative Procedures, any member of the Exchange notifies exchange officials of, or there otherwise comes to the attention of exchange officials, an alleged or apparent error in the Index due to any alleged or apparent error in the weighting of the price for any constituent stock of the Index first made since the publication of the closing Index figure on the last business day prior to the Last Trading Day, then exchange officials shall promptly investigate such alleged or apparent error. If in their opinion an error has been made, the Exchange shall as soon as reasonably practicable publish a correction to the Index and the EDSP shall be calculated using Index figures as so corrected. Save as allowed by term 6.02, no correction to the Index shall be made in respect of any error notified to exchange officials or coming to their attention after the time so specified in the Administrative Procedures.

6.02 If, not later than thirty minutes after the provisional EDSP for a particular delivery month is first published, any member of the Exchange notifies exchange officials of, or there otherwise come to the attention of exchange officials, an alleged or apparent error in the Index due to any cause whatsoever other than an error in the weighting of the price for any constituent stock of the Index, then exchange officials shall investigate such alleged or apparent error. If in their opinion an error has been made, they shall correct any Index figures affected thereby which have been or will be used to calculate the EDSP for that delivery month and shall calculate or re-calculate (as the case may be) the EDSP in accordance therewith. No correction of Index figures or recalculation of the EDSP shall be made in respect of any error notified to exchange officials or coming to their attention after the expiry of such thirty minute period.

6.03 No correction to the Index or re-calculation of the EDSP shall be made other than as may be allowed for in term 6.01 and 6.02.

6.04 Neither the Exchange nor exchange officials shall have any liability whatsoever in respect of any decision as to whether or not to correct Index figures or as to the amount of any correction, or as to whether or not to re-calculate the EDSP.

7. Emergency Provisions

7.01 If, at any time after the close of trading two business days prior to the day which would have been the Last Trading Day in respect of a delivery month, it becomes known to the Exchange that on the day which would have been the Last Trading Day either or both of the market and the Stock Exchange will not be open for business, then the business day next following such day shall become the Last Trading Day in respect of that delivery month and the Exchange shall post a notice to that effect in the market.

7.02 If, after the commencement of trading on the Last Trading Day in respect of a delivery month, either or both of the market and the Stock Exchange closes for business or FTSE International for any reason does not calculate or does not publish or ceases to publish the Index or for any reason the Exchange does not display the Index figure in the market, with the effect that trading in Contracts for that delivery month is, in the opinion of exchange officials, substantially prevented or hindered or that there are insufficient Index figures from which to calculate the EDSP in accordance with term 5.01 and the Administrative Procedures, then either:

(a) cessation of trading in Contracts for the current delivery month shall be postponed until such later time on that day as exchange officials may in their absolute discretion specify by notice posted in the market, in which case the EDSP shall be calculated in accordance with term 5.01 but using the Index figures during a period so specified in their absolute discretion by exchange officials and the provisional and final EDSPs shall be published at such times as exchange officials shall in their discretion determine, always allowing for the thirty minute period referred to in term 6.02; or

(b) if, in the opinion of exchange officials, the course described in paragraph (a) would be impossible, impracticable or for any reason undesirable, they may by notice posted in the market declare that day not to be the Last Trading Day and the next following business day, or any later business day chosen by them in their absolute discretion, to be the Last Trading Day in its place.

8. Payment

8.01 In respect of each lot comprised in a Contract the following payments shall be made by the time specified therefor in the Administrative Procedures:

(a) where the final EDSP exceeds the Contract price, payment by the Seller to the Clearing House and payment by the Clearing House to the Buyer; and

(b) where the Contract price exceeds the final EDSP, payment by the Buyer to the Clearing House and payment by the Clearing House to the Seller.

FTSE 100 Index

Member Handbook Volume 2 (30 June 1998) 4.1a.7

of an amount calculated by multiplying the difference in Value Points between the EDSP and the Contract price by the value per lot of one Value Point as specified in term 3.02.

9. Default

9.01 A Buyer or a Seller shall be in default where:

(a) he fails to fulfil his obligations under a Contract by the time and in the manner prescribed and in accordance with these terms, the Rules and the Administrative Procedures and the Regulations; or

(b) he fails to pay any sum due to the Clearing House in respect of a registered Contract by the time specified in these terms or in the Administrative Procedures or under the Regulations; or

(c) in the reasonable opinion of the Clearing House he is in default.

9.02 Subject to the default rules of the Clearing House, in the event of default by a Buyer or a Seller in respect of a registered Contract, the Board shall, at the request of the Clearing House, forthwith fix a price for invoicing back and each lot in issue shall be invoiced back at that price. Such price may at the Board's absolute discretion take account of any compensation the Board may consider should be paid by either party to the other.

10. Force Majeure

10.01 Subject to any steps taken at any time by the Board under emergency powers in the Rules, a Seller or a Buyer shall be liable to perform his obligations in respect of a lot comprised in a Contract by the due time therefore, notwithstanding that he may be or is likely to be prevented from so doing by any event beyond his reasonable control including, without limitation, any act of God, strike, lockout, war, armed conflict, use of force by authority of the United Nations, fire, riot or civil commotion, combination of workmen, act of terrorism, breakdown of machinery, unavailability or restriction of computer or data processing facilities or energy supplies or bank transfer systems.

11. Articles, Rules, Regulations, etc.

11.01 Every Contract shall be subject to the Articles and the Rules and the Regulations in so far as applicable notwithstanding that either or both of the parties to it be not a member of the Exchange or of the Clearing House.

11.02 In case of any conflict between the Administrative Procedures and these terms or the Rules, the provisions of these terms and the Rules shall prevail and, in the event of any conflict between these terms and the Rules, the Rules shall prevail.

12. Arbitration

12.01 Subject to term 12.02, any dispute arising from or in relation to a Contract shall be referred to arbitration under the Rules relating to arbitration and arbitration shall be held in accordance with the Rules in force at the time of such reference.

12.02 No dispute arising from or in relation to any invoicing back price fixed by the Board under these terms shall be referred to arbitration under the Rules.

13. Governing Law

13.01 Every Contract shall be governed by and construed in accordance with English law.

14. Non-registered Contracts

14.01 In respect of a Contract which is not a registered Contract ('non-registered Contract') these terms shall be modified by the parties thereto so as to require and allow that a Contract to be registered with the Clearing House under the Rules and the Regulations is capable of being so registered, and to facilitate performance of such Registered Contract (and of any intermediate

Contract) in accordance with these terms and the Administrative Procedures. Modifications may also be made to the terms of a non-registered Contract to permit performance of such non-registered Contract if, without such modifications, it may not be possible to perform such Contract by the applicable times specified in these terms and the Administrative Procedures. Without prejudice to the generality of the foregoing, all references in these terms to payment or dealing between the Buyer or the Seller and the Clearing House shall be modified so as to require a similar payment or dealing directly between the Buyer and the Seller party to such non-registered Contract.

15. Economic and Monetary Union

15.01 This term 15 shall not apply to delivery months up to and including December 1998.

15.02 The Board in its absolute discretion may from time to time vary, substitute or remove any of, or add to, the terms of this Exchange Contract in order to reflect the existence of, or to permit, require or facilitate payment in, the Single Currency or to reflect changes to the Index made pursuant to the participation of the United Kingdom in Economic and Monetary Union in the European Union.

15.03 Subject to term 15.01, any variation, substitution or removal of, or addition to, the terms of this Exchange Contract made pursuant to term 15.02 shall have such effect with regard to existing and/or new Contracts as the Board may determine.

15.04 Any determination by the Board to vary, substitute or remove any of, or add to, the terms of this Exchange Contract pursuant to terms 15.02 and 15.03 shall be the subject of a General Notice.

Issue Date: 5 December 1997.

FTSE 100 INDEX CONTRACT

Exchange Contract No. 29

Administrative Procedures

Price
The minimum price fluctuation shall be five Value Points.

Last Trading Day
09.15 hours The last time for notification to exchange officials under term 6.01 of any error or alleged error in the Index due to any error or alleged error in the weighting of the price for any constituent stock of the Index. No correction to the Index shall be made in respect of any such error which is first notified to exchange officials or which first comes to their attention after this time.

The Exchange shall publish any correction to the Index under term 6.01 as soon as reasonably practicable.

30 seconds after 10.30 hours Trading in Contracts for the relevant delivery month shall cease.

As soon as reasonably practicable after cessation of trading but no later than 15.00 hours The Exchange will publish a provisional EDSP.

Before calculating the provisional EDSP, exchange officials shall take the last eighty-one Index figures calculated, the last of such figures being the calculation made at 10.30 hours and the first being a calculation made not earlier than 10.05 hours, and shall exclude the twelve highest (or, in the event of equality, twelve of the highest) and the twelve lowest (or, in the event of equality, twelve of the lowest) of those eighty-one figures. The remaining fifty-seven shall be the Index figures used to calculate the EDSP in accordance with term 5.01.

The Exchange will, together with the provisional EDSP, publish the last eighty-one Index figures referred to above.

30 minutes after the publication of the provisional EDSP is the last time for notification to exchange officials of an error or alleged error in the Index of a kind falling to be dealt with under term 6.02.

In any investigation into an alleged or apparent error in the Index in accordance with term 6.02, exchange officials shall have regard, in reaching an opinion as to whether an error has been made, to the Ground Rules for the Management of the UK Series compiled by the FTSE Actuaries Share Indices Steering Committee in force at that time.

As soon as reasonably practicable after the expiry of the 30-minute period referred to above The Exchange will publish the final EDSP.

Settlement Day
By 10.00 hours All payments required by term 8.01 to be made by the Buyer and the Seller shall have been completed.

Issue Date: 12 February 1998.

Source: Euronext.liffe.

Appendix 2

Euronext.liffe listed option contracts

LIFFE individual equity option contracts (as at April 2004)

Company	LIFFE code	Tick Size
3i Group plc	III	0.5
Abbey National plc	ANL	0.5
Alliance & Leicester plc	LEI	0.5
Allied Domecq plc	ADQ	0.5
Amvescap plc	AVZ	0.5
Anglo American plc	AAM	0.5
ARM Holdings plc	ARM	0.5
AstraZeneca plc	AZA	0.5
Aviva plc	CUA	0.5
BAA plc	APT	0.5
BAE Systems plc	AER	0.25
Barclays plc	BBL	0.25
BG Group plc	BGG	0.5
BHP Billiton plc	BLT	0.5
BOC Group Plc	BOC	0.5
Boots Group plc	BOT	0.5
BP plc	BP	0.5
British Airways plc	AWS	0.25
British American Tobacco plc	TAB	0.5
British Sky Broadcasting Group plc	BSK	0.5
BT Group plc	BTG	0.25
Cable & Wireless plc	C + W	0.25
Cadbury Schweppes plc	CAD	0.5
Capita Group plc	CPI	0.5
Carlton Communications plc	CCM	0.5
Carnival plc	POC	0.5
Celltech Group plc	CCH	0.5
Centrica plc	CTR	0.5
Colt Telecom Group plc	CTM	0.25
Compass Group plc	CPG	0.5

Continued

LIFFE individual equity option contracts (as at April 2004)—cont'd

Company	LIFFE code	Tick Size
Corus Group plc	STL	0.25
Diageo plc	GNS	0.5
Dixons Group plc	DIX	0.5
EMAP plc	EMA	0.5
EMI Group plc	EMI	0.5
Gallaher Group plc	GAL	0.5
GlaxoSmithKline plc	GXO	0.5
GUS plc	GUS	0.5
HBOS plc	HAX	0.5
Hanson plc	HSN	0.5
Hilton Group plc	LDB	0.5
HSBC Holdings plc	HSB	0.5
Imperial Chemical Industries plc	ICI	0.5
Imperial Tobacco Group plc	IMP	0.5
International Power plc	IPR	0.5
InterContinental Hotels Group plc	IHG	0.5
Invensys plc	BRT	0.25
ITV plc	GME	0.5
Kingfisher plc	KGF	0.5
Land Securities Group plc	LS	0.5
Legal & General Group plc	LGE	0.25
Lloyds TSB Group plc	TSB	0.5
LogicaCMG plc	LOG	0.5
London Stock Exchange plc	LSE	0.5
Man Group Plc	EMG	0.5
Marks & Spencer Group plc	M + S	0.25
Mitchells & Butlers plc	MAB	0.5
mm02plc	OOM	0.25
Morrison (Wm) Supermarkets plc	MWR	0.25
National Grid Transco plc	NGG	0.5
Next Plc	NXT	0.5
Northern Rock plc	NKR	0.5
Pearson plc	PSO	0.5
Peninsular & Oriental Steam Navigation Co	PO	0.5
Prudential plc	PRU	0.5
Reckitt Benckiser plc	RB	0.5
Reed Elsevier plc	REI	0.5
Rentokil Initial plc	RTO	0.5
Reuters Group plc	RUT	0.5
Rio Tinto plc	RTZ	0.5
Rolls-Royce Group plc	RR	0.5
Royal & Sun Alliance Insurance Group plc	RYL	0.5
Royal Bank of Scotland Group plc	RBS	0.5
SABMiller Plc	SAB	0.5
Safeway plc	AYL	0.5
Sage Group plc	SGE	0.5
Sainsbury (J) plc	SAN	0.25
Scottish & Newcastle plc	SCN	0.5

LIFFE individual equity option contracts (as at April 2004)—cont'd

Company	LIFFE code	Tick Size
Scottish & Southern Energy plc	SSE	0.5
Scottish Power plc	SPW	0.5
Shell Transport & Trading Co plc	SHL	0.25
Shire Pharmaceuticals Group plc	SHP	0.5
Smith & Nephew plc	SNP	0.5
Standard Chartered plc	SCB	0.5
Tesco plc	TCO	0.25
Tomkins plc	TMK	0.5
Unilever plc	ULV	0.5
United Utilities plc	UUL	0.5
Vodafone Group plc[+]	VOD	0.25
Whitbread plc	WTB	0.5
WPP Group plc	WPP	0.5

Source: Euronext.liffe.

Appendix 3

IPE exchange for physicals

EXCHANGING FUTURES FOR PHYSICAL (EFPs)

IPE Brent Crude

The International Petroleum Exchange offers the facility for participants in oil markets to use the IPE Brent Crude futures contract to separate the pricing of crude oil from supply and at the same time enable counterparties in the delivery process to be known.

There are several ways in which EFPs can be useful for market participants, where they can be used to initiate futures positions, close futures positions and to directly swap a futures position for a similar physical position.

Exchanging Futures for Physical trades work on the basis that counterparties agree that they wish to complement their physical transaction with an accompanying futures transaction. They then advise their brokers operating on the Floor of the IPE to register their transactions with the Exchange.

When the EFPs are registered with the IPE the volume is attributed to that trading day but the price is not declared to the market.

The advantages are best illustrated by example. The following three scenarios enable oil market participants to trade with preferred physical counter parties, even if they have differing views of the future direction of market price.

Importantly, EFPs enable delivery of crude against the IPE Brent Crude contract, as in the first example.

For further information contact
IPE Oil Markets 00 44 (0) 207 265 3775

Using an EFP to directly swap a futures and physical position

Scenario

A **crude oil producer** has 2 million bbls of crude unsold. He believes the market to be undersupplied and that the price is going to increase.

A **refiner** needs to have 2 million bbls of crude available on the 10th of December. **He has bought 2000 December IPE Brent Crude futures contracts at $17** in the anticipation that the price of crude is going to rise between November and December.

Both participants are therefore long in a market where they expect the price to rise. However, the producer has not secured a buyer for his crude oil and the refinery buyer wants to be able to secure supply of the quality and delivery timing he needs.

The producer and refiner have done business together before.

They agree to exchange their respective positions in order to meet their needs, i.e. the seller wants to remain long in the market as he thinks the price is going up. The buyer wants to secure a price and the quality and delivery timing he needs.

How does the Exchange of Futures for Physical work?

On November 10th, the producer agrees to sell 2 million bbls of crude at the IPE December Brent Crude Futures Contract settlement price for that day's trading. The crude oil will be delivered on 10th December. The refiner's long futures position will be exchanged for this physical supply.

The two parties advise their brokers that they have agreed this EFP.

The two brokers then contact each other on the IPE trading floor and register with the Exchange that this EFP has been agreed and the price. The refiner's long December futures position is passed over to the producer's account at the IPE December Brent Contract settlement price for November 10th.

Positions after the EFP

The November 10th settlement price for the IPE December Brent contract is $17.50 barrel.

Producer

Short 2 million barrels of crude	$17.50
Long 2000 December Brent futures	$17.50
Sale of crude not priced until producer sells futures	

Refiner

Long 2000 December Brent futures	$17.00
Sold 2000 December Brent futures	$17.50
	$00.50 profit
Long 2 million bbls crude at	$17.50
December delivery has been fixed at $17.00	

Because both participants believe the price is going to increase the EFP has suited both their needs, enabling security of supply without commitment to a price on behalf of the Producer.

Using an EFP to open a futures position

Scenario

Assume that neither party has an existing open position in IPE Brent Crude futures.

A **crude oil producer** has been approached by one of his long standing customers, who wishes to purchase 500,000 bbls for loading in 15 days time. He would like to supply the customer but does not want to commit to a price because he believes the price is going to rise.

The **buying customer** wants to secure supply from the producer to minimise freight on a VLCC, but does not want to commit to the price as he believes the price is going to fall.

The producer and customer agree to do business via an EFP so that they can retain exposure to the price of crude oil but secure each other's delivery requirements. They agree to take equal and opposite futures positions to that which they are transacting in the physical deal.

How does the Exchange of Futures for Physical Work?

On October 1st, the producer agrees to sell 500,000 bbls of crude oil to the customer at the IPE November Brent Crude Futures Contract settlement price for that day's trading. The crude oil will be delivered on October 16th. They will also take out equal and opposite positions in the November Brent Crude Futures Contract at the same price.

The two parties advise their brokers that they have agreed this EFP.

The two brokers then contact each other on the IPE trading floor and register with the Exchange that this EFP has been agreed and the price. A long position of 500 lots is opened for the producer and a short position of 500 lots is opened for the customer.

Positions after the EFP

The October 1st settlement price for the IPE November contract is $16.00

Producer

Short 500,000 bbls crude oil	$16.00
Long 500 lots November Brent futures	$16.00
Crude Oil not priced until futures sold	

Customer

Long 500,000 bbls crude oil	$16.00
Short 500 lots November Brent futures	$16.00
Crude Oil is not priced until futures bought	

Because equal and opposite positions in the November futures contract have been exchanged for the physical positions, both parties remain exposed to the price of crude oil as they were before the physical trade was completed. Thus the pricing of the transaction has been separated from the physical trade itself.

It is now up to the refiner and customer to separately decide when is the best time for them to price the transaction, which will occur when they close the futures positions they hold.

Using an EFP to close futures positions

Scenario

A **producer** has 2 million bbls of crude oil in tank. In anticipation of the price going down before he has sold the crude, **he has previously sold 2000 May IPE Brent Crude futures at $17.00**. The price has fallen $0.50/bbl since then.

A **refiner** wants to buy the crude from the producer but is concerned that the price of oil is going to fall further.

How does the Exchange of Futures for Physical Work?

On April 5th, the producer agrees to sell 2 million bbls to the customer at the IPE May Brent Crude futures contract settlement price for that trading day, plus 20c barrel to reflect the quality of the crude oil. They agree to EFP the trade and take equal and opposite futures positions to that which they have physically traded.

The two parties advise their brokers that they have agreed this EFP. The two brokers then contact each other on the IPE trading floor and register with the Exchange that this EFP has been agreed and the price. The producers's existing short 2000 May futures position is closed. The customer has a position opened of 2000 short May futures.

Positions after the EFP

The April 5th settlement price for the IPE May Brent futures contract is $16.50

Producer

Short 2000 May Futures at	$17.00
Long 2000 May Futures at	$16.50
	$00.50 profit
Short 2 million bbls crude at	$16.70 (settlement + 20c)
Producer's selling price to customer fixed at	$17.20

Customer

Long 2 million bbls crude	$16.70
Short 2000 May Futures	$16.50

Crude is not priced until futures are bought back

Because both parties believe the price is going further down, the EFP has enabled them to detach pricing from supply, meeting both their pricing and physical supply requirements.

The customer can price the product at any time by buying back the 2000 May futures contracts.

Source: IPE.

Appendix 4

IPE expiry dates

IPE CONTRACT EXPIRY DATES 1995/96

Delivery Month	Brent Crude futures	Gas Oil futures	Brent Crude options	Gas Oil options
January 1995	Thursday 15th December	Thursday 12th January 1995	Monday 12th December	Thursday 5th January 1995
February	Monday 16th January 1995	Friday 10th February	Wednesday 11th January 1995	Friday 3rd February
March	Monday 13th February	Friday 10th March	Wednesday 8th February	Friday 3rd March
April	Thursday 16th March	Wednesday 12th April	Monday 13th March	Wednesday 5th April
May	Wednesday 12th April	Thursday 11th May	Friday 7th April	Wednesday 3rd May
June	Tuesday 16th May	Monday 12th June	Thursday 11th May	Monday 5th June
July	Thursday 15th June	Wednesday 12th July	Monday 12th June	Wednesday 5th July
August	Friday 14th July	Thursday 10th August	Tuesday 11th July	Thursday 3rd August
September	Wednesday 16th August	Tuesday 12th September	Friday 11th August	Tuesday 5th September
October	Thursday 14th September	Thursday 12th October	Monday 11th September	Thursday 5th October
November	Monday 16th October	Friday 10th November	Wednesday 11th October	Friday 3rd November
December	Wednesday 15th November	Tuesday 12th December	Friday 10th November	Tuesday 5th December
January 1996	Thursday 14th December	Thursday 11th January 1996	Monday 11th December	Thursday 4th January 1996
February	Tuesday 16th January 1996	Monday 12th February	Thursday 11th January 1996	Monday 5th February
March	Wednesday 14th February	Tuesday 12th March	Friday 9th February	Tuesday 5th March
April	Thursday 14th March	Thursday 11th April	Monday 11th March	Tuesday 2nd April
May	Monday 15th April	Friday 10th May	Wednesday 10th April	Thursday 2nd May
June	Thursday 16th May	Wednesday 12th June	Monday 13th May	Wednesday 5th June
July	Thursday 13th June	Thursday 11th July	Monday 10th June	Thursday 4th July
August	Tuesday 16th July	Monday 12th August	Thursday 11th July	Monday 5th August
September	Thursday 15th August	Thursday 12th September	Monday 12th August	Thursday 5th September
October	Friday 13th September	Thursday 10th October	Tuesday 10th September	Thursday 3rd October
November	Wednesday 16th October	Tuesday 12th November	Friday 11th October	Tuesday 5th November
December	Thursday 14th November	Thursday 12th December	Monday 11th November	Thursday 5th December

IPE CONTRACT EXPIRY DATES 1996/97

Delivery Month	Brent Crude futures	Gas Oil futures	Brent Crude options	Gas Oil options
January 1996	Thursday 14th December	Thursday 11th January 1996	Monday 11th December	Thursday 4th January 1996
February	Tuesday 16th January 1996	Monday 12th February	Thursday 11th January 1996	Monday 5th February
March	Wednesday 14th February	Tuesday 12th March	Friday 9th February	Tuesday 5th March
April	Thursday 14th March	Thursday 11th April	Monday 11th March	Tuesday 2nd April
May	Monday 15th April	Friday 10th May	Wednesday 10th April	Thursday 2nd May
June	Thursday 16th May	Wednesday 12th June	Monday 13th May	Wednesday 5th June
July	Thursday 13th June	Thursday 11th July	Monday 10th June	Thursday 4th July
August	Tuesday 16th July	Monday 12th August	Thursday 11th July	Monday 5th August
September	Thursday 15th August	Thursday 12th September	Monday 12th August	Thursday 5th September
October	Friday 13th September	Thursday 10th October	Tuesday 10th September	Thursday 3rd October
November	Wednesday 16th October	Tuesday 12th November	Friday 11th October	Tuesday 5th November
December	Thursday 14th November	Thursday 12th December	Monday 11th November	Thursday 5th December
January 1997	Monday 16th December	Friday 10th January 1997	Wednesday 11th December	Friday 3rd January 1997
February	Thursday 16th January 1997	Wednesday 12th February	Monday 13th January 1997	Wednesday 5th February
March	Thursday 13th February	Wednesday 12th March	Monday 10th February	Wednesday 5th March
April	Friday 14th March	Thursday 10th April	Tuesday 11th March	Thursday 3rd April
May	Tuesday 15th April	Monday 12th May	Thursday 10th April	Friday 2nd May
June	Thursday 15th May	Thursday 12th June	Monday 12th May	Thursday 5th June
July	Friday 13th June	Thursday 10th July	Tuesday 10th June	Thursday 3rd July
August	Wednesday 16th July	Tuesday 12th August	Friday 11th July	Tuesday 5th August
September	Thursday 14th August	Thursday 11th September	Monday 11th August	Thursday 4th September
October	Monday 15th September	Friday 10th October	Wednesday 10th September	Friday 3rd October
November	Thursday 16th October	Wednesday 12th November	Monday 13th October	Wednesday 5th November
December	Thursday 13th November	Thursday 11th December	Monday 10th November	Thursday 4th December

IPE CONTRACT EXPIRY DATES 1997/98

Delivery Month	Brent Crude futures	Gas Oil futures	Brent Crude options	Gas Oil options	Natural Gas futures
January 1997	Monday 16th December	Friday 10th January 1997	Wednesday 11th December	Friday 3rd January 1997	–
February	Thursday 16th January 1997	Wednesday 12th February	Monday 13th January 1997	Wednesday 5th February	–
March	Thursday 13th February	Wednesday 12th March	Monday 10th February	Wednesday 5th March	27th February 1997
April	Friday 14th March	Thursday 10th April	Tuesday 11th March	Thursday 3rd April	26th March
May	Tuesday 15th April	Monday 12th May	Thursday 10th April	Friday 2nd May	29th April
June	Thursday 15th May	Thursday 12th June	Monday 12th May	Thursday 5th June	29th May
July	Friday 13th June	Thursday 10th July	Tuesday 10th June	Thursday 3rd July	27th June
August	Wednesday 16th July	Tuesday 12th August	Friday 11th July	Tuesday 5th August	30th July
September	Thursday 14th August	Thursday 11th September	Monday 11th August	Thursday 4th September	28th August
October	Monday 15th September	Friday 10th October	Wednesday 10th September	Friday 3rd October	29th September
November	Thursday 16th October	Wednesday 12th November	Monday 13th October	Wednesday 5th November	30th October
December	Thursday 13th November	Thursday 11th December	Monday 10th November	Thursday 4th December	27th November
January 1998	Tuesday 16th December	Monday 12th January 1998	Thursday 11th December	Monday 5th January 1998	30th December
February	Thursday 15th January 1998	Thursday 12th February	Monday 12th January 1998	Thursday 5th February	29th January 1998
March	Thursday 12th February	Thursday 12th March	Monday 9th February	Thursday 5th March	26th February
April	Monday 16th March	Wednesday 8th April	Wednesday 11th March	Wednesday 1st April	30th March
May	Wednesday 15th April	Tuesday 12th May	Wednesday 8th April	Tuesday 5th May	29th April
June	Thursday 14th May	Thursday 11th June	Monday 11th May	Thursday 4th June	28th May
July	Monday 15th June	Friday 10th July	Wednesday 10th June	Friday 3rd July	29th June
August	Thursday 16th July	Wednesday 12th August	Monday 13th July	Wednesday 5th August	30th July
September	Friday 14th August	Thursday 10th September	Tuesday 11th August	Thursday 3rd September	28th August
October	Tuesday 15th September	Monday 12th October	Thursday 10th September	Monday 5th October	29th September
November	Thursday 15th October	Thursday 12th November	Monday 12th October	Thursday 5th November	29th October
December	Friday 13th November	Thursday 10th December	Tuesday 10th November	Thursday 3rd December	27th November

IPE CONTRACT EXPIRY DATES 1999/2000

Delivery Month	Brent Crude futures	Brent Crude options	Gas Oil futures	Gas Oil options	Natural Gas futures	Natural Gas BOM
Jan-99	Wed 16 Dec 98	Fri 11 Dec 98	Tuesday 12 Jan	Tuesday 5 Jan	Wed 30 Dec 98	Thursday 28 Jan
Feb	Thursday 14 Jan	Monday 11 Jan	Thursday 11 Feb	Thursday 4 Feb	Thursday 28 Jan	Thursday 25 Feb
March	Thursday 11 Feb	Monday 8 Feb	Thursday 11 Mar	Thursday 4 Mar	Thursday 25 Feb	Friday 26 Mar
April	Tuesday 16 Mar	Thursday 11 Mar	Monday 12 Apr	Thursday 1 Apr	Tuesday 30 Mar	Tuesday 27 Apr
May	Thursday 15 Apr	Monday 12 Apr	Wednesday 12 May	Wednesday 5 May	Thursday 29 Apr	Thursday 27 May
June	Friday 14 May	Tuesday 11 May	Thursday 10 June	Thursday 3 June	Thursday 27 May	Friday 25 June
July	Tuesday 15 June	Thursday 10 June	Monday 12 July	Monday 5 July	Tuesday 29 June	Wednesday 28 July
Aug	Thursday 15 July	Monday 12 July	Thursday 12 Aug	Thursday 5 Aug	Thursday 29 July	Thursday 26 Aug
September	Monday 16 Aug	Wednesday 11 Aug	Friday 10 Sep	Friday 3 Sep	Friday 27 Aug	Monday 27 Sep
October	Wednesday 15 Sept	Friday 10 Sept	Tuesday 12 Oct	Tuesday 5 Oct	Wednesday 29 Sep	Thursday 28 Oct
November	Thursday 14 Oct	Monday 11 Oct	Thursday 11 Nov	Thursday 4 Nov	Thursday 28 Oct	Thursday 25 Nov
December	Monday 15 Nov	Wednesday 10 Nov	Friday 10 Dec	Friday 3 Dec	Monday 29 Nov	Friday 24 Dec
Jan-00	Thursday 16 Dec	Monday 13 Dec	Wednesday 12 Jan	Wednesday 5 Jan	Wednesday 29 Dec	Thursday 27 Jan
Feb	Friday 14 Jan	Tuesday 11 Jan	Thursday 10 Feb	Thursday 3 Feb	Friday 28 Jan	Thursday 24 Feb
March	Monday 14 Feb	Wednesday 9 Feb	Friday 10 Mar	Friday 3 Mar	Monday 28 Feb	Tuesday 28 Mar
April	Thursday 16 Mar	Monday 13 Mar	Wednesday 12 Apr	Wednesday 5 Apr	Thursday 30 Mar	Thursday 27 Apr
May	Thursday 13 Apr	Monday 10 Apr	Thursday 11 May	Thursday 4 May	Thursday 27 Apr	Thursday 25 May
June	Tuesday 16 May	Thursday 11 May	Monday 12 June	Monday 5 June	Tuesday 30 May	Tuesday 27 June
July	Thursday 15 June	Monday 12 June	Wednesday 12 July	Wednesday 5 July	Thursday 29 June	Thursday 27 July
Aug	Friday 14 July	Tuesday 11 July	Thursday 10 Aug	Thursday 3 Aug	Friday 28 July	Friday 25 Aug
September	Wednesday 16 Aug	Friday 11 Aug	Tuesday 12 Sep	Tuesday 5 Sep	Wednesday 30 Aug	Wednesday 27 Sep
October	Thursday 14 Sep	Monday 11 Sep	Thursday 12 Oct	Thursday 5 Oct	Thursday 28 Sep	Thursday 26 Oct
November	Monday 16 Oct	Wednesday 11 Oct	Friday 10 Nov	Friday 3 Nov	Monday 30 Oct	Monday 27 Nov
December	Wednesday 15 Nov	Friday 10 Nov	Tuesday 12 Dec	Tuesday 5 Dec	Wednesday 29 Nov	Thursday 28 Dec

IPE CONTRACT EXPIRY DATES 2001/2002

Delivery Month	Brent Crude futures	Brent Crude options	Gas Oil futures	Gas Oil options	Natural Gas futures	Natural Gas BOM
Jan-01	Thursday 14 Dec	Monday 11 Dec	Thursday 11 Jan	Thursday 4 Jan	Thursday 28 Dec 00	Friday 26 Jan
Feb	Tuesday 16 Jan	Thursday 11 Jan	Monday 12 Feb	Monday 5 Feb	Tuesday 30 Jan	Friday 23 Feb
March	Tuesday 13 Feb	Thursday 8 Feb	Monday 12 Mar	Monday 5 March	Tuesday 27 Feb	Wednesday 28 Mar
April	Thursday 15 Mar	Monday 12 Mar	Wednesday 11 Apr	Wednesday 4 Apr	Thursday 29 Mar	Thursday 26 Apr
May	Wednesday 11 Apr	Friday 6 Apr	Thursday 10 May	Wednesday 2 May	Friday 27 Apr	Friday 25 May
June	Wednesday 16 May	Friday 11 May	Tuesday 12 June	Tuesday 5 June	Wednesday 30 May	Wednesday 27 June
July	Thursday 14 June	Monday 11 June	Thursday 12 July	Thursday 5 July	Thursday 28 June	Thursday 26 July
Aug	Monday 16 July	Wednesday 11 July	Friday 10 Aug	Friday 3 Aug	Monday 30 July	Tuesday 28 Aug
September	Thursday 16 Aug	Monday 13 Aug	Wednesday 12 Sep	Wednesday 5 Sep	Thursday 30 Aug	Thursday 27 Sep
October	Thursday 13 Sep	Monday 10 Sep	Thursday 11 Oct	Thursday 4 Oct	Thursday 27 Sep	Friday 26 Oct
November	Tuesday 16 Oct	Thursday 11 Oct	Monday 12 Nov	Monday 5 Nov	Tuesday 30 Oct	Tuesday 27 Nov
December	Thursday 15 Nov	Monday 12 Nov	Wednesday 12 Dec	Wednesday 5 Dec	Thursday 29 Nov	Thursday 27 Dec
Jan-02	Friday 14 Dec	Tuesday 11 Dec	Thursday 10 Jan	Thursday 3 Jan	Friday 28 Dec	Monday 28 Jan
Feb	Wednesday 16 Jan	Friday 11 Jan	Tuesday 12 Feb	Tuesday 5 Feb	Wednesday 30 Jan	Monday 25 Feb
March	Wednesday 13 Feb	Friday 8 Feb	Tuesday 12 Mar	Tuesday 5 Mar	Wednesday 27 Feb	Wednesday 27 Mar
April	Thursday 14 Mar	Monday 11 Mar	Thursday 11 Apr	Thursday 4 Apr	Wednesday 27 Mar	Thursday 25 Apr
May	Monday 15 Apr	Wednesday 10 Apr	Friday 10 May	Thursday 2 May	Monday 29 Apr	Tuesday 28 May
June	Thursday 16 May	Monday 13 May	Wednesday 12 June	Wednesday 5 June	Thursday 30 May	Thursday 27 June
July	Thursday 13 June	Monday 10 June	Thursday 11 July	Thursday 4 July	Thursday 27 June	Friday 26 July
Aug	Tuesday 16 July	Thursday 11 July	Monday 12 Aug	Monday 5 Aug	Tuesday 30 July	Wednesday 28 Aug
September	Thursday 15 Aug	Monday 12 Aug	Thursday 12 Sep	Thursday 5 Sep	Thursday 29 Aug	Thursday 26 Sep
October	Friday 13 Sep	Tuesday 10 Sep	Thursday 10 Oct	Thursday 3 Oct	Friday 27 Sep	Monday 28 Oct
November	Wednesday 16 Oct	Friday 11 Oct	Tuesday 12 Nov	Tuesday 5 Nov	Wednesday 30 Oct	Wednesday 27 Nov
December	Thursday 14 Nov	Monday 11 Nov	Wednesday 12 Dec	Thursday 5 Dec	Thursday 28 Nov	Tuesday 24 Dec

IPE CONTRACT EXPIRY DATES 2003/2004

Delivery Month	Brent Crude futures	Brent Crude options	Gas Oil futures	Gas Oil options	Natural Gas futures	Natural Gas BOM
Jan-03	16-Dec-02	11-Dec-02	10-Jan-03	3-Jan-03	30-Dec-02	28-Jan-03
Feb	16-Jan-03	13-Jan-03	12-Feb	5-Feb	30-Jan-03	25-Feb-03
March	13-Feb	10-Feb	12-Mar	5-Mar	27-Feb-03	27-Mar-03
April	14-Mar	11-Mar	10-Apr	3-Apr	28-Mar-03	25-Apr-03
May	15-Apr	10-Apr	12-May	2-May	29-Apr-03	28-May-03
June	15-May	12-May	12-Jun	5-Jun	29-May-03	26-Jun-03
July	13-Jun	10-Jun	10-Jul	3-Jul	27-Jun-03	28-Jul-03
Aug	16-Jul	11-Jul	12-Aug	5-Aug	30-Jul-03	28-Aug-03
September	14-Aug	11-Aug	11-Sep	4-Sep	28-Aug-03	25-Sep-03
October	15-Sep	10-Sep	10-Oct	3-Oct	29-Sep-03	28-Oct-03
November	16-Oct	13-Oct	12-Nov	5-Nov	30-Oct-03	27-Nov-00
December	13-Nov	10-Nov	11-Dec	4-Dec	27-Nov-03	24-Dec-00
Jan-04	16-Dec	11-Dec	12-Jan-04	5-Jan-04	30-Dec-03	28-Jan-04
Feb	15-Jan-04	12-Jan-04	12-Feb	5-Feb	29-Jan-04	26-Feb-04
March	12-Feb	9-Feb	11-Mar	4-Mar	26-Feb-04	26-Mar-04
April	16-Mar	11-Mar	8-Apr	1-Apr	30-Mar-04	27-Apr-04
May	15-Apr	8-Apr	12-May	5-May	29-Apr-04	27-May-04
June	14-May	11-May	10-Jun	3-Jun	27-May-04	25-Jun-04
July	15-Jun	10-Jun	12-Jul	5-Jul	29-Jun-04	28-Jul-04
Aug	15-Jul	12-Jul	12-Aug	5-Aug	29-Jul-04	26-Aug-04
September	16-Aug	11-Aug	10-Sep	3-Sep	27-Aug-04	27-Sep-04
October	15-Sep	10-Sep	12-Oct	5-Oct	29-Sep-04	28-Oct-04
November	14-Oct	11-Oct	11-Nov	4-Nov	28-Oct-04	25-Nov-04
December	15-Nov	10-Nov	10-Dec	3-Dec	29-Nov-04	24-Dec-04

IPE CONTRACT EXPIRY DATES 2005/2006

Delivery Month	Brent Crude futures	Brent Crude options	Gas Oil futures	Gas Oil options	Natural Gas futures	Natural Gas BOM
Jan-05	16-Dec-04	13-Dec-04	12-Jan-05	5-Jan-05	30-Dec-04	27-Jan-05
Feb	14-Jan-05	11-Jan-05	10-Feb	3-Feb	28-Jan-05	24-Feb-05
March	11-Feb	8-Feb	10-Mar	3-Mar	25-Feb-05	24-Mar-05
April	16-Mar	11-Mar	12-Apr	5-Apr	30-Mar-05	27-Apr-05
May	14-Apr	11-Apr	12-May	5-May	28-Apr-05	26-May-05
June	16-May	11-May	10-Jun	3-Jun	27-May-05	27-Jun-05
July	15-Jun	10-Jun	12-Jul	5-Jul	29-Jun-05	28-Jul-05
Aug	14-Jul	11-Jul	11-Aug	4-Aug	28-Jul-05	25-Aug-05
September	16-Aug	11-Aug	12-Sep	5-Sep	30-Aug-05	27-Sep-05
October	15-Sep	12-Sep	12-Oct	5-Oct	29-Sep-05	27-Oct-05
November	14-Oct	11-Oct	10-Nov	3-Nov	28-Oct-05	25-Nov-05
December	15-Nov	10-Nov	12-Dec	5-Dec	29-Nov-05	28-Dec-05
Jan-06	15-Dec-05	12-Dec-05	12-Jan-06	5-Jan-06	29-Dec-05	26-Jan-06
Feb	16-Jan-06	11-Jan-06	10-Feb-06	3-Feb-06	30-Jan-06	23-Feb-06
March	13-Feb-06	8-Feb-06	10-Mar-06	3-Mar-06	27-Feb-06	28-Mar-06
April	16-Mar-06	13-Mar-06	12-Apr-06	5-Apr-06	30-Mar-06	27-Apr-06
May	12-Apr-06	7-Apr-06	11-May-06	4-May-06	27-Apr-06	25-May-06
June	16-May-06	11-May-06	12-Jun-06	5-Jun-06	30-May-06	27-Jun-06
July	15-Jun-06	12-Jun-06	12-Jul-06	5-Jul-06	29-Jun-06	27-Jul-06
Aug	14-Jul-06	11-Jul-06	10-Aug-06	3-Aug-06	28-Jul-06	25-Aug-06
September	16-Aug-06	11-Aug-06	12-Sep-06	5-Sep-06	30-Aug-06	27-Sep-06
October	14-Sep-06	11-Sep-06	12-Oct-06	5-Oct-06	28-Sep-06	26-Oct-06
November	16-Oct-06	11-Oct-06	10-Nov-06	3-Nov-06	30-Oct-06	27-Nov-06
December	15-Nov-06	10-Nov-06	12-Dec-06	5-Dec-06	29-Nov-06	28-Dec-06

IPE CONTRACT EXPIRY DATES 2007/2008

Delivery Month	Brent Crude futures	Brent Crude options	Gas Oil futures	Gas Oil options	Natural Gas futures	Natural Gas BOM
Jan-07	14-Dec-06	11-Dec-06	11-Jan-07	4-Jan-07	28-Dec-06	26-Jan-07
Feb	16-Jan-07	11-Jan-07	12-Feb-07	5-Feb-07	30-Jan-07	23-Feb-07
March	13-Feb-07	8-Feb-07	12-Mar-07	5-Mar-07	27-Feb-07	28-Mar-07
April	15-Mar-07	12-Mar-07	12-Apr-07	3-Apr-07	29-Mar-07	26-Apr-07
May	13-Apr-07	10-Apr-07	10-May-07	2-May-07	27-Apr-07	25-May-07
June	16-May-07	11-May-07	12-Jun-07	5-Jun-07	30-May-07	27-Jun-07
July	14-Jun-07	11-Jun-07	12-Jul-07	5-Jul-07	28-Jun-07	26-Jul-07
Aug	16-Jul-07	11-Jul-07	10-Aug-07	3-Aug-07	30-Jul-07	28-Aug-07
September	16-Aug-07	13-Aug-07	12-Sep-07	5-Sep-07	30-Aug-07	27-Sep-07
October	13-Sep-07	10-Sep-07	11-Oct-07	4-Oct-07	27-Sep-07	26-Oct-07
November	16-Oct-07	12-Oct-07	12-Nov-07	5-Nov-07	30-Oct-07	27-Nov-07
December	15-Nov-07	12-Nov-07	12-Dec-07	5-Dec-07	29-Nov-07	27-Dec-07
Jan-08	14-Dec-07	11-Dec-07	10-Jan-08	3-Jan-08	28-Dec-07	28-Jan-08
Feb	16-Jan-08	11-Jan-08	12-Feb-08	5-Feb-08	30-Jan-08	26-Feb-08
March	14-Feb-08	11-Feb-08	12-Mar-08	5-Mar-08	28-Feb-08	27-Mar-08
April	14-Mar-08	11-Mar-08	10-Apr-08	3-Apr-08	28-Mar-08	25-Apr-08
May	15-Apr-08	10-Apr-08	12-May-08	2-May-08	29-Apr-08	28-May-08
June	15-May-08	12-May-08	12-Jun-08	5-Jun-08	29-May-08	26-Jun-08
July	13-Jun-08	10-Jun-08	10-Jul-08	3-Jul-08	27-Jun-08	28-Jul-08
Aug	16-Jul-08	11-Jul-08	12-Aug-08	5-Aug-08	30-Jul-08	28-Aug-08
September	14-Aug-08	11-Aug-08	11-Sep-08	4-Sep-08	28-Aug-08	25-Sep-08
October	15-Sep-08	10-Sep-08	10-Oct-08	3-Oct-08	29-Sep-08	28-Oct-08
November	16-Oct-08	13-Oct-08	12-Nov-08	5-Nov-08	30-Oct-08	27-Nov-08
December	13-Nov-08	10-Nov-08	11-Dec-08	4-Dec-08	27-Nov-08	24-Dec-08

IPE CONTRACT EXPIRY DATES 2009/2010

Delivery Month	Brent Crude futures	Brent Crude options	Gas Oil futures	Gas Oil options	Natural Gas futures	Natural Gas BOM
Jan-09	16-Dec-08	11-Dec-08	12-Jan-09	5-Jan-09	30-Dec-08	28-Jan-08
Feb	15-Jan-09	12-Jan-09	12-Feb-09	5-Feb-09	29-Jan-09	25-Feb-08
March	12-Feb-09	9-Feb-09	12-Mar-09	5-Mar-09	26-Feb-09	26-Mar-09
April	16-Mar-09	11-Mar-09	8-Apr-09	1-Apr-09	30-Mar-09	27-Apr-09
May	15-Apr-09	8-Apr-09	12-May-09	5-May-09	29-Apr-09	28-May-09
June	14-May-09	11-May-09	11-Jun-09	4-Jun-09	28-May-09	25-Jun-09
July	15-Jun-09	10-Jun-09	10-Jul-09	3-Jul-09	29-Jun-09	28-Jul-09
Aug	16-Jul-09	13-Jul-09	12-Aug-09	5-Aug-09	30-Jul-09	27-Aug-09
September	14-Aug-09	11-Aug-09	10-Sep-09	3-Sep-09	27-Aug-09	25-Sep-09
October	15-Sep-09	10-Sep-09	12-Oct-09	5-Oct-09	29-Sep-09	28-Oct-09
November	15-Oct-09	12-Oct-09	12-Nov-09	5-Nov-09	29-Oct-09	26-Nov-09
December	13-Nov-09	10-Nov-09	10-Dec-09	3-Dec-09	27-Nov-09	24-Dec-09
Jan-10	16-Dec-09	11-Dec-09	12-Jan-10	5-Jan-10	30-Dec-09	28-Jan-10
Feb	14-Jan-10	11-Jan-10	11-Feb-10	4-Feb-10	28-Jan-10	25-Feb-10
March	11-Feb-10	8-Feb-10	11-Mar-10	4-Mar-10	25-Feb-10	26-Mar-10
April	16-Mar-10	11-Mar-10	12-Apr-10	1-Apr-10	30-Mar-10	27-Apr-10
May	15-Apr-10	12-Apr-10	12-May-10	5-May-10	29-Apr-10	27-May-10
June	14-May-10	11-May-10	10-Jun-10	3-Jun-10	27-May-10	25-Jun-10
July	15-Jun-10	10-Jun-10	12-Jul-10	5-Jul-10	29-Jun-10	28-Jul-10
Aug	15-Jul-10	12-Jul-10	12-Aug-10	5-Aug-10	29-Jul-10	26-Aug-10
September	16-Aug-10	11-Aug-10	10-Sep-10	3-Sep-10	27-Aug-10	27-Sep-10
October	15-Sep-10	10-Sep-10	12-Oct-10	5-Oct-10	29-Sep-10	28-Oct-10
November	14-Oct-10	11-Oct-10	11-Nov-10	4-Nov-10	28-Oct-10	25-Nov-10
December	15-Nov-10	10-Nov-10	10-Dec-10	3-Dec-10	29-Nov-10	24-Dec-10

IPE CONTRACT EXPIRY DATES 2011/2012

Delivery Month	Brent Crude futures	Brent Crude options	Gas Oil futures	Gas Oil options
Jan-11	16-Dec-10	13-Dec-10	12-Jan-11	5-Jan-11
Feb	14-Jan-11	11-Jan-11	10-Feb-11	3-Feb-11
March	11-Feb-11	8-Feb-11	10-Mar-11	3-Mar-11
April	16-Mar-11	11-Mar-11	12-Apr-11	5-Apr-11
May	14-Apr-11	11-Apr-11	12-May-11	5-May-11
June	16-May-11	11-May-11	10-Jun-11	3-Jun-11
July	15-Jun-11	10-Jun-11	12-Jul-11	5-Jul-11
Aug	14-Jul-11	11-Jul-11	11-Aug-11	4-Aug-11
September	16-Aug-11	11-Aug-11	12-Sep-11	5-Sep-11
October	15-Sep-11	12-Sep-11	12-Oct-11	5-Oct-11
November	14-Oct-11	11-Oct-11	10-Nov-11	3-Nov-11
December	15-Nov-11	10-Nov-11	12-Dec-11	5-Dec-11
Jan-12	15-Dec-11	12-Dec-11	12-Jan-12	5-Jan-12
Feb	16-Jan-12	11-Jan-12	10-Feb-12	3-Feb-12
March	14-Feb-12	9-Feb-12	12-Mar-12	5-Mar-12
April	15-Mar-12	12-Mar-12	12-Apr-12	3-Apr-12
May	13-Apr-12	10-Apr-12	10-May-12	3-May-12
June	16-May-12	11-May-12	12-Jun-12	5-Jun-12
July	14-Jun-12	11-Jun-12	12-Jul-12	5-Jul-12
Aug	16-Jul-12	11-Jul-12	10-Aug-12	3-Aug-12
September	16-Aug-12	13-Aug-12	12-Sep-12	5-Sep-12
October	13-Sep-12	10-Sep-12	12-Oct-12	5-Oct-12
November	16-Oct-12	11-Oct-12	12-Nov-12	5-Nov-12
December	15-Nov-12	12-Nov-12	12-Dec-12	5-Dec-12

Appendix 5

LME copper brands

Country	Brand	Producer
Australia	ISA	Mount Isa Mines Ltd
	OLYDA	WMC (Olympic Dam Corporation) Pty Ltd
Austria	BRX	Montanwerke Brixlegg Aktiengesellschaft
Belgium	OLEN	n.v. Umicore Copper s.a.
	SME	Metallo-Chemique International NV
Brazil	CbM	Caraiba Metais SA
Canada	FKA	Falconbridge Ltd
	NORANDA (produced after October 1999)	Noranda Inc.
	ORC	Inco Ltd
Chile	ABRA	Sociedad Contractual Minera El Abra
	AE	Corporacion Nacional del Cobre de Chile
	AE SX EW	Corporacion Nacional del Cobre de Chile
	CCC	Corporacion Nacional del Cobre de Chile
	CCC-SBL	Corporacion Nacional del Cobre de Chile
	cCc-SX-EW	Corporacion Nacional del Cobre de Chile
	CDA	Compañia Minera Carmen de Andacollo
	CHUQUI-P	Corporacion Nacional del Cobre de Chile
	CMCC	Compañia Minera Cerro Colorado Ltda
	COLLAHUASI (produced after December 1998)	Compania Minera Dona Ines De Collahuasi SCM
	ENM	Empresa Nacional de Mineria
	ESOX (produced after April 1999)	Minera Escondida Limitada
	LBF	Compania Minera Falconbridge Lomas Bayas
	MET	Minera El Tesoro
	MIC-P	Minera Michilla S.A
	MIC-T	Minera Michilla S.A
	MB	Empresa Minera de Mantos Blancos SA
	MV	Empresa Minera de Mantos Blancos SA
	RT	Corporacion Nacional del Cobre de Chile
	ZALDIVAR	Compania Minera Zaldivar

Continued

Country	Brand	Producer
China	GUIYE	Jiangxi Copper Company Ltd
	JINTUN (produced after 31/8/97)	Jinlong Copper Co., Ltd
	TIE FENG	Yunnan Copper Industry Co., Ltd
	TG	Anhui Tongdu Copper Stock Co., Ltd
Finland	OKM	Harjavalta Copper Oy
Germany	HK	Norddeutsche Affinerie AG
	NA-ESN	Norddeutsche Affinerie AG
India	BIRLA COPPER	Hindalco Industries Limited
	STERLITE	Sterlite Industries (India) Ltd
Indonesia	GRESIK	PT Smelting
Japan	DOWA	Dowa Mining Co., Ltd
	HM	Nippon Mining and Metals Co., Ltd
	MITSUBISHI	Mitsubishi Materials Corporation
	MITSUI	Mitsui Mining & Smelting Co., Ltd
	OSR	Onahama Smelting & Refining Co., Ltd
	SR	Nippon Mining and Metals Co., Ltd
	SUMIKO N	Sumitomo Metal Mining Co., Ltd
	SUMIKO T	Sumitomo Metal Mining Co., Ltd
	TAMANO	Mitsui Mining & Smelting Co., Ltd
Korea (South)	CHANGHANG	LG-Nikko Copper Inc.
	ONSAN	LG-Nikko Copper Inc.
	ONSAN II	LG-Nikko Copper Inc.
Myanmar	MONYWA S&K	Myanmar Ivanhoe Copper Company Ltd
Norway	FHG	Falconbridge Nikkelverk A/S
Oman	OMCO	Oman Mining Co., LLC
Peru	SMCV	Cyprus Amax Minerals Company
	SPCC-ILO	Southern Peru Copper Corporation
	SPCC-SXEW	Southern Peru Copper Corporation
Philippines	PASAR	Philippine Associated Smelting and Refining Corporation
Poland	HMG-B	KGHM Polska Miedz SA
	HMG-S	KGHM Polska Miedz SA
	HML	KGHM Polska Miedz SA
South Africa	PMC	Palabora Mining Company Ltd
Spain	ERCOSA	Elmet SL
	FMS	Atlantic Copper SA
Sweden	BK	Boliden Mineral AB
USA	ATR	ASARCO Incorporated
	BHP COPPER**	BHP Copper Inc.
	CB* CC	Cyprus Amax Minerals Company
	CMMC ER	Cyprus Amax Minerals Company
	CTB	Cyprus Amax Minerals Company
	KUC	Kennecott Utah Copper Corporation

Country	Brand	Producer
	MAGMA*	BHP Copper Inc.
	P* D	Phelps Dodge Sales Co Incorporated
	RAY	ASARCO Incorporated
Zambia	MCM	Mopani Copper Mines Plc
	REC	Konkola Copper Mines plc

* Not good for delivery if placed on warrant after 31.01.97.

** Not good for delivery if placed on warrant after 26.10.01.

Source: London Metal Exchange.

Appendix 6

FSA derivatives and warrants risk warning

Warrants and derivatives risk warning notice (E)

E

Table   This table belongs to ■ COB 5.4.6 E.

This notice is provided to you, as a private customer, in compliance with the rules of the Financial Services Authority (FSA). Private customers are afforded greater protections under these rules than other customers are and you should ensure that your firm tells you what this will mean to you. This notice cannot disclose all the risks and other significant aspects of warrants* and/or derivative* products such as futures*, options*, and contracts for differences* (* delete as appropriate). You should not deal in these products unless you understand their nature and the extent of your exposure to risk. You should also be satisfied that the product is suitable for you in the light of your circumstances and financial position. Certain strategies, such as a 'spread' position or a 'straddle', may be as risky as a simple 'long' or 'short' position.

Although warrants and/or derivative instruments can be utilised for the management of investment risk, some of these products are unsuitable for many investors. Different instruments involve different levels of exposure to risk and in deciding whether to trade in such instruments you should be aware of the following points. (Include or delete as appropriate).

1. Warrants

A warrant is a time-limited right to subscribe for shares, debentures, loan stock or government securities and is exercisable against the original issuer of the underlying securities. A relatively small movement in the price of the underlying security results in a disproportionately large movement, unfavourable or favourable, in the price of the warrant. The prices of warrants can therefore be volatile.

It is essential for anyone who is considering purchasing warrants to understand that the right to subscribe which a warrant confers is invariably limited in time with the consequence that if the investor fails to exercise this right within the predetermined time-scale then the investment becomes worthless.

You should not buy a warrant unless you are prepared to sustain a total loss of the money you have invested plus any commission or other transaction charges.

2. Off-exchange warrant transactions

Transactions in off-exchange warrants may involve greater risk than dealing in exchange traded warrants because there is no exchange market through which to liquidate your position, or to assess the value of the warrant or the exposure to risk. Bid and offer prices need not be quoted, and even where they are, they will be established by dealers in these instruments and consequently it may be difficult to establish what is a fair price. Your firm must make it clear to you if you are entering into an off-exchange transaction and advise you of any risks involved.

3. Securitised derivatives

These instruments may give you [a time-limited right (Note 1)] [an absolute right (Note 2)] to acquire or sell one or more types of investment which is normally exercisable against someone other than the issuer of that investment. Or they may give you rights under a contract for differences which allow for speculation on fluctuations in the value of the property of any description or an index, such as the FTSE 100 index. In both cases, the investment or property may be referred to as the 'underlying instrument'.

These instruments often involve a high degree of gearing or leverage, so that a relatively small movement in the price of the underlying investment results in a much larger movement, unfavourable or favourable, in the price of the instrument. The price of these instruments can therefore be volatile.

These instruments have a limited life, and may (unless there is some form of guaranteed return to the amount you are investing in the product) expire worthless if the underlying instrument does not perform as expected.

You should only buy this product if you are prepared to sustain a [total loss (Note 3)] [substantial loss (Note 4)] [loss (Note 5)] of the money you have invested plus any commission or other transaction charges.

You should consider carefully whether or not this product is suitable for you in light of your circumstances and financial position, and if in any doubt please seek professional advice.

Notes (these notes are not part of the notice):

1. Use for instruments such as covered warrants where there is some form of exercise required by the investor.

2. Use for instruments such as linked notes, or some certificates where there is no form of exercise required by the investor.

3. Use for instruments such as covered warrants where the return payable to the investor is totally dependant upon the performance of the underlying instrument/s to which the product is linked and there is not another form of payment due to the investor (for example the repayment of capital).

4. Use for instruments such as linked notes where there is a form of return paid to the investor irrespective of the performance of the underlying instrument/s to which the product is linked, but the return is low.

5. Use for instruments such as linked notes where there is a form of return paid to the investor irrespective of the performance of the underlying instrument/s to which the product is linked, but the return is high but less than 100 per cent of the amount paid for the product.

4. Futures

Transactions in futures involve the obligation to make, or to take, delivery of the underlying asset of the contract at a future date, or in some cases to settle the position with cash. They carry a high degree of risk. The 'gearing' or 'leverage' often obtainable in futures trading means that a small deposit or down payment can lead to large losses as well as gains. It also means that a relatively small movement can lead to a proportionately much larger movement in the value of your investment, and this can work against you as well as for you. Futures transactions have a contingent liability, and you should be aware of the implications of this, in particular the margining requirements, which are set out in paragraph 9.

5. Options

There are many different types of options with different characteristics subject to the following conditions.

Buying options:

Buying options involves less risk than selling options because, if the price of the underlying asset moves against you, you can simply allow the option to lapse. The maximum loss is limited to the premium, plus any commission or other transaction charges. However, if you buy a call option on a futures contract and you later exercise the option, you will acquire the future. This will expose you to the risks described under 'futures' and 'contingent liability investment transactions'.

Writing options:

If you write an option, the risk involved is considerably greater than buying options. You may be liable for margin to maintain your position and a loss may be sustained well in excess of the premium received. By writing an option, you accept a legal obligation to purchase or sell the underlying asset if the option is exercised against you, however far the market price has moved away from the exercise price. If you already own the underlying asset which you have contracted to sell (when the options will be known as 'covered call options') the risk is reduced. If you do not own the underlying asset ('uncovered call options') the risk can be unlimited. Only experienced persons should contemplate writing uncovered options, and then only after securing full details of the applicable conditions and potential risk exposure.

Traditional options:

Certain London Stock Exchange member firms under special exchange rules write a particular type of option called a 'traditional option'. These may involve greater risk than other options. Two-way prices are not usually quoted and there is no exchange market on which to close out an open position or to effect an equal and opposite transaction to reverse an open position. It may be difficult to assess its value or for the seller of such an option to manage his exposure to risk.

Certain options markets operate on a margined basis, under which buyers do not pay the full premium on their option at the time they purchase it. In this situation you may subsequently be called upon to pay margin on the option up to the level of your premium. If you fail to do so as required, your position may be closed or liquidated in the same way as a futures position.

6. Contracts for differences

Futures and options contracts can also be referred to as contracts for differences. These can be options and futures on the FTSE 100 index or any other index, as well as currency and interest rate swaps. However, unlike other futures and options, these contracts can only be settled in cash. Investing in a contract for differences carries the same risks as investing in a future or an option and you should be aware of these as set out in paragraphs 4 and 5 respectively. Transactions in contracts for differences may also have a contingent liability and you should be aware of the implications of this as set out in paragraph 9.

7. Off-exchange transactions in derivatives

It may not always be apparent whether or not a particular derivative is arranged on exchange or in an off-exchange derivative transaction. Your firm must make it clear to you if you are entering into an off-exchange derivative transaction.

While some off-exchange markets are highly liquid, transactions in off-exchange or 'non transferable' derivatives may involve greater risk than investing in on-exchange derivatives because there is no exchange market on which to close out an open position. It may be impossible to liquidate an existing position, to assess the value of the position arising from an off-exchange transaction or to assess the exposure to risk. Bid prices and offer prices need not be quoted, and, even where they are, they will be established by dealers in these instruments and consequently it may be difficult to establish what is a fair price.

8. Foreign markets
Foreign markets will involve different risks from the UK markets. In some cases the risks will be greater. On request, your firm must provide an explanation of the relevant risks and protections (if any) which will operate in any foreign markets, including the extent to which it will accept liability for any default of a foreign firm through whom it deals. The potential for profit or loss from transactions on foreign markets or in foreign denominated contracts will be affected by fluctuations in foreign exchange rates.

9. Contingent liability investment transactions
Contingent liability investment transactions, which are margined, require you to make a series of payments against the purchase price, instead of paying the whole purchase price immediately.

If you trade in futures contracts for differences or sell options, you may sustain a total loss of the margin you deposit with your firm to establish or maintain a position. If the market moves against you, you may be called upon to pay substantial additional margin at short notice to maintain the position. If you fail to do so within the time required, your position may be liquidated at a loss and you will be responsible for the resulting deficit. Even if a transaction is not margined, it may still carry an obligation to make further payments in certain circumstances over and above any amount paid when you entered the contract.

Save as specifically provided by the FSA, your firm may only carry out margined or contingent liability transactions with or for you if they are traded on or under the rules of a recognised or designated investment exchange. Contingent liability investment transactions which are not so traded may expose you to substantially greater risks.

10. Limited liability transactions
Before entering into a limited liability transaction, you should obtain from your firm or the firm with whom you are dealing a formal written statement confirming that the extent of your loss liability on each transaction will be limited to an amount agreed by you before you enter into the transaction.

The amount you can lose in limited liability transactions will be less than in other margined transactions, which have no predetermined loss limit. Nevertheless, even though the extent of loss will be subject to the agreed limit, you may sustain the loss in a relatively short time. Your loss may be limited, but the risk of sustaining a total loss to the amount agreed is substantial.

11. Collateral
If you deposit collateral as security with your firm, the way in which it will be treated will vary according to the type of transaction and where it is traded. There could be significant differences in the treatment of your collateral depending on whether you are trading on a recognised or designated investment exchange, with the rules of that exchange (and the associated clearing house) applying, or trading off-exchange. Deposited collateral may lose its identity as your property once dealings on your behalf are undertaken. Even if your dealings should ultimately prove profitable, you may not get back the same assets which you deposited, and may have to accept payment in cash. You should ascertain from your firm how your collateral will be dealt with.

12. Commissions
Before you begin to trade, you should obtain details of all commissions and other charges for which you will be liable. If any charges are not expressed in money terms (but, for example, as a percentage of contract value), you should obtain a clear and written explanation, including appropriate examples, to establish what such charges are likely to mean in specific money terms. In the case of futures, when commission is charged as a percentage, it will normally be as a percentage of the total contract value, and not simply as a percentage of your initial payment.

13. Suspensions of trading
Under certain trading conditions it may be difficult or impossible to liquidate a position. This may occur, for example, at times of rapid price movement if the price rises or falls in one trading session to such an extent that under the rules of the relevant exchange trading is suspended or restricted. Placing a stop-loss order will not necessarily limit your losses to the intended amounts, because market conditions may make it impossible to execute such an order at the stipulated price.

14. Clearing house protections
On many exchanges, the performance of a transaction by your firm (or third party with whom he is dealing on your behalf) is 'guaranteed' by the exchange or clearing house. However, this guarantee is unlikely in most circumstances to cover you, the customer, and may not protect you if your firm or another party defaults on its obligations to you. On request,

your firm must explain any protection provided to you under the clearing guarantee applicable to any on-exchange derivatives in which you are dealing. There is no clearing house for traditional options, nor normally for off-exchange instruments which are not traded under the rules of a recognised or designated investment exchange.

15. Insolvency

Your firm's insolvency or default, or that of any other brokers involved with your transaction, may lead to positions being liquidated or closed out without your consent. In certain circumstances, you may not get back the actual assets which you lodged as collateral and you may have to accept any available payments in cash. On request, your firm must provide an explanation of the extent to which it will accept liability for any insolvency of, or default by, other firms involved with your transactions.

[name of firm]
[on duplicate for signature by private customer]
I/We have read and understood the risk warning set out above.

Date
[Signature of the customer]
[Signature of joint account holder]
Note to firms

Paragraphs 1–15 may be deleted when they relate to particular kinds of business which will not be carried out with or for the customer.

This notice may be incorporated as part of a two-way customer agreement, but the customer must sign separately that he has read and understood the risk warnings.

Source: FSA.

Appendix 7

Useful websites and suggested further reading

Useful websites

www.afma.com	Australian Financial Markets Association
www.asx.com.au	Australian Stock Exchange
www.bba.org.uk	British Bankers Association
www.bis.org	Bank for International Settlement
www.cbl-ltd.co.uk	Computer Based Learning Ltd
www.cboe.com	Chicago Board Options Exchange
www.cbot.com	Chicago Board of Trade
www.cftc.com	Commodities Future Trading Commission
www.clearingcorp.com	Clearing Corporation
www.clearstream.com	Clearstream
www.cme.com	Chicago Mercantile Exchange
www.crestco.co.uk	CREST
www.dce.com.cn	Dalian Commodity Exchange
www.dscportfolio.com	The Derivatives and Securities Consultancy Ltd
www.dtc.org	Depository Trust Company
www.ecsda.com	European Central Securities Depositories Association
www.eurexchange.com	Eurex
www.euroclear.com	Euroclear
www.euronext.com	Euronext
www.foa.co.uk	Futures and Options Association
www.futuresindustry.org	Futures Industry Association
www.fsa.go.jp	Financial Services Agency Japan
www.fsa.gov.uk	Financial Services Authority
www.hkex.com.hk	Hong Kong Exchanges and Clearing
www.isda.org	International Swaps and Derivatives Association
www.iseoptions.com	International Securities Exchange
www.isma.co.uk	International Securities Markets Association

www.theipe.com	International Petroleum Exchange
www.issanet.org	International Securities Services Association
www.intcx.com	Intercontinental Exchange
www.lchclearnet.co.uk	LCH.Clearnet
www.liffe.com	Euronext.liffe (London International Financial Futures & Options Exchange)
www.lme.co.uk	London Metal Exchange
www.londonstockexchange.com	London Stock Exchange
www.nasdaq.com	NASDAQ
www.nseindia.com	National Stock Exchange of India
www.norex.com	Norex Alliance
www.nymex.com	NYMEX
www.nyse.com	New York Stock Exchange
www.ose.or.jp	Osaka Securities Exchange
www.risk.ifci.ch	G30 Recommendations
www.sec.gov	Securities Exchange Commission (US)
www.sfe.com.au	Sydney Futures Exchange
www.sgx.com	Singapore Exchange
www.tiffe.or.jp	Tokyo International Financial Futures Exchange
www.tocom.or.jp	Tokyo Commodity Exchange
www.tse.or.jp	Tokyo Stock Exchange
www.swx.com	SWX Swiss Exchange

Suggested further reading

General books

- Understanding The Financial Markets*
- Managing Technology in the Operations Function*
- Clearing, Settlement and Custody*
- Controls Procedures and Risk*
- Relationship and Resource Management in Operations*.

Published by Butterworth-Heinemann.

Foreign exchange and currency

- Mastering Treasury Operations
- Understanding Foreign Exchange and Currency Options.

Published by FT Prentice Hall.

Derivatives settlement and management

- Global Operations Management*
- Advanced Global Operations Management*

- Exchange Traded Derivatives Administration**
- OTC Derivative Administration**.

Published by The Securities Institute.

e-learning – visUlearn^{TM} series of CD-ROMS*

- Equities & Bonds
- Derivatives & Commodities
- Operations – Clearing, Settlement & Custody
- An Overview of the Financial Services Industry.

Operational risk management

- Managing Derivatives Risk – Guidelines for End-Users.

Published by The Futures and Options Association.

Periodicals

- Futures and OTC World – published by Metal Bulletin.
- Futures Industry – published by FIA.

* Order from www.dscportfolio.com or call 0207 403 8383 quoting websites/reading for a major discount.

** Investment Administration Qualification Workbooks-order at the Securities and Investment Institute website.

Appendix 8

Euronext.liffe corporate action policy

Corporate events policy

The following extracts from the Euronext.liffe Corporate Action Policy will help readers to understand how the exchange approaches dealing with a corporate action on an underlying and how it affects the derivatives listed.

It is important to understand the process and to make sure clients understand process and the changes that might occur to their positions, indeed reference is made to this in the exchange document the full version of which is available at the Euronext.liffe website.

Policy

When shares become ex entitlement in respect of a Corporate Event, a holding in cum entitlement shares is, in effect, transformed into the ex entitlement shares and the Relevant Entitlement. For example, in the case of a rights issue, a holding in cum entitlement shares is transformed into ex entitlement shares and nil paid rights in the appropriate proportions. In some cases, e.g. share splits, subdivisions and consolidations, the ex entitlement shares may cease to exist, leaving only the entitlement.

The methodology detailed in this Policy Document is based on the principle that, when the shares underlying an Individual Equity Option Contract (which has not been exercised) or a Universal Stock Futures Contracts (cash settlement) and Universal Stock Futures Contracts (physical delivery) become ex entitlement, contracts on such shares should be amended to reflect in economic terms (as far as practicable) a holding equivalent to ex entitlement shares and the Relevant Entitlement. This could be achieved in a number of ways, e.g. by modifying the underlying security to become a package consisting of ex entitlement shares and the value of the entitlement or, as is usually the case, by altering the exercise prices of Individual Equity Option Contracts, or the price used as the base to determine variation margin flow for Universal Stock Futures Contracts (cash settlement) and Universal Stock Futures Contracts (physical delivery), (i.e. the previous day's daily settlement price) (hereafter the '**reference price**'), and/or the lot size of the contracts. If contracts are amended in line with this principle, those with open positions should not be unduly advantaged or disadvantaged economically by the Corporate Event.

The next section explains the methodology, which the Board shall, in most situations, follow to determine what adjustments (if any) will be made to Individual Equity Option Contracts, Universal Stock Futures Contracts (cash settlement) and Universal Stock Futures Contracts (physical delivery) to cater for special dividends, bonus/scrip issues, rights issues and demergers. In cases where it is inappropriate or impossible to adjust contracts in line with this methodology, or in cases where the Corporate Event is an event other than a special dividend, bonus/scrip issue, rights issue or demerger, the Exchange will have regard, as far as practicable, to the principle detailed above in determining the appropriate adjustment.

Methodology: Adjustments

As noted, the Board retains the right to determine how any particular Corporate Event will be reflected in contract adjustments. However, as a general rule:

Demergers

In the case of **demergers which create two substantial new companies** the 'package method' will be used. The Board shall use the following guideline in this context: a company shall be considered to be 'substantial' if the market capitalisation is likely to represent 20 per cent or more of the market capitalisation of the original company. In the case of a multiple demerger, this guideline may not be appropriate or readily applicable, and the Board will have regard to the particular nature of the demerger and its timing in determining contract adjustments. Where a demerger applies to an Individual Equity Option Contract, the company shares should be readily available for settlement in the UK.

In the case of **Individual Equity Option Contracts**, the 'package method' does not entail alterations to either the lot size or the exercise price of a contract. On exercise, Delivery Sellers are required to deliver the number of ex entitlement shares they have contracted to sell together with the proportionate number of entitlements.

In the case of **Universal Stock Futures Contracts (cash settlement)**, the 'package method' does not entail alterations to either the lot size or the reference price of a contract. Futures contracts will become contracts on the package of the ex entitlement shares and the proportionate number of entitlements. The Exchange will determine the EDSP as the value of this package.

In the case of **Universal Stock Futures Contracts (physical delivery)**, the 'package method' does not entail alterations to either the lot size or the reference price of a contract. Futures contracts will become contracts on the package of the ex entitlement shares and the proportionate number of entitlements. On the last trading day, Delivery Sellers are required to deliver the number of ex entitlement shares they have contracted to sell together with the proportionate number of entitlements.

Bonus/Scrip Issues

In the case of **bonus/scrip issues**, the 'ratio method' will be used. This method entails creating a ratio (and corresponding inverse ratio) of the number of post event shares in issue to the pre-event shares in issue.

In the case of **Individual Equity Option Contracts**, the ratio and inverse ratio are used to alter the lot size (by multiplying the lot size by the ratio) and the exercise price of each series (by multiplying the exercise price by the inverse ratio). On exercise, Delivery Sellers are required to deliver the adjusted number of ex entitlement shares in return for a consideration of the adjusted exercise price multiplied by the adjusted lot size.

In the case of **Universal Stock Futures Contracts (cash settlement)**, the ratio and inverse ratio are used to alter the lot size (by multiplying the lot size by the ratio) and the reference price of each contract (by multiplying the reference price by the inverse ratio).

In the case of **Universal Stock Futures Contracts (physical delivery)**, the ratio and inverse ratio are used to alter the lot size (by multiplying the lot size by the ratio) and the reference price of each contract (by multiplying the reference price by the inverse ratio). On the last trading day, Delivery Sellers are required to deliver the number of ex entitlement shares they have contracted to sell together with the proportionate number of entitlements.

Rights Issues, Cash and Non-Cash Special Dividends and Demergers Not Creating Two Substantial Companies

In the case of **rights issues, cash and non-cash special dividends** and **demergers which do not create two substantial companies:**

In the case of **Individual Equity Option Contracts:**

(i) the ratio method will be used if the application of this method would result in an increase in the lot size of more than 20 shares where the standard contract size is 1,000 shares, or more than 2 shares where the standard lot size is 100 shares. This method entails creating a ratio (and corresponding inverse ratio) of the cum entitlement share price to the ex entitlement share price. The lot size will be multiplied by the ratio and the exercise price will be multiplied by the inverse ratio; otherwise (ii) the 'reduction in strikes method' will be used. This method entails reducing the exercise price of each series by the value of the entitlement. On exercise, Delivery Sellers will be required to deliver the number of ex entitlement shares they have contracted to sell in return for a consideration of the adjusted exercise price multiplied by the standard lot size. It should be noted that, in the case of cash special dividends, exercise prices will be reduced by the net amount of the special dividend.

In the case of **Universal Stock Futures Contracts (cash settlement) and Universal Stock Futures Contracts (physical delivery)**:

(i)   the ratio method will be used if the application of this method would result in an increase in the lot size of more than 20 shares where the standard contract size is 1,000 shares, or more than 2 shares where the standard lot size is 100 shares; otherwise

(ii)   the 'reduction method' will be used. This method entails reducing the reference price of each contract by the value of the entitlement. It should be noted that, in the case of cash special dividends, the reference price will be reduced by the net amount of the special dividend.

Note: Complex capital adjustments could necessitate the use of a combination of the above methods.

Ordinary Dividends

It should be noted that the Board will not adjust contracts to cater for ordinary dividends. The Board will use the following criteria for deciding whether a dividend should be considered to be a special dividend:

(a)   the declaration by a company of a dividend additional to those dividends declared as part of the company's normal results and dividend reporting cycle; merely an adjustment to the timing of the declaration of a company's expected dividend would not be considered as a special dividend circumstance; or

(b)   the identification of an element of a cash dividend paid in line with a company's normal results and dividend reporting cycle as an element that is unambiguously additional to the company's normal payment.

Methodology: Prices used as the basis for adjustments

Certain methods of adjustment require a valuation of one or more of the following in order to determine the appropriate level of adjustment: the cum entitlement share price; the ex entitlement share price; and the Relevant Entitlement. The Board's approach regarding the prices used as the basis for adjustments is set out below.

The Board will seek to determine any adjustments after the determination of the daily settlement price on the last day of trading of the relevant share cum entitlement (such adjustments will not become effective until the start of trading of the contract on the first day of trading of the share ex entitlement).

This will be feasible if no valuation is required, or if it is in practice possible to carry out a valuation accurately at or around the time of the determination of the daily settlement price on the last day of trading of the relevant share cum entitlement.

However, this is not always possible and it may be necessary to carry out the valuation when the underlying stock market opens on the first day of trading of such share ex entitlement. In the case of Individual Equity Option Contracts, this will entail a suspension of trading, potentially for the entire trading session, for the necessary contract adjustments to be made. In contrast, in the case of Universal Stock Futures Contracts (cash settlement) and Universal Stock Futures Contracts (physical delivery), **trading will continue in the relevant futures contract on a 'cum entitlement' basis**, with the necessary contract adjustments being made after the close of business on the first day the share is trading ex entitlement.

As stated above, the Board retains the right to determine how contracts should best be adjusted. However, as a general rule in the case of rights issues, cash and non-cash special dividends and demergers:

(a)   if it is possible to carry out a reliable valuation of the relevant components on the underlying stock market at or around the time of determination of daily settlement prices on the last day of trading of the relevant share cum entitlement, adjustments will be determined after the close of business on that day; and

(b)   if it is not possible to carry out a reliable valuation on the underlying stock market at or around the time of determination of daily settlement prices on the last day of trading of the relevant share cum entitlement, adjustments will be determined on the basis of opening prices of the relevant components on the first day of trading of such shares ex entitlement. As stated above, this will necessitate suspending trading in the relevant Individual Equity Option Contract, potentially for the entire session.

It should be noted that in limited circumstances it may be appropriate or necessary to use 'when issued' prices as the basis for adjustments. Such prices will only be used if the Board, in its judgement, considers them to reflect reliably the value of the relevant components.

It should also be noted that the timing of an announcement by a company of a Corporate Event may result in the Exchange not being able to effect the appropriate contract adjustments before the start of trading on the first day the shares trade ex entitlement. In such circumstances, the Exchange will suspend trading of the relevant Individual Equity Option Contract, potentially for the entire trading session, until the necessary contract adjustments have been made. In contrast, in order to provide market access for the greatest period of time, Universal Stock Futures Contracts (cash settlement) and Universal Stock Futures Contracts (physical delivery) will open for trading **on a 'cum entitlement' basis for that trading session**, and necessary contract adjustments will be made after the close of business of the first day on which the share trades ex entitlement.

Furthermore, it should be noted that the timing of an announcement by a company of a Corporate Event may occur during the trading session where, exceptionally, such Corporate Event also becomes effective during that same trading session. In such circumstances, the Exchange will suspend trading in the Individual Equity Option Contract, potentially for the remainder of that trading session, for the necessary contract adjustments to be made. **In contrast, Universal Stock Futures Contracts (cash settlement) and Universal Stock Futures Contracts (physical delivery) will remain open for trading on a 'cum entitlement' basis for the remainder of the trading session,** and the necessary contract adjustments will be made after the close of business.

Member firms should draw to the attention of changes created by the provisions in the Policy to their clients given that for instance a Universal Stock Futures Contract (cash settlement) and Universal Stock Futures Contract (physical delivery) would be trading 'cum entitlement' when the underlying share would be trading 'ex entitlement'.

Takeovers

The Board reserves the right to determine how contracts should best be adjusted in the event that a company is the subject of a takeover offer.

However, as a general rule the Board will make such a determination on the basis described below. In the case of **Individual Equity Option Contracts,** Delivery Contracts shall be performed as follows:

(a)   before the offer has been declared 'wholly unconditional', by requiring Delivery Sellers to deliver the number of shares in 'non-assented' form that they have contracted to sell; and

(b)   once the offer is declared wholly unconditional, in respect of Delivery Contracts to be settled through CREST, by requiring the matching and settlement of the components of the headline offer for the takeover in appropriate proportions.

The Settlement Day may be postponed until the acquiring company distributes the consideration for the takeover, in which case The London Clearing House may continue to call delivery margin until settlement is completed.

In the case of **Universal Stock Futures Contracts (cash settlement)**, the EDSP shall be calculated as follows:

(a)   before the offer has been declared 'wholly unconditional', by using the Relevant Reference Price for the contract, as defined in the List of Contract Details, (i.e. the price by reference to which the EDSP shall be calculated) based on the valuation of 'non-assented' shares; and

(b)   once the offer is declared wholly unconditional, by using a valuation representative of the components of the headline offer for the takeover in appropriate proportions. The Board will seek to ensure that the timing of the calculation of the EDSP is unaffected by the outcome of the takeover offer.

In the case of **Universal Stock Futures Contracts (physical delivery)**, Delivery Contracts shall be performed as follows:

(a) before the offer has been declared 'wholly unconditional', by requiring Delivery Sellers to deliver the number of shares in 'non-assented' form that they have contracted to sell; and

(b) once the offer is declared wholly unconditional, in respect of Delivery Contracts to be delivered through CREST or Euroclear, by requiring the matching and settlement of the components of the headline offer for the takeover in appropriate proportions.

The Settlement Day may be postponed until the acquiring company distributes the consideration for the takeover, in which case The London Clearing House may continue to call delivery margin until settlement is completed.

Equity Shares Contracts

Where a contract is created in the terms of Exchange Contract No. 211 at a time when the shares are cum entitlement, but the delivery of shares takes place on or after the ex entitlement date, the Exchange will require that both the ex entitlement shares and the Relevant Entitlement are delivered. The ex entitlement shares and the Relevant Entitlement should be delivered in quantities reflecting the original bargain size. Shares and entitlements should be delivered in exchange for an unadjusted amount of consideration per bargain.

In the case of takeovers, where contracts are made prior to the takeover being declared wholly unconditional, the Seller will be required to deliver shares not assented to the offer, or any alternative offer. The Buyer should be able to direct the acceptance of the offer, if required, prior to the settlement date.

The following attachement to the Policy gives examples of adjustments

Attachment to Corporate Events Policy
EXAMPLES OF ADJUSTMENTS TO CATER FOR CORPORATE EVENTS

Example 1

Company BBB announces its intention to demerge by granting 2 shares in the new company, CCC (which is a substantial company and is to be listed on the London Stock Exchange), to existing shareholders for every one share in BBB held. BBB shares are due to commence trading ex entitlement on 25 August. The options on BBB shares are adjusted such that delivery contracts which arise as a result of exercise on and from 25 August are settled by delivery of 1000 BBB shares and 2000 CCC shares.

The cash settlement futures on BBB shares are adjusted such that the EDSP will be calculated as the combined value of 1 BBB share and 2 CCC shares. The physical delivery futures on BBB shares are adjusted such that delivery contracts which arise on the last trading day are settled by delivery of 1000 BBB shares and 2000 CCC shares.

Example 2

Company DDD announces a 1 for 3 bonus issue. This would mean that post event there would be 4/3 as many shares in issue as pre event.

Before the market opens on 8 September:

(a)   the lot size of the DDD options is multiplied by 4/3 and the exercise prices are multiplied by 3/4; and

(b)   the lot size of the DDD cash settlement and physical delivery futures is multiplied by 4/3 and the reference price for determining variation margin (i.e. the previous night's settlement price) is multiplied by 3/4.

Example 3

Company EEE announces a redeemable two part rights issue to fund a potential acquisition on the basis of one unit for every 20 shares held. The price for each unit is payable in two instalments. Money is repayable to the extent that it is not used for the acquisition. EEE shares are due to commence trading ex entitlement on 6 December. It is not possible to formulate a reliable theoretical value for the ex entitlement share price due to uncertainty as to whether the acquisition will proceed, and it is therefore necessary to delay the opening of the market in EEE options on the first day of trading ex entitlement to carry out a valuation. The ex entitlement share price is 400p and the price of the unit is 240p.

The theoretical cum entitlement share price is:

$$\frac{240}{20} + 400 = 412$$

The ratio of the theoretical cum entitlement share price to the ex entitlement share price is:

$$\frac{412}{400} = 1.03$$

Before the market in EEE options opens on 6 December, the lot size of the EEE options is multiplied by 1.03 and the exercise prices are divided by 1.03. (NB: it may be necessary for the market in EEE options to remain suspended for the entire trading session.)

Both cash settlement and physical delivery futures contracts on EEE continue to trade on a 'cum entitlement' basis on 6 December. Before the market opens on the following business day, the lot size of EEE futures is multiplied by 1.03 and the reference price (i.e. the previous night's settlement price) is divided by 1.03.

Source: LIFFE Corporate Action Policy Document.

Appendix 9

SPAN

What is SPAN®

Standard Portfolio Analysis of Risk (SPAN®) is a margining system used by LCH.Clearnet to calculate initial margins due from and to its clearing members. SPAN® is a computerised system which calculates the effect of a range of possible changes in price and volatility on portfolios of derivatives. The worst probable loss calculated by the system is then used as the initial margin requirement.

Initial margin

All of Euronext.liffe's London exchange traded products are centrally cleared by LCH.Clearnet which acts as the central counterparty to all trades. LCH.Clearnet guarantees the fulfillment of all trades transacted on Euronext.liffe and as such assumes the risk of carrying all open positions forward. This risk is hedged by charging margin on the risk exposure faced by LCH.Clearnet to its clearing members. For LCH.Clearnet accurately to assess this risk, and therefore the margin that they will charge their clearing members, it needs an accurate means of assessing the potential risk it faces, for both single and portfolios of derivative positions. LCH.Clearnet uses London SPAN® for this purpose.

Identifying overall risk

The objective of SPAN® is to identify the overall risk inherent in a portfolio of futures and options derivative contracts. SPAN® treats both futures and options uniformly, while recognising the unique exposures associated with options portfolios. Critically, SPAN® also recognises inter-month and inter-commodity risk relationships, where the holding of one position may offset the risk associated with holding another position and vice-versa.

London SPAN®'s overriding objective is to determine the largest loss (risk) that a portfolio of derivative positions might be reasonably expected to suffer over a period of time (worst probable loss). For Euronext.liffe, LCH.Clearnet is responsible for determining what is a 'reasonable' worst possible loss, and for setting the basic SPAN® parameters accordingly which will be used to cal-culate margin requirements on its clearing members' portfolios.

SPAN® methodology

To identify the worst probable one-day loss on a portfolio, SPAN® con-structs a series of scenarios of changing underlying prices and volatilities for each derivative instrument in the portfolio, these 'risk arrays' are cen-tral to the SPAN® methodology, from this the worst probable outcome – the scanning loss – is selected. SPAN® will then add up all the scanning losses for the portfolio, add any inter-month spread charges and subtract any inter-commodity credits. This is then compared to the 'short option mini-mum charge' and whichever is the greater is the initial margin. This can be represented by:

$$\text{Initial margin} = \text{scanning loss} + \text{inter-month spread charge} - \text{Inter-commodity charge credit}$$

or; the short option minimum charge, whichever is the greater.

This is explained in greater detail below.

Scanning loss and risk arrays

The SPAN® risk array represents how a specific derivative contract (e.g. a future or option on a future, or an option on a stock) will react (gain or lose value), from the current point in time to a specific point in time in the future (usually the following day), to a specific set of market conditions over this time duration. The time duration is typically one trading day as SPAN® is primarily concerned with assessing the worst probable loss which may occur from one trading day to another.

The market conditions that are evaluated are called 'risk scenarios'. There are sixteen risk scenarios and these are defined in terms of:

• how much the price of the underlying is expected to change over the time duration;
• how much the volatility of the underlying will change over the time duration.

The results of this calculation for each risk scenario – the amount by which the derivative contract will gain or lose value over the time duration – is called the risk array value. The set of risk array values for the specific contract under the full set of risk scenarios constitutes the risk array. The scanning range, that is the range at which SPAN® scans up and down from the current underlying market price, is set and reviewed by LCH.Clearnet.

SPAN® uses the risk arrays to scan underlying market price changes and volatility changes for all contracts in a portfolio in order to determine value gains and losses at the portfolio level. The largest loss recorded from this process is used as the 'scanning loss' for the portfolio.

Inter-month spread charge

SPAN® assumes that price moves correlate perfectly across contract months. However, since price moves across contract months rarely exhibit perfect correlation, SPAN® adds an Inter-Month Spread Charge to the Scanning Loss associated with each instrument. Effectively, this Inter-month Spread Charge covers the inter-month basis risk that may exist for portfolios containing futures and options with different expirations.

For each futures contract or other underlying instrument in which the portfolio has positions, SPAN® identifies the net delta associated with it. SPAN® then creates spreads using these net deltas. As these spreads are created, SPAN® keeps track of each tier (a set of consecutive futures contracts) of how much delta has been consumed by spreading the tier, and how much remains. For each spread formed, SPAN® assesses a charge per spread, the total of all these charges for a particular commodity constitutes the inter-month spread charge for that commodity.

Strategy spreads

A new feature of London SPAN® version 4 is its 'Strategy Spread functionality'. Here, consecutive Butterfly and Condor strategies with in a portfolio are identified and processed at an appropriate rate, reflecting their lower risk profile before the calculation of the inter-month spread charge. As such, portfolios containing these strategies under London SPAN® version 4 will benefit from the more accurate assessment of their risk.

These strategies are automatically identified by London SPAN® version 4 even if these positions were not created as a strategy.

Inter-commodity credits

Price movements tend to correlate fairly well between related underlying instruments. As a result, gains from positions in one derivatives instrument will sometimes offset losses in another related instrument. Therefore to recognise the risk reducing aspects of portfolios that contain positions in related derivative instruments, SPAN® will form inter-commodity spreads for these positions. These spreads produce credits that in the final calculation of the initial margin, may reduce that margin.

Each spread formed by SPAN® generates a percentage saving from the total initial margin requirement for the underlying instrument. SPAN® applies these percentages to the outright initial margin requirements and in most cases derives a lower initial margin requirement for the specific instrument. SPAN® uses delta information to generate spreads, and the more of a portfolio's delta which is allocated to spreads, the greater the spread credit for the portfolio.

Short options minimum charge

Short options positions in extremely out-of-the-money strikes may appear to have little or no risk across the entire scanning range. However, in the event that the underlying market conditions change significantly these options may move into-the-money and may generate large losses for holders of short positions in these options. To cover this risk, SPAN® allocates a minimum requirement for each short option contained in a portfolio. The Short Option Minimum Charge acts as the lower boundary to the risk requirement for each underlying instrument. The risk requirement for the instrument in question cannot fall below this level.

Definitions

Initial margin   The returnable deposit required by LCH.Clearnet from its members when opening certain futures and options positions. Initial margin is usually calculated by taking the worst probable loss that the position could sustain, and can be paid in either cash or collateral.

Scanning loss   A term used to describe the initial margin calculated by SPAN®. The scanning loss will be the worst-case potential risk in a portfolio of derivatives across a range of changes in price and volatility as calculated by the SPAN® system.

Source: LCH.Clearnet.

Appendix 10

TIMS

Risk exposure is a focal point of vital importance for all international markets and clearing organizations. As world financial derivatives markets expand and counterparty credit risk increases in size and complexity, an organization's ability to assess its exposure to credit risk has become even more critical. The Options Clearing Corporation's Theoretical Intermarket Margin System (TIMS) provides this capability.

The Options Clearing Corporation (OCC) is the first clearing organization in the world to have implemented a risk-based margin methodology for the U.S. listed securities options markets. OCC's TIMS methodology is a sophisticated system for measuring the monetary risk inherent in portfolios containing options, futures and options on futures positions.

TIMS allows clearing institutions to measure, monitor and manage the level of risk exposure of their members' portfolios. TIMS can calculate risk exposure at different account levels and for different account types. In addition, TIMS uses advanced portfolio theory to margin all positions relating to the same underlying product and combines the risk of closely related products into integrated portfolios. This portfolio aspect of TIMS is integral for the recognition of hedges used by market participants in increasingly interrelated markets.

By Introducing TIMS, OCC responded to the growing need for a risk-based margin system that is cost effective, hardware independent and capable of interfacing with an existing clearing system. TIMS is becoming an international standard for assessing risk in derivatives markets.

Methodology

TIMS uses advanced pricing models to project the liquidation value of each portfolio given changes in the price of each underlying product. These models generate a set of theoretical values based on various factors including current prices, historical prices and market volatility. Based on flexible criteria established by a clearinghouse, statistically significant hedges receive appropriate margin offsets. TIMS also is used to predict a member's potential intra-day risk under varying sets of assumptions regarding market behavior.

TIMS organizes all classes of options and futures relating to the same underlying asset into class groups and all class groups whose underlying assets exhibit close price correlation into product groups. The daily margin requirement for a clearing member is calculated based on its entire position within a class group and various product groups. The margin requirement consists of two components, a mark to market component and an additional margin component.

Premium Margin

The mark to market component takes the form of a premium margin calculation that provides margin debits or requirements for net short positions and margin credits for net long positions. The margin debits and credits are netted to determine the total premium margin requirement or credit for each class group. The premium margin component represents the cost to liquidate the portfolio at current prices by selling the net long positions and buying back the net short positions.

Additional Margin

The additional margin component, the portion of the margin requirement that covers market risk, is calculated using price theory in conjunction with class group margin intervals. TIMS projects the theoretical cost of liquidating a portfolio of positions in the event of an assumed worst case change in the price of the underlying asset. Theoretical values are used to determine what a position will be worth when the underlying asset value changes. Given a set of input parameters (i.e., option contract specifics, interest rates, dividends and volatility), the pricing model will predict what the position should theoretically be worth at a specified price for the underlying instrument.

The class group margin interval determines the maximum one day increase in the value of the underlying asset (upside) and the maximum one day decrease in the value of the underlying asset (downside) that can be expected as a result of historical volatility. The methodology used to determine class group margin intervals and product groups can be specified by each clearing institution. OCC's methodology for determining class group margin intervals is based on ongoing statistical analysis. For each class group, the standard deviation is computed and a margin interval is calculated which covers a predetermined percentage specified by the clearinghouse. This approach provides both a confidence level and historical perspective on volatility and accounts for any non-normal price distribution patterns. TIMS also calculates theoretical values at equal intervals between the two endpoints (upside and downside) and at the current market value to protect against certain trading strategies that may have their largest loss between these two endpoints.

OCC's methodology for determining which class groups comprise a product group and the appropriate percentage deduction to account for the lack of perfect correlation between class groups is also based on ongoing statistical analysis. For each pair of class groups, TIMS computes a coefficient of determination. TIMS assigns class groups to a product group when the value of the coefficient between the class groups is within policy limits established by the clearinghouse. The product group percentage or offset is established based on the lowest coefficient of determination among all of the class groups included in the product group. When calculating an account's total margin requirement, this specified percentage of any margin credits at the class group level is used to offset margin requirements generated by other class groups in the same product group.

Source: Option Clearing Corporation.

Index

Page numbers in italics refers to tables and figures.